Robert Wilbert

Ennobling the Ordinary

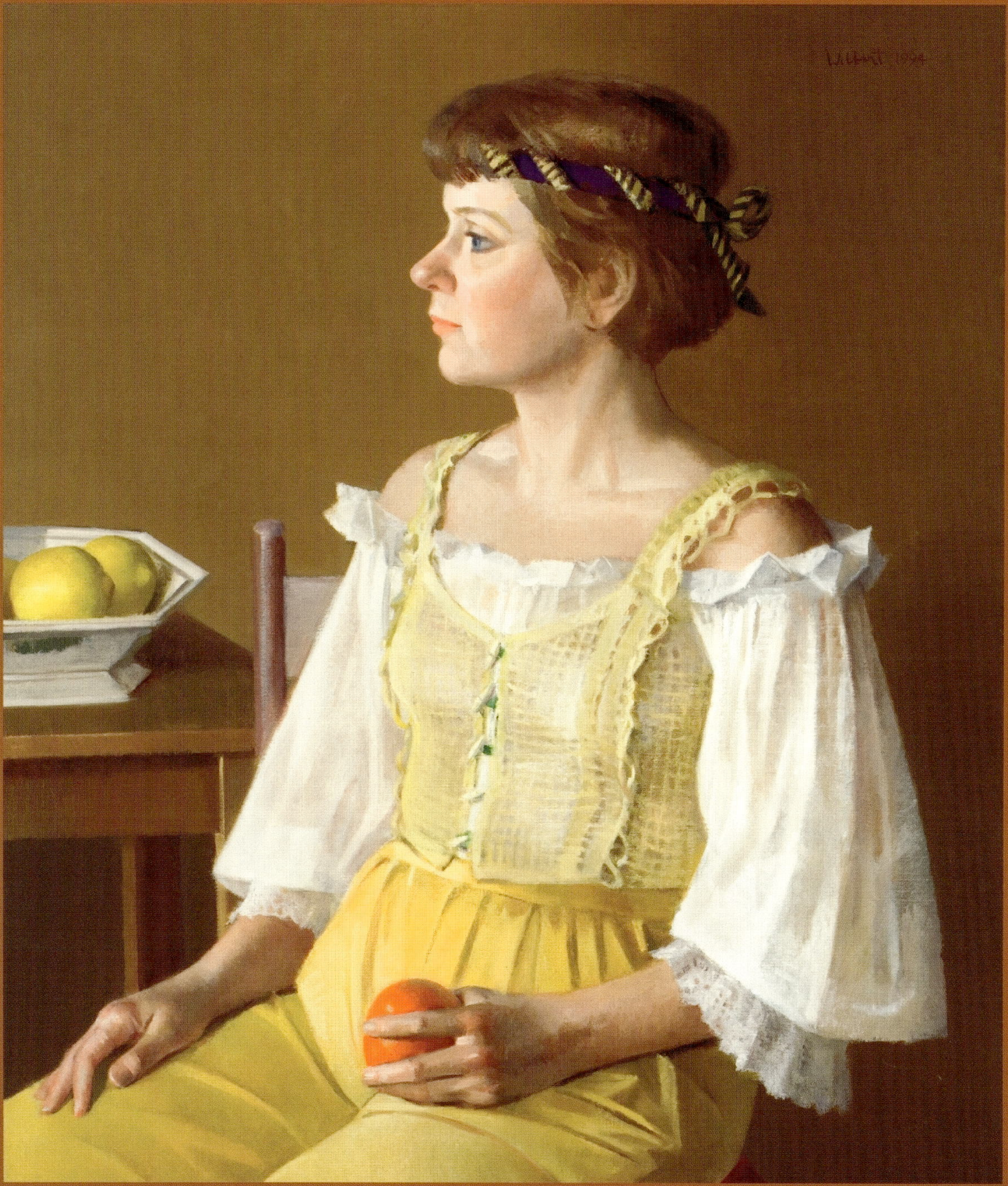

Robert Wilbert

Ennobling the Ordinary

Gere Baskin, Editor

Detroit Focus, 2011

Frontispiece: 1994, Oil on canvas
Mary with Orange 46 × 40 inches
Collection of the Artist

Unless otherwise indicated below, photographs of Robert Wilbert's work were taken by Dirk Bakker.
Figures with Folding Screen, page 102: Peter Harholdt
Yellow Gladioli with Figured Vase, page 105; *Flowers in a Green Vase*, page 110; and *Zinnias with Hat and Mask*, page 114: Robert Hensleigh
Mime with Drum, page 95; and *Tulips with Indian Club and Blue Dish*, page 91: Tom Van Eynde

P.O. Box 843
Royal Oak, MI 48068
www.detroitfocus.org

Funds in support of this publication were received from the National Endowment for the Arts and the Michigan Council for the Arts (now the Michigan Council for Arts and Cultural Affairs), as well as from the generous donors listed at the end of this volume.

ISBN: 978-0-615-45383-5

Book design and production: Savitski Design
Manuscript editor: Cynthia Newman Edwards

NATIONAL ENDOWMENT FOR THE ARTS
A great nation deserves great art.

michigan council for arts and cultural affairs

Contents

Preface and Acknowledgments

Robert Wilbert: Ennobling the Ordinary was conceived as a publication under the auspices of Detroit Focus, which has a thirty-two–year history as a nonprofit artist organization in the greater Detroit area. Detroit Focus has produced numerous art exhibitions, catalogues, public sculpture, and site-specific installations; it has commissioned art work and for fourteen years published *Detroit Focus Quarterly*. The group also developed a Visiting Artists Program in the Detroit Public Schools. In November 2000, under the leadership of director Michael Sarnacki, Detroit Focus organized the largest visual arts event in the city's history. Detroit Focus 2000 consisted of over one hundred photography exhibitions and dozens of lectures, special events, and the creation of an artists portfolio which was acquired for the collections of the Detroit Institute of Arts, the University of Michigan Museum of Art, the Mira Goddard Center for Photography at Ryerson University, Toronto, and Kresge Art Museum, Michigan State University.

The primary mission of Detroit Focus has always been to serve artists and educate the community. Publishing a book about an artist is certainly a new project for the organization and is an endeavor that has been different than any other. Robert Wilbert was selected because he is an artist whose paintings have had a significant impact on other artists and the greater community. Young artists seeking a place in the broad spectrum of the art world can gain much from this study. It defines a career carefully considered in terms of discovering possibilities for artistic development and characterized by numerous contributions to the community as an artist, educator, mentor, advocate for the arts, and devoted family man. These values and attitudes, particularly when combined with Robert Wilbert's innate talent and intellect, offer thoughtful building blocks for a career in the arts.

Relationship is a key word in trying to understand all the facets of Robert Wilbert and his work. The history that accompanies these relationships unfolds into a fascinating tale of the art world over the last fifty years in Metropolitan Detroit. During the course of thirty-eight years on the faculty of the Department of Art and Art History at Wayne State University, Wilbert was instrumental, as coordinator of the painting area, in bringing the program to prominence, both locally and nationally. While at Wayne, he helped to establish a collegial atmosphere that nurtured generations of students who have gone on to successful careers, contributing to the arts in very positive ways as artists, writers, educators, curators, and art dealers. His relationships became deep friendships that have sustained him and his wife Gretchen in their later years.

Robert Wilbert's work has been collected by numerous institutions, including the Detroit Institute of Arts and several national corporations. Among his many commissions are the design of the 1987 U.S. postage stamp commemorating Michigan's sesquicentennial, the official portrait of James Blanchard, governor of Michigan (1983–91), and that of Irvin D. Reid, president of Wayne State University (1997–2008). The latter painting was completed and dedicated in May 2010. Wilbert continues to produce new work in oil and watercolor. After years of teaching advanced painting at the Birmingham Bloomfield Art Center, in January 2011 he left the center to return to his studio full time to explore new ideas.

Robert Wilbert has said that he has been blessed

in his career and by this community. That blessing has been ours to have been given the opportunity to appreciate a great talent and the impact of his wisdom on so many in the community.

In 2008 an application for grant money in support of this publication was made to the Michigan Council for Arts and Cultural Affairs (MCACA), which judged the project worthy of funding (the awarded funds include money from the National Endowment for the Arts [NEA]). The application was supported by Professor Gilda Snowden, Fine Arts Department, College for Creative Studies; Jane Linn, President and CEO, Birmingham Bloomfield Art Center; Sandra Schemske, Coordinator, University Art Collection, Wayne State University; and MaryAnn Wilkinson, Curator of Modern Art, Detroit Institute of Arts. Also crucial to the project's success was the enthusiastic support of the Detroit Focus Board of Directors: Michael Sarnacki, President; Marcia Freedman, Secretary; and Stanley Freedman, Treasurer.

Further discussion developed a core group of individuals who believed the project was very important and who have remained steadfast in their dedication to the process of creating this publication. They are Florence Morris, Donald Morris Gallery; Susanne Hilberry, Susanne Hilberry Gallery; Marsha Miro, Founding Director of the Museum of Contemporary Art Detroit (MOCAD); Peter Williams, Professor of Art, University of Delaware; Ellen Phelan, artist and recent recipient of the Smithsonian Archives of American Art Medal; Dirk Bakker, former Head of Photography, Detroit Institute of Arts; John McKinnon, Program Coordinator, Society for Contemporary Art, Art Institute of Chicago; and Cynthia Newman Edwards, freelance editor and former Managing Editor at both the Detroit Institute of Arts and the J. Paul Getty Museum.

All the aforementioned individuals have been professionally recognized for their contributions to the arts, both nationally and in Michigan. They have worked diligently with me to bring the project to fruition, and I am grateful to them for their commitment and for sharing their broad knowledge and experience. Particular praise must go to Gretchen Wilbert, Robert's wife, as a wonderful repository of fact and a great friend. Robert himself, despite his modesty, was a primary source of information and a joy to work with.

Images for the publication were selected by Florence Morris, Susanne Hilberry, Dirk Bakker, Gere Baskin, and Robert Wilbert. Photography for the book was done by Dirk Bakker, Robert Hensleigh, Tom Van Eynde, and Peter Harholdt. John Lacko provided additional assistance. Many people helped locate paintings and bibliographic materials. My thanks to Hazel Blake of Susanne Hilberry Gallery, Ferndale, Michigan; David Klein of David Klein Gallery; Artspace II Inc.; Roger Ramsay of Roger Ramsay Gallery, Chicago; Jason Molchanow, Associate Curator, The JPMorgan Chase Art Collection, Chicago; Don Walsh of Royal Insurance Company of America; Catherine Scandalis, Administrative Assistant, Metropolitan Museum of Art, New York; Tami Miller, Director of Exhibitions and Collections, Krasl Art Center, St. Joseph, Michigan; Kim Hoffmann, Curator of Collections, South Bend Regional Museum of Art; Denise Neil-Binion, Researcher/Registrar, Ball State University Museum of Art; Cindy Medley Buckner, Research Curator and Supervisor of the Works on Paper Study, Grand Rapids Art Museum; Cheryl Leibold, Archivist, Pennsylvania Academy of the Fine Arts; Barbara Heller, Conservator, Detroit Institute of Arts; Maria R. Ketcham, Head Librarian, Research Library and Archive, Detroit Institute of Arts; Regina Schreck, Registrar, Detroit Institute of Arts; Hanne Fuglsang Nielsen, Archivist, Pewabic Pottery, Detroit; Pat McCormick, Archives, The Butler Institute of American Art, Youngstown, Ohio; Christina Hicks, Registrar, Oklahoma City Museum of Art; Linda Richer, Research Librarian, W. E. Upjohn Institute for Employment Research, Kalamazoo, Michigan; Judy Dyki, Library Director, Cranbrook Academy of Art Library, Bloomfield Hills, Michigan; Michelle Perron, Director, Center Galleries, College of Creative Studies, Detroit; Marge Sikora, Registrar/Volunteer Coordinator, Birmingham Bloomfield Art Center, Birmingham, Michigan; Peter Ott, Registrar, Flint Museum of Art; and Kathryn Wildfong, Editor in Chief, Wayne State University Press. I also owe great gratitude to Max Mikles of COMPSERVICE*plus* for solving all computer problems.

My personal thanks to my husband Sid Baskin for his patience, "black pen," and unquestionable support of this book.

Gere Baskin, January 2011

Introduction

Why create a book about Robert Wilbert? The easy answer is, of course, the quality of the paintings he has produced over his lifetime. The more difficult answer is as nuanced as the slight variations of tone in those paintings. While the essays and interviews in this volume provide insights into Wilbert's career and where his work fits in the context of a particular moment in history, it is only by examining the works themselves that we can truly appreciate his achievement as an artist.

Robert's talent revealed itself at an early age and was encouraged by his family and friends. By the time he was ten he was involved in classes at the Art Institute of Chicago and traveled there weekly on public transportation. As an undergraduate of the University of Illinois, in the summer of 1950, he attended painting classes offered by the University of Denver and was taught by Julio de Diego, in Central City, Colorado. During that time he met C. E. Van Duzer, who later became director of the Flint Institute of Arts in Michigan. Van Duzer influenced Wilbert's decision to take his first job as an educational assistant to the director at the Flint Institute from 1954 to 1956.

When he was a graduate student at the University of Illinois in 1952 he was encouraged to apply for a national competitive exhibition, "American Water Colors, Drawings and Prints," which was to be held at the Metropolitan Museum of Art in New York. It is interesting to note that among the national jurors were Mauricio Lasansky from Iowa, Andrew Wyeth from Pennsylvania, and a number of artists from New York, such as Stuart Davis, Karl Knath, Charles Burchfield, Reginald Marsh, Yasuo Kuniyoshi, and Abraham Rattner. Representing every region of the country, these were the luminaries of the time. Wilbert's watercolor titled *Toadstool* was accepted by the Regional Jury of Selection in Chicago and was shown in the exhibition. He also exhibited the following year at the Art Institute of Chicago.

How an artist attains regional or national recognition is one of the most problematic issues in the profession. During the early years of Robert's career there were very few galleries in which to exhibit around the country, certainly not the plethora of galleries and other opportunities to put one's work before the public that exist today. The exhibition history included here reveals some clues to Robert's success. He participated in State Fairs and regional exhibitions in Michigan, Illinois, and Indiana. A variety of university art galleries and museums offered annual exhibition opportunities. He participated in annual exhibitions in Philadelphia, Oklahoma, Indiana, North Carolina, Kentucky, Ohio, Illinois, and Michigan. From participating in these venues he obtained recognition and many awards.

After his two-year stay in Flint, Robert joined the faculty at Wayne State University (in 1956) as an assistant professor and began a thirty-eight–year career as an artist/teacher that has brought him wide respect and reverence in his chosen field. Shortly after arriving in Detroit, he conceived the idea of using empty space in a frame shop to begin the AAA Gallery, which he directed and for which he curated many exhibitions. The quality of these exhibitions was superior; invited artists included Gerome Kamrowski (associated with Abstract Surrealism, initiated the Hylozist Group in the 1960s), Allen Leepa (Abstract Expressionist painter), Jens Plum (representational artist associated with Michigan State University), Stefan Davidek (highly regarded abstract painter from Flint), and many others. Newspaper reviews of this venue were consistently positive and lauded the initiative of the artists involved. The gallery was active from 1958 to 1960.

In 1961, Robert began an enduring and very important relationship with Donald and Florence Morris of the Donald Morris Gallery (the gallery remained active in the Detroit metropolitan environs until 1995). Although Donald died in 2004, Robert's friendship with Florence and her sons continues. The gallery no longer has physical space in this area; however, it is still active in Detroit and New York. A new era began in 1997, when his long-time friend and colleague Susanne Hilberry undertook to represent his work at the Susanne Hilberry Gallery, Ferndale, Michigan.

Self-Portrait 1989, Oil on canvas
Figure 1 34 × 36 inches
Collection of the Artist

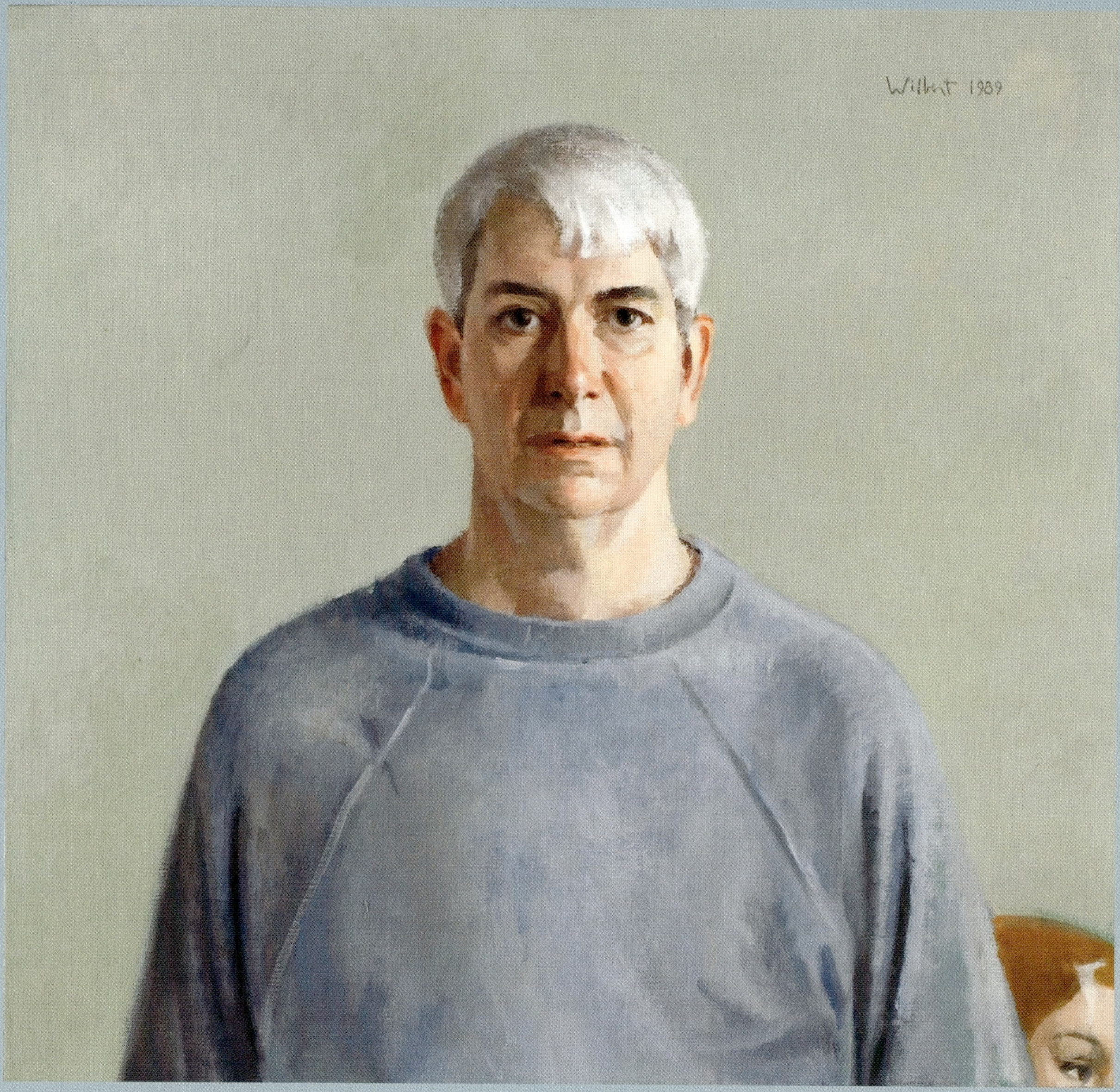

John McKinnon

On the Edge of Reality

Robert Wilbert is known as a painter's painter and "Detroit's Manet"[1] because of his ongoing exploration of painterly inventions within the traditional genres of still life, the human figure, and the landscape. Wilbert's artwork is situated at the heart of the perpetual dispute between representation and abstraction that can be traced back to Aristotle and Plato. What we think of as modern art arose from new explorations of representing form in space. According to a conventional art historical view, modernism was first expressed in the archetypal paintings by Edouard Manet and Paul Cézanne that did not act as windows to the world. Historians often credit the flat spatial planes of Manet and Cézanne as the first instances of the abstract painterly techniques that later evolved into the radical use of space within movements such as Cubism and Color Field painting. In the mid-twentieth century, as a renewed interest in realism[2] became pitted against the gesture-filled movement known as Abstract Expressionism, the debate between representation and abstraction was rekindled. That debate remains vital today across a huge range of media and pluralistic methods of production, as contemporary artists such as Wilbert challenge the age-old polemic by claiming new painterly territory. Throughout his career of over forty years, Wilbert has dedicated himself to observations of the real, never claiming complete allegiance either to the subject matter depicted or to painting as pure form. Instead, he forged his own path, explaining, "I found other ways to be modern."[3]

"Nothing is more abstract than reality."
— Giorgio Morandi[4]

Among the influences Wilbert acknowledges is the twentieth-century Italian painter Giorgio Morandi, who over a fifty-year career, coolly analyzed the same hand-constructed cardboard boxes, aged milk bottles, banal decanters, and humble glasses to generate luscious still-life paintings (see fig. 2). Morandi's dedication to a seemingly modest subject matter made him a conservative, yet radical, artist within the context of the mid-twentieth century. He believed that the visual world could not be accurately translated into words, but that it could be captured in a painting after meticulous study.[5] Like Morandi, Wilbert considers reality a starting point for his paintings.

Wilbert builds his compositions around realistic forms—nude models, fresh flowers, chairs, tables, mannequins, and various second-hand objects from thrift stores and antique shops. His studio is a workplace, but it also serves as a constant backdrop against which a revolving cast of characters are directed. For example, the head of a female mannequin appears, barely visible, in the lower right corner of a *Self-Portrait* from 1989 (fig. 1) and is featured prominently in *Gladioli with Mannequin* (1995; fig. 3). A bust of Saint Anthony looks peacefully over Wilbert's shoulder in *Self-Portrait with Statue* (1989; fig. 4) and stands next to a

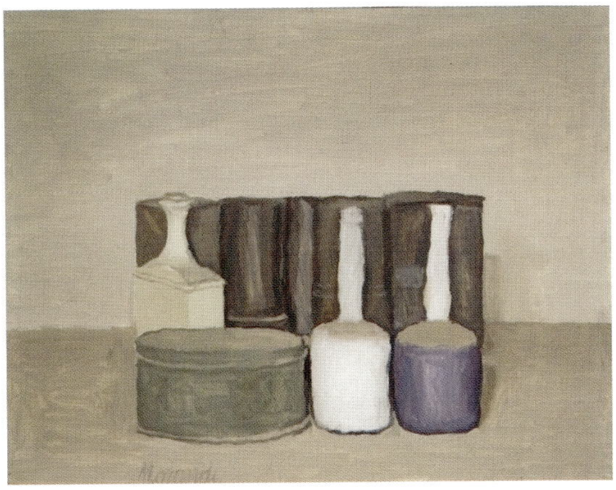

Still Life
Giorgio Morandi
(Italian, 1890–1964)
Figure 2
(see p. 13)

1954, Oil on canvas
14 x 18¼ in. (35.56 x 46.35 cm)
Smith College Museum of Art, Northampton, Massachusetts, Purchase SC 1954:62

Gladioli with Mannequin
Figure 3

1995, Oil on canvas
47 × 34 inches
Collection of the Artist

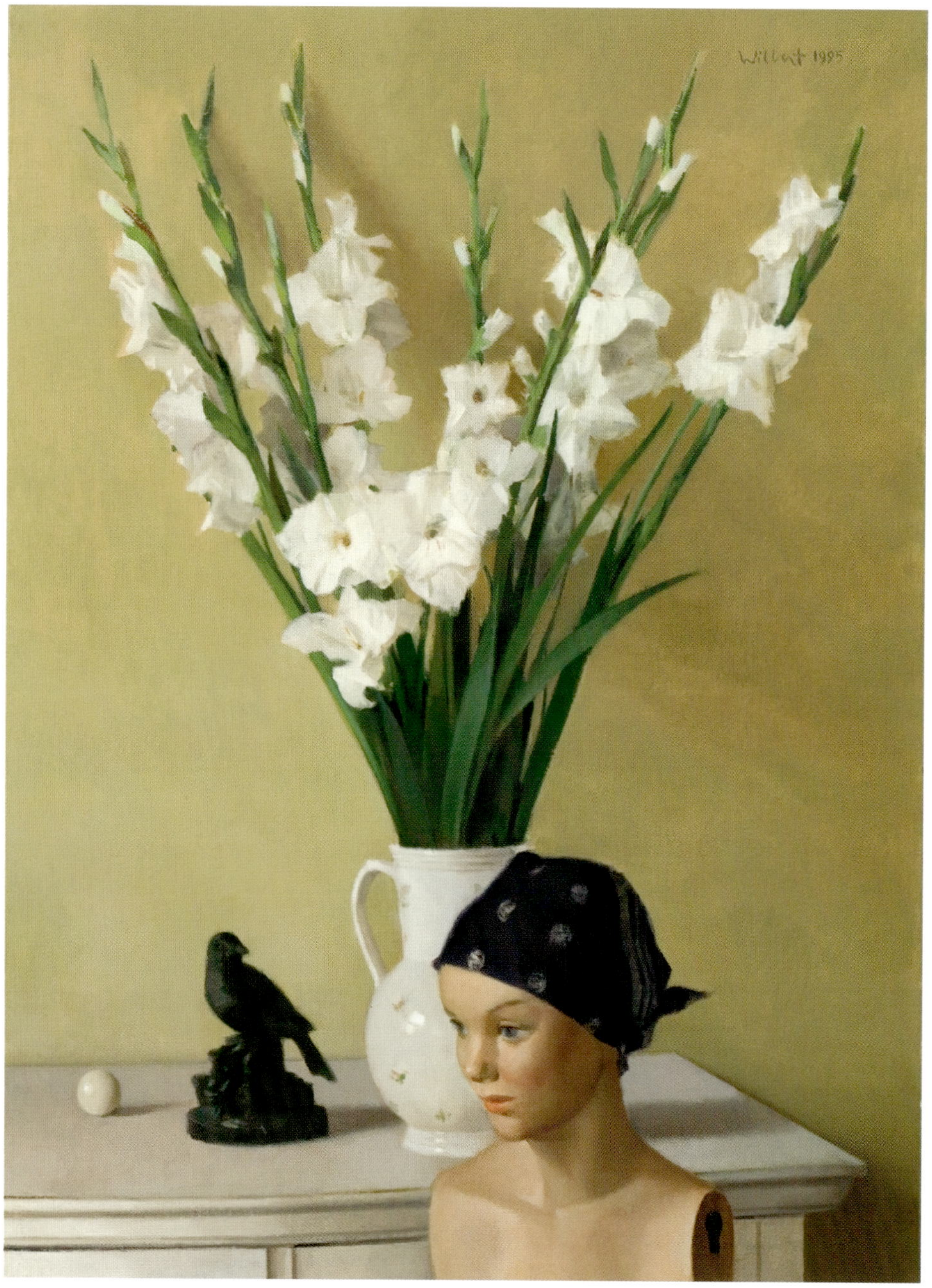

Self-Portrait with Statue
Figure 4

1989, Oil on canvas
56 × 40 inches
Collection of Marcia and Howard Parven

Performer with Religious Figure
Figure 5

1995, Oil on canvas
50 × 40 inches
Collection of Gordon and Hannah Moss

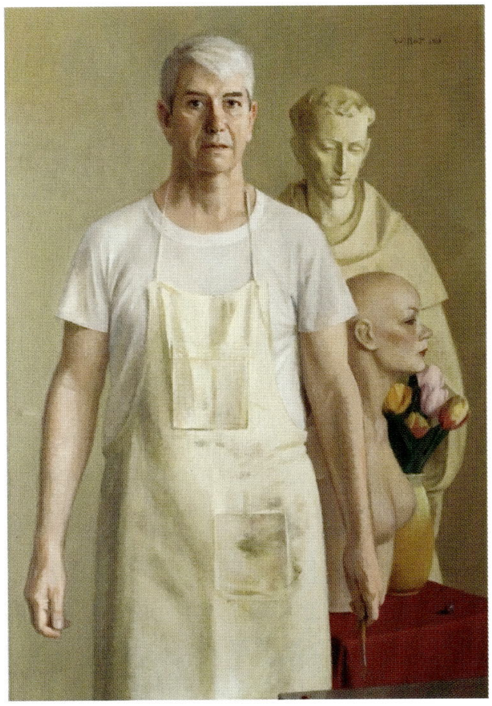

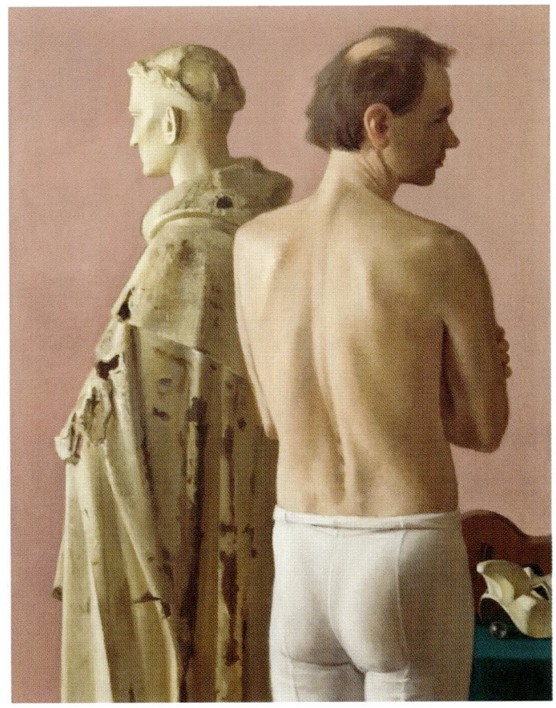

balding male in *Performer with Religious Figure* (1995; fig. 5). This bust and many of the other objects memorialized in Wilbert's paintings are still in his studio, worn from constant reshuffling and the passage of time, much as Morandi's often reused containers became layered with soft, velvety dust.

Wilbert's studio is an active place of object connoisseurship and contemplation, but it is also a regular setting for live figure models. Like the inanimate objects, these individuals move within the confines of his studio, politely sitting in kitchen chairs, lounging in old lawn furniture, and posing among the artist's collection of objects. Throughout his career, Wilbert has repeatedly painted the same friends, family members, and acquaintances. While the artist is personally attached to these individuals, he nevertheless treats them as another pictorial variable.[6] The integration of human figures into his paintings allows him to create new visual possibilities by adjusting scale, perspective, and compositional relationships within the studio. For instance, a figure may pose within a carefully articulated still-life arrangement or relax on an isolated chaise lounge. Whether the subject is an apple, a human, or an old fan, Wilbert gives it the same attention, concentrating on its shape, color, line, and form as compositional elements.

From the unassuming corner of his studio, Morandi devoted himself to the arrangement of simplified forms with restricted subject matter, but he never ventured into pure abstraction. Wilbert has similarly dedicated himself to painting a narrow subject matter grounded in the real with a variety of inventive techniques. He remains faithful to the original subject but does not focus on microscopic details. Wilbert's primary concern is not to make realistic or stylized representations of his subjects but rather, like a dedicated composer, to deftly organize his subjects into lyrical compositions. Wilbert is keenly aware of the object's physical properties, including the spaces found between the objects, and he pursues their truth with diligence and tenacity. With focused concentration, diligent rigor, and a constant methodology, Wilbert seeks to discover the essence of real objects. To this end,

Excavation
Willem de Kooning (American, born in the Netherlands, 1904–1997)
Figure 6

1950, Oil on canvas
81 x 100¼ in. (205.7 x 254.6 cm)
Art Institute of Chicago, Mr. and Mrs. Frank G. Logan Purchase Prize Fund; restricted gifts of Edgar J. Kaufmann, Jr., and Mr. and Mrs. Noah Goldowsky, Jr., 1952.1
Photo: © The Art Institute of Chicago
Painting: © 2011 The Willem de Kooning Foundation / Artists Rights Society (ARS), New York

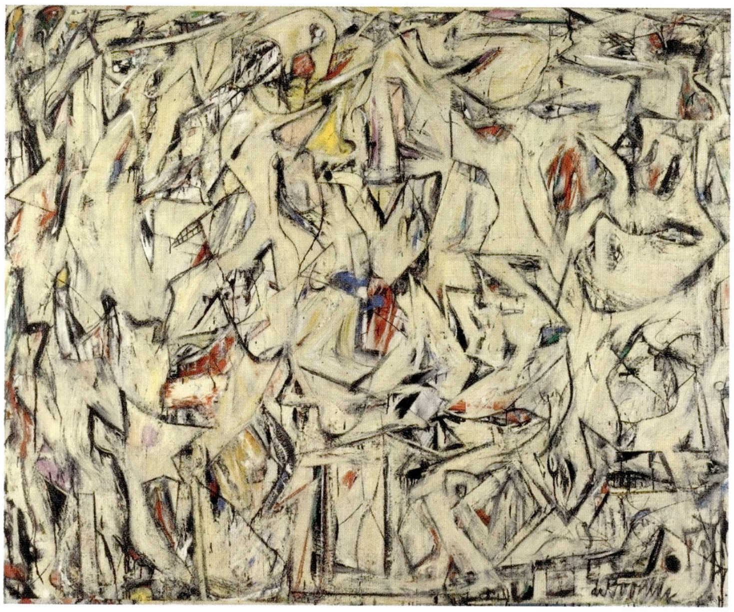

he uses various structural compositions, color ranges, and a careful consideration of the amount of detail in the painting—some of the same pictorial concerns addressed by pure abstract painters.

"One day, some painter used 'Abstraction' as a title for one of his paintings. It was a still life."
— Willem de Kooning[7]

In the 1950s, Willem de Kooning and Jackson Pollock were the central artists in the prevailing movement of Abstract Expressionism. The public embrace of de Kooning and Pollock revolutionized the art world. They enjoyed a celebrity-like status that presented a new and exciting model of the American artist.

De Kooning's 1951 symposium paper for the Museum of Modern Art, "What Abstract Art Means to Me," attacked *abstract* as a term that originated from the ivory tower of philosophers. He campaigned against the broadly accepted idea of abstraction and advocated that an individual artist's creative process was of paramount importance. He claimed that *Abstraction* is a "very tricky title" for a still life and asserted that it "wasn't really a very good one."[8] Despite de Kooning's criticism, many artists and historians understand abstract formalism as having evolved out of representation, including the rich painterly tradition of still-life subjects. In addition, the spatial construction of an object within an artist's studio and subsequent representation on canvas present a painter with an infinite number of problems to solve. Wilbert, like de Kooning, sees the structural complexities that lie within any assemblage of real space—within his arranged objects he sees light, shapes, space, and color.

As a student at the University of Illinois in the 1950s, Wilbert was exposed to a range of painterly interests. It was an exciting time to be a student as the New York School Abstract Expressionists were making waves in the international art scene. Wilbert, and other young artists, saw in the careers of Pollock and de Kooning the potential to reach the heights that European artists had reached in the past. Wilbert's formative work was inspired by de Kooning's *Excavation* (1950; fig. 6), a painting that he studied during visits to the Art Institute of Chicago. *Excavation,* a tension-filled painting, created with masterful brushwork and organic shapes, exemplifies de Kooning's virtuoso style and compositional approach. The anatomical forms (originating from a film of a woman working in a rice field) are layered and abstracted, taking on new properties as the paint swims across the surface of the work. Wilbert was attracted to the free-associative and all-over composition of *Excavation,* an approach he emulated for several years. One of the unique aspects of Wilbert's paintings during this period is the interchangeability between representation and abstraction. The same source material could easily become a complex composition of abstract lines and shapes on canvas or a recognizable landscape or still life. For example, the lines within *Expressway* (1959; fig. 7) give shape to a cityscape and complex highway system but also stand on their own as formal elements.

Wilbert then shifted to a figurative style with active brushstrokes that may have been influenced by de Kooning's *Women* series. The central figure of *Woman, I* (1950–52) differs drastically from the complex organization of spatial relationships

Expressway
Figure 7

1959, Oil on canvas
36 × 48 inches
Collection of W.E. Upjohn Institute for Employment Research

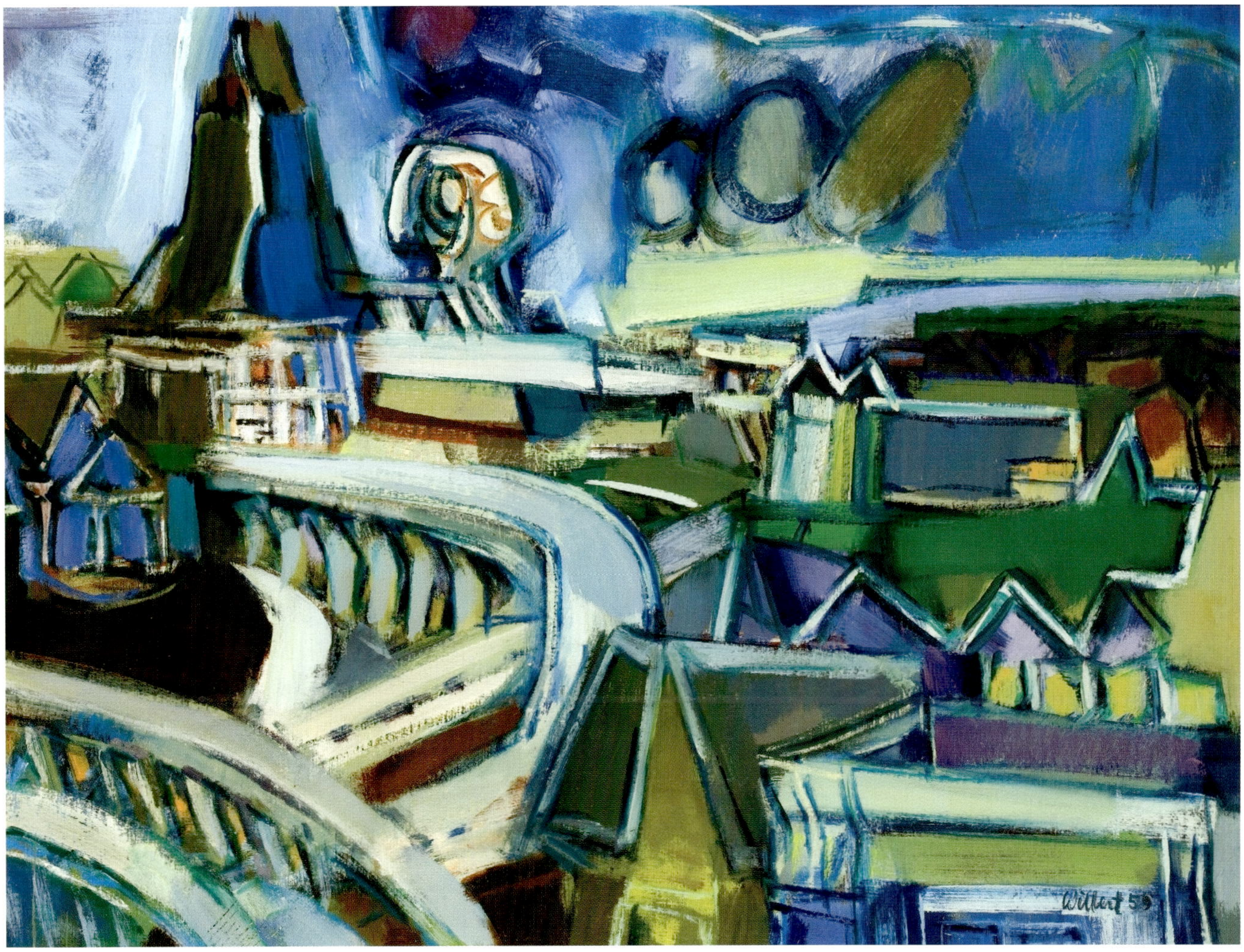

Skin Divers 1961, Oil on canvas
Figure 8 36 × 48 inches
Collection of the Artist

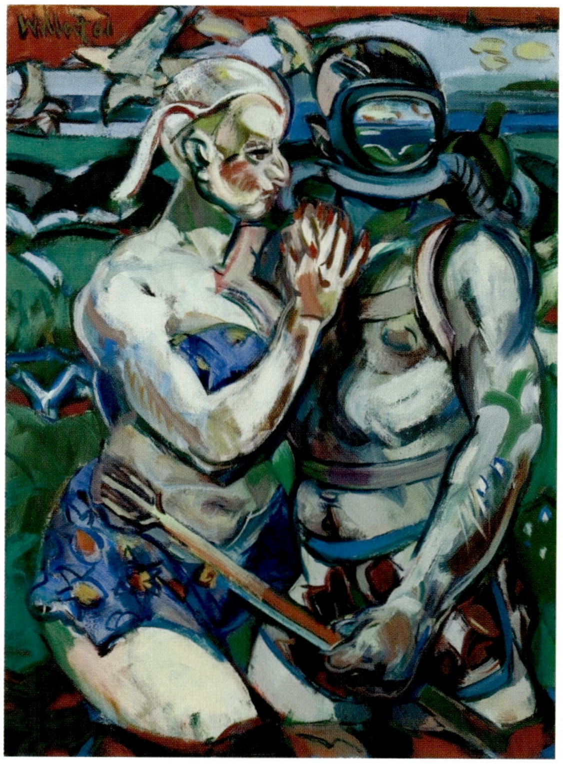

found in de Kooning's previous work. Scandalously, the figure was the most prominent aspect of the painting, as evidenced by the decipherable body parts and face. De Kooning had used figurative elements in his earlier work, but this piece was seen as a dramatic and contentious return to the figure.[9] *Woman, I* became one of the most reproduced images of the period, influenced many younger artists, and gave artists permission to challenge the dominance of pure abstraction. Wilbert's portraits made in the early 1960s, such as *Skin Divers* (1961; fig. 8) and *Seated Tennis Player* (1962; fig. 9), treat the figure as the most important compositional element and are typified by active brushstrokes and a liberal use of color. Wilbert eventually streamlined his figurative and still-life paintings into a more crisp representational style, but he continued to be concerned with formal issues of abstraction. While his work after 1962 is detached from the bold gestures of the Abstract Expressionists, it nevertheless contains some of the primary concerns of the movement, among them the use of pictorial logic, material concerns of paint, and an individual vision.

"I like to seize the one sharp instant in Nature, to imprison it by means of ordered shapes and space relationships."
— Milton Avery[10]

For over thirty years, beginning in 1961, Wilbert was represented by the preeminent gallery in the Detroit area, the Donald Morris Gallery. He exhibited his work alongside artists such as Milton Avery, Alexander Calder, Willem de Kooning, Joan Miro, and Philip Pearlstein. Through his relationship with the gallery, Wilbert was given national and international exposure as well as an opportunity to study works by other artists, both in exhibitions and in the gallery's back room.

Wilbert readily admits that he was influenced by the color and flatness of Milton Avery's work. While Avery used the fleeting attributes of his immediate environment to begin an exploration of painterly surfaces, the representation of

Seated Tennis Player
Figure 9

1962, Oil on canvas
36 × 30 inches
Collection of the Artist

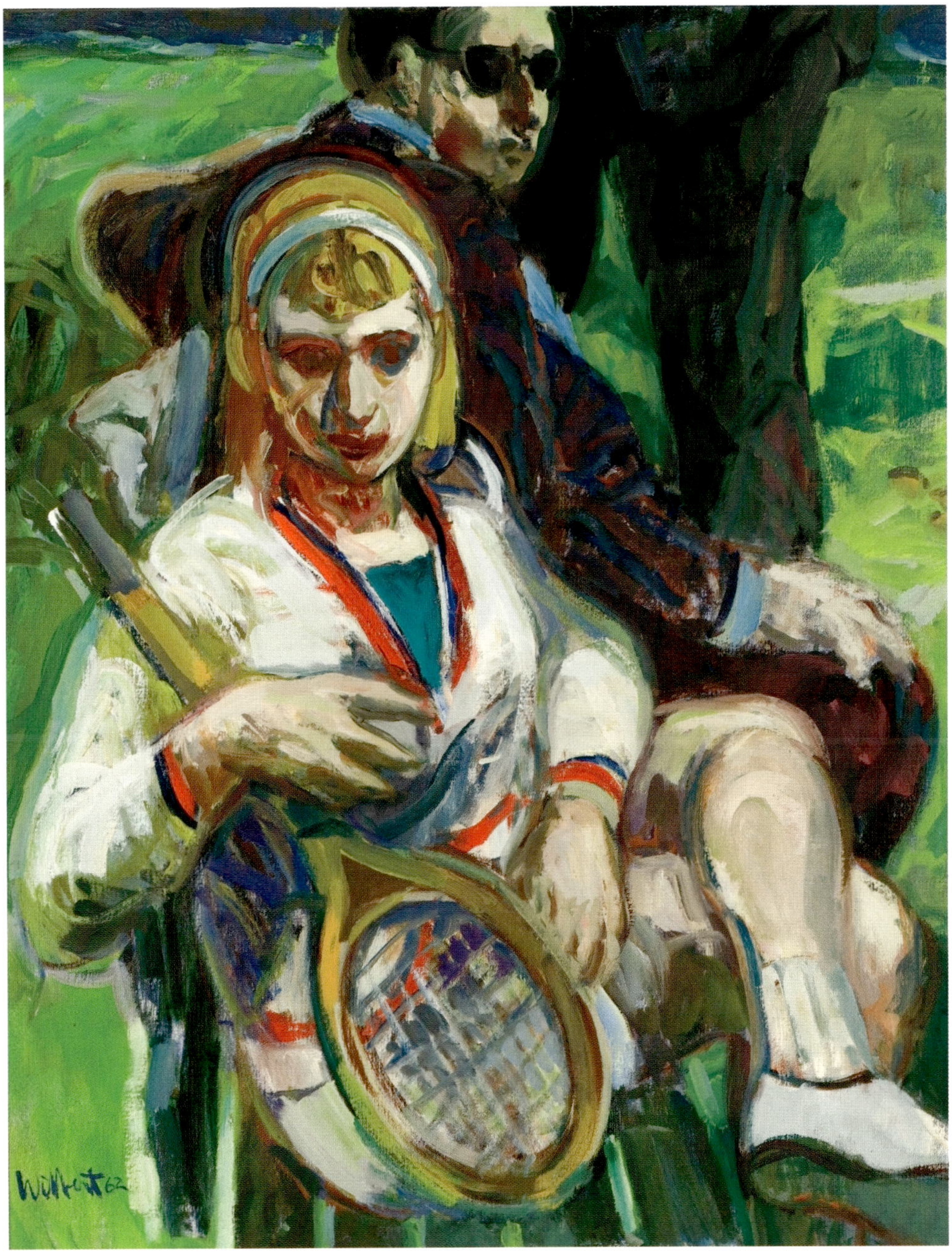

The Card Players
Milton Avery (American, 1885–1965)
Figure 10

1945, Oil on canvas, 50 x 34 in. (127 x 86.36 cm)
Milwaukee Art Museum, Gift of Mrs. Harry Lynde Bradley M1977.199
Photo: P. Richard Eells

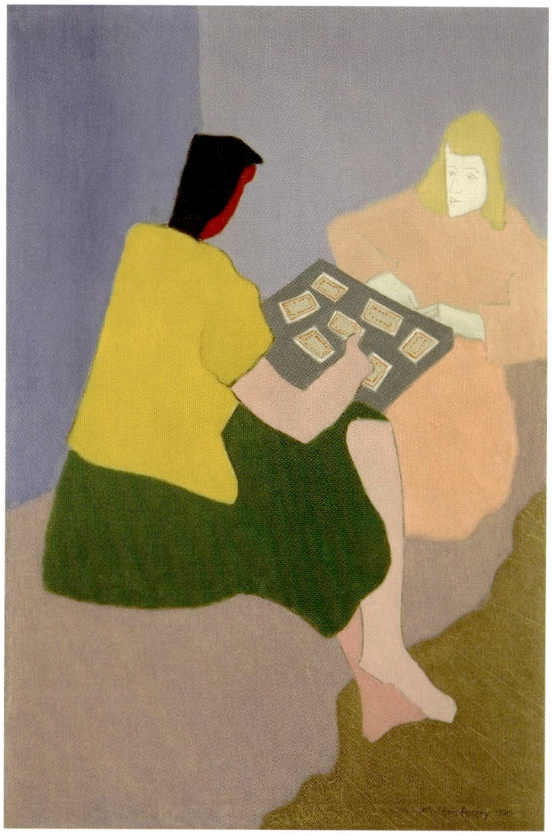

nature was not his primary concern. Instead of reproducing every nuanced detail of his subjects, he acknowledged the reality of the canvas as a flat, plastic, and artificial painting surface. He flattened figures, exaggerated forms, compacted perspectives, and invented new color schemes to create simplified, interlocking shapes that capture "the purity and essence of the idea—expressed in its simplest form."[11] For example, in *The Card Players* (1945; fig. 10), he economically uses line and shape to render an interior space, cards, a table, figures, and facial features. The pale white skin of the far player and the bright red face of the near competitor are not used to evoke mood but rather to create pictorial tension. Avery's studied formalist painting technique resulted in painted forms that can be viewed as abstractions, independent of his original sources. While Avery's painting process made nature flat and artificial, Wilbert's approach depicts artificially constructed studio arrangements with volumetric accuracy. Wilbert claims that the artificiality of his process reaches much deeper than the surface of the canvas. He admits, "What is shown in my paintings is an 'arrangement,' but more than that, an arrangement of things in the studio and not part of the everyday world."[12] For example, *Still Life with Toy Car and Game Board* (1979; fig. 11) contains a chair, musical instrument, toy car, game board, a bunch of bananas, and other objects that would not ordinarily be found together. The position of each visual element is meticulously planned and works in concert with the others to form a complex composition. The painting would be a very different one without the diagonal red box or the vertically oriented blue game board on which it rests. Making a consistent challenge to himself, Wilbert looks upon the subjects of his studio through a different lens than the casual observer. With each subtle change, Wilbert deftly organizes his arrangements into a constant visual ballet. Like Avery, his focused concentration on the depiction of common objects demonstrates his keen sense of balance and pictorial tension.

Wilbert's process of picture making is also deliberately calculated, from the first choice of store-bought items to the considered decision of what color to make the background. The main subjects of Wilbert's paintings are carefully articulated in advance to create dynamic color relationships (see, for example, *Tulips on Green*, 1999; fig. 12). Wilbert takes small liberties with the actual colors of an object in order to create better color harmonies. He explains, "Calibrating the color is a means of controlling the work's dramatic tension."[13] Wilbert paints his backgrounds in various color ranges and degrees of flatness, both to create balance and to provide contrast to the dimensional objects in the foreground (see, for example, the self-portraits, figs. 1, 3, 17, and page 116, all painted in his studio). He does not choose these colors to express his feelings or to create a mood. Rather, each color was chosen as a painterly variable in constructing a new

Still Life with Toy Car and Game Board
Figure 11

1979, Oil on canvas
60 × 48 inches
Collection of the Artist

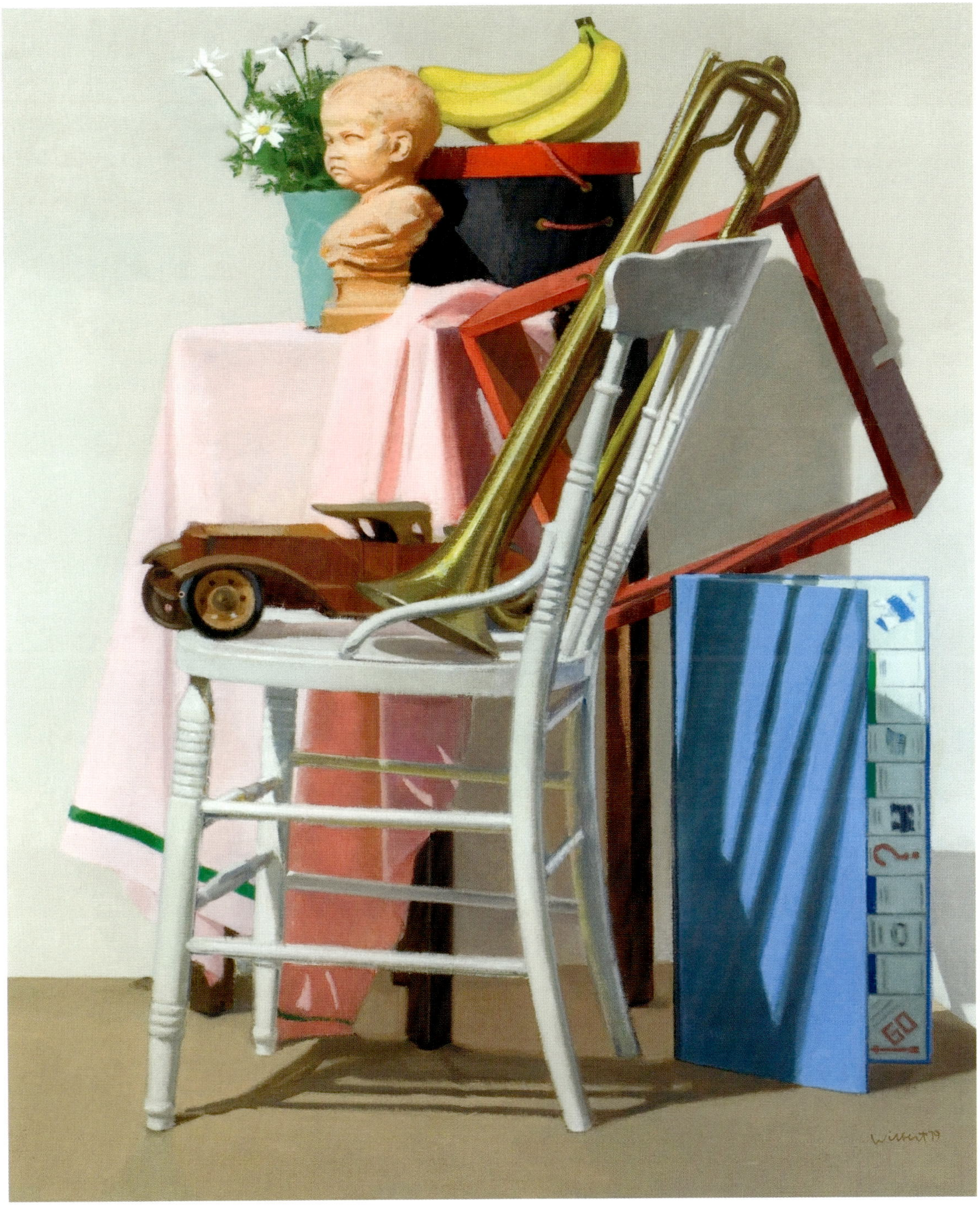

Tulips on Green
Figure 12

1999, Oil on canvas
22 × 18 inches
Collection of the Artist

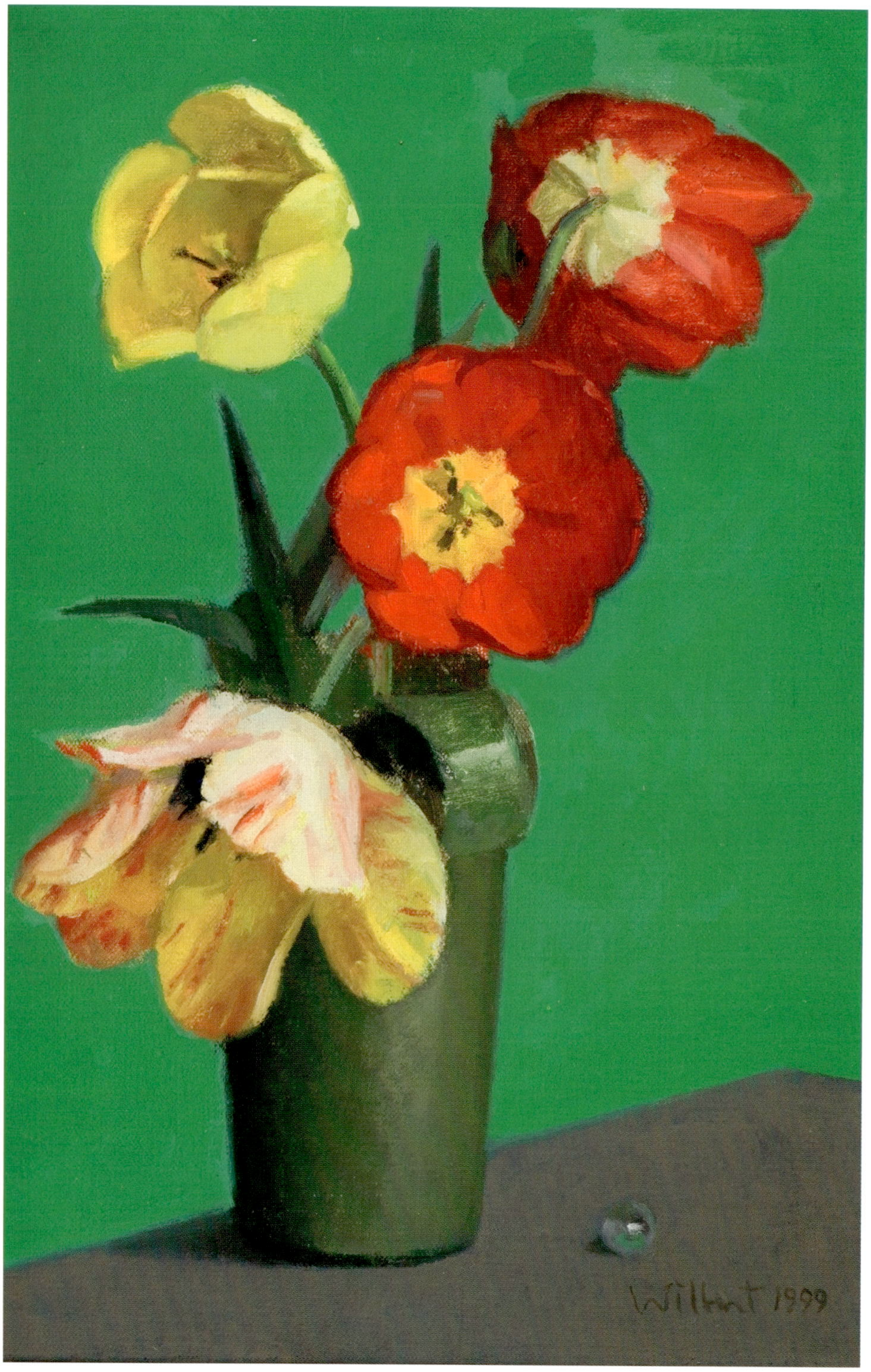

Two Nudes with Red Drape
Philip Pearlstein (American, b. 1924)
Figure 13

1965, Oil on canvas
53¾ x 70⅛ in. (136.53 x 178.12 cm)
Houston Museum of Fine Arts PP12574
Photo: Courtesy of Betty Cuningham Gallery

formal relationship because, like Avery, Wilbert is very sensitive to the final painted surface.

> *"While remaining faithful to his intention to record his visual experience, the artist working from a model is guided by his particular interests to concentrate on the forms, or on their spatial relationships, or on light and color."— Philip Pearlstein*[14]

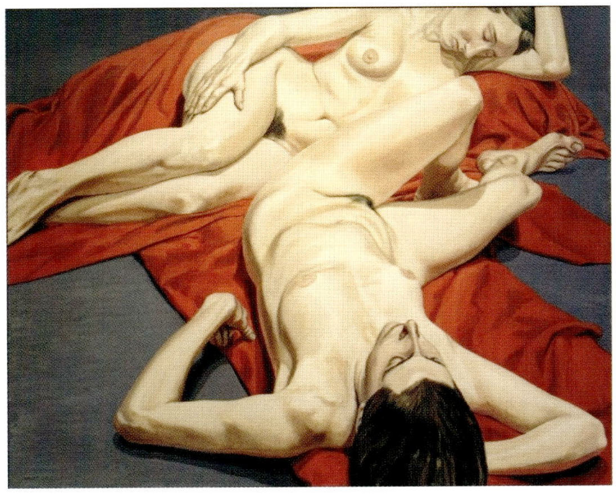

Another influence on Wilbert was Philip Pearlstein, a radical and outspoken artist who advocated for the place of observational painting against the dominance of Abstract Expressionism. In "Figure Paintings Today Are Not Made in Heaven," written in 1962, Pearlstein claimed that a straightforward realist approach to depicting the visible world was viable because elements of abstraction were still present within natural forms. His representational paintings are notable for their fidelity to the appearance of life models and studio interiors. Ironically, his work was viewed both as regressive and as a breakthrough.

Both Pearlstein and Wilbert are adamant in maintaining that their paintings have no narrative intent and that they do not purposefully incorporate a psychological edge nor are they expressive of the human condition. Further, they do not use figurative subject matter for social or political uses—their approach as artists being primarily based on formal decisions. Pearlstein's subject is the nude figure, chosen because, lacking clothing or outside references, it enables him to avoid constructing a narrative within the painting (fig. 13). Instead, he concentrates on the shapes and compositional forces caused by the posture of the figures and the shape of the ordinary objects in his studio. He claims that by placing realistic forms in juxtaposition to one another, he and other artists interested in representation are capable of creating tension-filled compositions that are equivalent to the flat planes of completely abstract works. Wilbert's practice of direct observation is similar. He combines seemingly unrelated objects such as high-heeled shoes and apples for their compositional forms and with the desire to avoid an obvious narrative. Wilbert views the objects and models in his studio as utilitarian. In fact, he refers to both as "props."[15] This potentially de-humanizing term also has a dramatic connotation, which is fitting because Wilbert admits that, "theatricality is something I accept."[16] Costumes are present throughout Wilbert's paintings, from the hat on his wife in *Gretchen with Veiled Hat* (1972; see fig. 15) to the many paintings of Gerry the Fool (see pages 94 and 95). When making decisions in his studio, Wilbert often chooses new and unexpected props, but he wants to be "careful not to be too entertaining."[17]

Pearlstein's positional text of 1962 summarized a new movement composed of painters who were working with representation in direct opposition to the mythic ideals of abstraction. They were consciously attempting to deal with the champions of abstraction, de Kooning and Pollock, whose influence was omnipresent. These artists, among them Chuck Close, Richard Estes, and the sculptor Duane Hanson, were generically labeled "realists." Much like Close, Wilbert paints with a crisp representational style but doesn't identify his work as realist. He remains faithful to a real subject but does not focus on microscopic details, as do Hanson or Estes, whose extraordinary, hyperreal representations fall in the realm of trompe l'oeil. Instead of using a fine, one-hair paintbrush

Male Nude with Glasses
Figure 14

1981, Oil on canvas
48 × 88 inches
Collection of the Artist

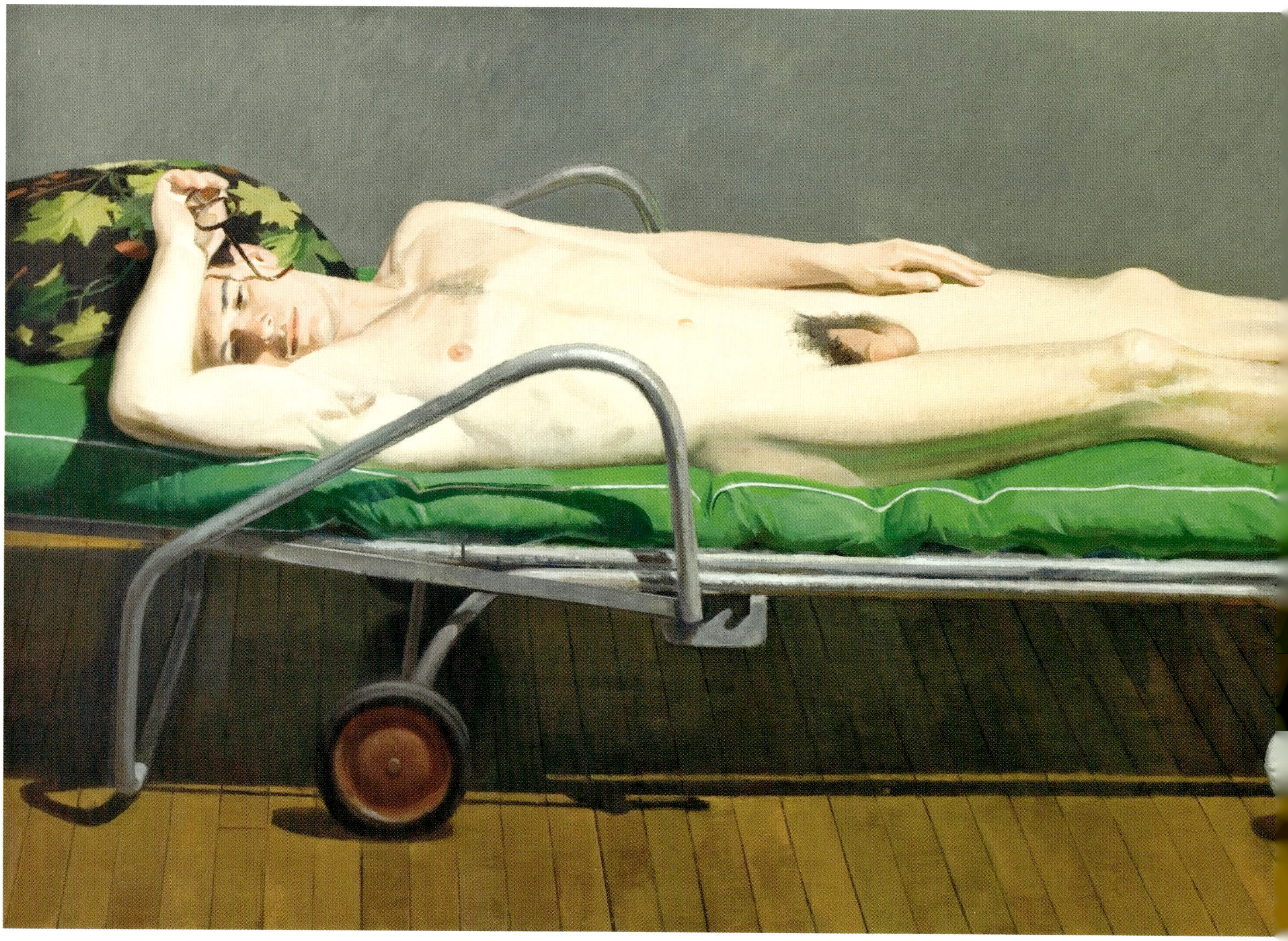

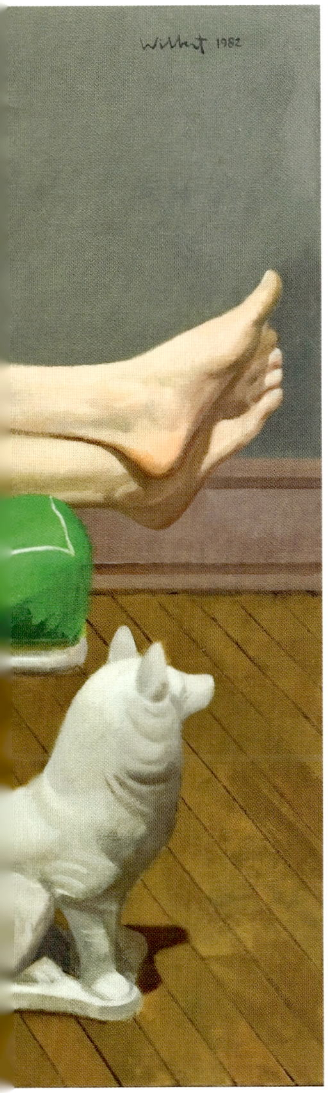

to hide the process of its creation, Wilbert carefully articulates each subject with a variety of brushstrokes. A quick glance at the large painting *Male Nude with Glasses* (1981; fig. 14) reveals that different types of mark making are used to depict the figure and the accompanying objects, whether a green lawn chair or wooden floorboards. The subject is real, but the treatment acknowledges the "truth" of the flat surface, demonstrating how Wilbert captures the equivalence between the multiple aspects of a painting and thus eludes categorization as a realist.

The investigation of the figure, landscape, and still life has occupied artists throughout the long trajectory of art history, and despite contemporary concerns with social commentary or political statements, these traditional genres remain fruitful territory for exploration. Like other painters throughout history, Wilbert yearns for a new perspective and better pictorial solutions. He sees it as his personal challenge to continually ruminate on the same forms, while orchestrating an original composition that is neither formulaic nor predetermined. By constantly repositioning himself in relationship to the same figures and objects, the artist discovers new truths about his immediate environment. Through the perpetual act of making innumerable formal decisions in depicting the same humble subject matter, Wilbert navigates a representational painting territory on the edge of reality.

Notes

1. Elizabeth Murray, quoted in Giovanna Constantini, "Life Painter," *Hour,* April 2000, p. 68.
2. This movement was sometimes called Photorealism. Some artists who took the aims of realism further were called Hyperrealists.
3. Robert Wilbert, quoted in Constantini, p. 68.
4. An interview with Morandi, recorded on April 25, 1957, by the Voice of America for the United States Information Service (Presto Recording Corporation, Paramus, New Jersey).
5. "The feelings and images aroused by the visible world are very difficult to express and are perhaps inexpressible with words because they are determined by forms, colors, space, and light": Georgio Morandi, quoted by Renato Miracco, "Nothing Is More Abstract Than Reality," in *Morandi: 1890–1964,* ed. Maria Cristina Bandera and Renato Miracco (Milan: Skira Editore S.p.A., 2009), p. 295.
6. Wilbert does not completely detach himself from human interaction with his models. He chooses people not only because they are interesting to look at but also because they are individuals he can spend hours talking to.
7. Willem de Kooning, "What Abstract Art Means to Me," written for a symposium held at the Museum of Modern Art on February 5, 1951; reprinted from *Museum of Modern Art Bulletin* 28, no. 3 (Spring 1951) and reproduced in Thomas B. Hess, *Willem de Kooning* (New York: Museum of Modern Art, 1968), pp. 143–44.
8. Ibid, p. 144.
9. Willem de Kooning and Jackson Pollock had both referenced male and female symbols through their work of the 1940s. But after de Kooning's *Women* series was exhibited, Pollock told de Kooning he abandoned "it," meaning abstraction.
10. Milton Avery, quoted in *Contemporary American Painting,* exh. cat. (Urbana, IL: College of Fine and Applied Art, University of Illinois, 1952), n. p.
11. Ibid.
12. Robert Wilbert, quoted in *Still Working: Underknown Artists of Age in America*, ed. Stuart Shedletsky (Seattle and London: University of Washington Press, 1994), p. 78.
13. Robert Wilbert, in an interview with Gere Baskin, December 2010.
14. Philip Pearlstein, "Figure Paintings Today Are Not Made in Heaven," *Art News* 61, no. 4 (Summer 1962): 39, 51–52. Reproduced in *Theories and Documents of Contemporary Art: A Sourcebook of Artists' Writings*, ed. Kristine Stiles and Peter Selz (Berkeley, CA: University of California Press, 1996), pp. 229–32.
15. Robert Wilbert, in an interview with the author, May 22, 2010.
16. Ibid.
17. Ibid.

Gere Baskin

The Donald Morris Gallery Years 1961–95: Interview with Florence and Steven Morris

When major art galleries first began to appear in Detroit in the late 1950s and early 1960s, they filled a large cultural void. The Donald Morris Gallery played an important role in this development and had a wide-ranging and significant effect on the city's art community. Donald and Florence Morris saw their mission as educational and sought to create an informal space in which artists and a population interested in art history and connoisseurship could interact. They hoped to develop an informed audience that would discover new meaning and fulfillment in their lives through exposure to major artists and exhibitions. Not only was the gallery a resource for artists and scholars, who were welcome to use its extensive library and files, it was also a Saturday afternoon gathering place for discussions about art (and University of Michigan football) and a place to meet internationally recognized artists such as Clement Meadmore, Philip Pearlstein, and Al Held, not to mention the venue for intimate musical soirees. The Morrises believed that one of the gallery's primary functions was to nurture and promote artists, not only by exhibiting their art but also by publishing catalogues of their work and otherwise documenting it for posterity.

Among the artists catalogued and exhibited at the Donald Morris Gallery were Milton Avery, David Barr, Alexander Calder, Joseph Cornell, Willem de Kooning, Jean Dubuffet, Al Held, Lester Johnson, Joan Miro, Picasso, Philip Pearlstein, and Robert Wilbert.

The Morrises embraced Robert Wilbert as an artist, friend, and intellectual equal, and there can be no doubt of their impact on his career. At an early juncture, Robert found in Donald and Florence both encouragement and a profound belief in his ideas. Perhaps just as importantly, as the gallery gained national and international recognition, Wilbert was afforded access to the work of many emerging artists who would play major roles in the world of contemporary art, and his own art was given wide exposure, beyond the success he already enjoyed among Michigan collectors.

With the task of marketing his new work being handled by the gallery, Wilbert was now better able to focus on developing his artistic ideas and abilities. Another boon was that Donald and Florence did not pressure him to constantly produce new work but rather worked to establish a relationship of mutual respect, trusting that Robert would be most productive if allowed to work at his own pace—an approach that proved beneficial to both the artist and the gallery and that is particularly consistent with Robert's basic personality, which is one of measured decision making. For Wilbert, life in all its aspects—creative, intellectual, everyday—is a slow, dignified dance.

This is particularly true in the studio, where the structure of a painting is constantly being compared to reality, whether that is a model, a still life, or a landscape. The vigorous scrutiny necessary to place all the elements of a painting into a cohesive, but not necessarily realistic, whole is palpable in his works. Surprise always exists in the placement of disparate elements, in their spatial relationships, and in the choice of color.

The following tape-recorded interview with Florence Morris and her son Steven regarding their relationship with Robert Wilbert took place in October 2008. It focuses on the period from 1961 to 1995, when the Donald Morris Gallery represented his work.

Gretchen with Veiled Hat
Figure 15

1972, Oil on canvas
48 × 48 inches
Collection of the Detroit Institute of Arts
Gift of Susanne Feld Hilberry in memory of her grandmother, Sara Wolf Kraus, F82.27

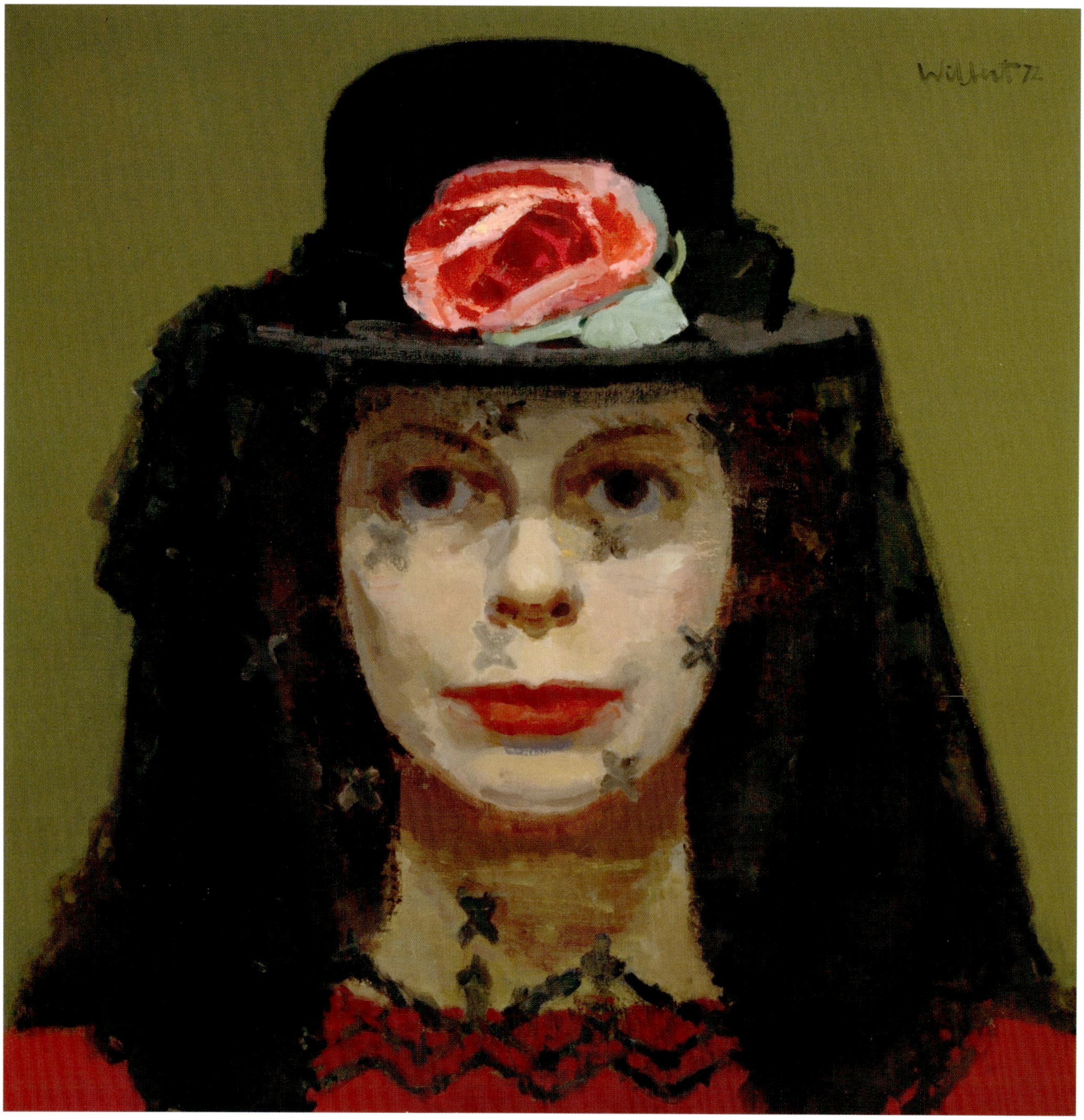

GB Gere Baskin, *interviewer*
FM Florence Morris
SM Steven Morris

GB

How did the relationship with Robert Wilbert begin?

FM

Well, he came to the gallery. He never said, I'm an artist and I want to show you my work—never. We liked him and then we found out that he taught art and that he had been showing his work at this gallery that was in a frame shop. Anyway, we suggested coming to look at his work. So we went to his apartment in Highland Park, this is around '62, '63, I think '62 [Wilbert's relationship with the gallery actually began in 1961 when he participated in a group exhibition], and we loved his paintings. I just thought he was a good artist. I liked his vision and his attitude and...everything about him. And so did Donald. We really felt a great rapport with him and his wife Gretchen. He was a very sophisticated artist visually—and very knowledgeable.

There were never any signed agreements. It was like the shake of a hand and we would then represent him. To this day, our relationship is so important, as is my belief in him. I think he was inspired by our attitude, too. Robert is not just an artist we represented. We had a firm commitment to his work. We had a belief in what his goals were, what he was about as an artist. We worked with his judgment of readiness. We never said, can we come up to your studio and see what you're doing? We knew Robert would invite us when he was ready.

Robert never produced large quantities of work so we couldn't exhibit him frequently. There were periods when we had enough for a watercolor exhibit, but not a painting show. We respected him for that, because he didn't release work from his studio that he didn't feel was ready. He edited his work.

GB

I think he still has that integrity. When I started cataloguing Robert's paintings in 2006, I came across so many works that were unsigned and I said, "Robert, this is of one of your sons. Why didn't you ever sign it?" He said, "Well, I always think I'm going to get him back in here."

FM

At the time he wouldn't release them because he was not confident enough that they were what he was trying to attain. I remember going into the studio and we thought he was finished with something, but he said "no, it's not finished yet." I respect that. He's not going to knock something out. A portrait has to be a work of art first to Robert. I have so much respect for him. We had a demand for the work and a lot of dealers would have been a little impatient. We wanted him to show in New York, but there were very few paintings to prepare for New York because his exhibits at our gallery [in Detroit] sold out.

GB

That was when Robert was awarded a National Endowment for the Arts Fellowship and took a leave of absence from Wayne State University from 1977 to 1979 and moved to New York with his family.

GB

Did you send Robert's work to other dealers?

FM

We did send work to the Roger Ramsay Gallery in Chicago and also sent a solo exhibit to John C. Stoller & Company, an excellent dealer in Minneapolis.

GB

What was the response of other dealers to him?

FM

There was a great deal of interest and respect for the work. Dealers thought he was a master painter and recognized, as we did, a psychological aspect that is very subtle. I don't think Robert's fully aware of it. I've never discussed it with him. I see that intensity in the portraits of Gretchen. My favorite is in the Detroit Institute of Arts collection, *Gretchen with Veiled Hat* [1972]. It is also apparent in his figure paintings, which include objects that create a psychological tension and mystery.

GB

What other elements do you see in his paintings?

FM

Oh, I think he's a great colorist and composer. There is a restraint and directness. Nothing in the paintings is superficial or superfluous.

GB

What artists do you think influenced him?

FM

I think that everyone has...as Picasso said, a mother and a father. I think that he has great admiration for [Max] Beckmann, and I saw some of Beckmann's influence on him.

GB

What about Cézanne?

FM

Cézanne is the father of most twentieth-century artists. I mean, you cannot get away from it. Cézanne teaches everyone! I think that American painting has had a great influence on Robert. People like Sargent and [Walter] Kuhn.

GB

Who else would you say he was influenced by? Sargent, Kuhn, Cézanne, who else?

(Steven Morris joins the conversation)

SM

Manet...and American painters like Sargent, Eakins, and...[Robert] Henri. Not the ashcan aesthetic, but American, late nineteenth-century European-American. I think it's subliminally there. I don't think it's a conscious thing. I think consciously, he's looking at Manet; he's looking at Sargent and Fantin Latour. He's looking at all art.

FM

Absolutely, and as time goes by I think Manet, Velázquez, and [Georgio] Morandi. One of the great influences is Chardin.

SM

Chardin, that's right. I'm sure he looked at our Balthus show. If you look at Bob's work after the Balthus show, the surfaces of his paintings are a little changed. He tries to mediate, not the '50s or early '60s work, but the work that we carried, committing to a kind of representational realism.

GB

But he does not think of himself as a realist?

SM

He's a realist, but he's interested in abstract issues. Rather than focusing on subjectivity of the figure, he's interested in it as a tool for addressing visual spatial issues.

FM

There's a mutual respect between Pearlstein and Wilbert.

SM

Like Pearlstein, Bob is much more concerned with visual spatial tension. As he has developed, he has more in common with the later black-and-white work of Al Held. It's about space. Originally when Pearlstein committed to the realism of the figure, it was about trying to focus on the figure and delineation...Bob is more traditional than Pearlstein. He is more accepting of the modernist premise, from Manet to current times. He's much more adherent to the modernist dictum. Pearlstein breaks the dictum by opening space up again, illusionistic space. Bob is not interested in illusionistic space, although there is illusion in his work.

FM

Do you feel the tension in Robert's figurative work?

SM

Different kinds of tension, I think, in terms of how he's studying his figure, his objects in space. There are metaphysical and atmospheric elements. Bob could make a very realistic figure...in other words like photorealism or the realism of the academy. He could paint a three-dimensional object in space. He's not interested in that. Bob wants to stay within the space and only round out the figure, the flesh of the face or the arm. He won't use sharp highlights, but just enough that you understand what's being portrayed as a three-dimensional object. He's interested in the shapes and the use of negative space, the contours and moving your eye through negative and positive space. The objects in the negative areas—they're so well-knitted. That's traditional art. He's interested in color, maybe a little like Avery.

FM

He's said it several times, "you know Avery just gets better and better." Did you hear that from him?

GB

Yes

SM

The other thing is he doesn't get juicy in his painting. He doesn't get oily-juicy. He also doesn't get dry and pasty and frescolike, like Balthus did in the late '50s and early '60s. Like every artist, he's exploring and trying to mine out a space that is a visual experience.

SM

Here's the difference between an academic painter and Bob, or an illustrator and Bob. The illustrator could have a sense of quickness in capturing a moment—Bob doesn't do that. An academic will make everything be really perfect and delineated—reproduce...that's not Bob either. He establishes the object and does it until it's right. If you look at Picasso and Matisse, they only do what's necessary to get the job done. Once it's done, that's it. They don't over-finish. That's not Bob. He's getting it until it's there. If there is illusion, color, and shadow to give form to the flower or any object, that's enough.

GB

Watercolor was one of the first classes Robert taught at Wayne State University. He has continued to revert to that medium throughout his career. What are your thoughts in regard to that body of work?

SM

The Lake Huron seascapes are very physical. Bob is actually in front of the sunrise at 4 a.m., ready to go and getting it down and changing things. They're really paintings. They are not just pictures. Lesser artists make pictures about how beautiful it is. He is communing with nature, like Avery. That's why Bob and Avery are poets. They're communing with nature, and they're integrating what they see. Poets are often quiet, or let me put it this way, their poetry is quiet.

FM

That's what Van Gogh did. He was capturing the moment.

SM

An emotional moment. That's why Bob is closer to Matisse in just putting what's necessary down. He's a little fussier because he wants to delineate things a little more, but that's American.

SM

Once there was a client who was interested in a Wilbert painting—interested on a lot of levels. He had some experience in the arts, but his experience went only so deep. He was looking at a painting of Bob's and one part bothered him. The color—"why did he make that line green?" One of the things that the client didn't understand was that he was projecting what he wanted the painting to look like. He was projecting what he thought was the right composition, the right color. These were his projections. Now, Bob's world is an ordered, settled world. He does things to move your eye. That's why he's a modern artist, not a traditional artist. So visually he's going to bring you to one place, and as soon as you're focused on this spot, he's moves to the next area, integrating everything together. He's working in this tension of what's called space and form, art and color. The ribbon or ball or odd color is stopping you, making the scene a little more awkward than normal. Only a little, because Bob usually hones his hue balances pretty tightly. The client was looking at objects as pictures. He was not looking at them as paintings. He was not deep enough into the craft of looking. He had only gone to the level of what a picture looks like, or what he likes. He did not have, emotionally, a deep enough understanding of what Bob is creating to comprehend it.

SM

Bob is an observer and there's a detachment and objectivity. At the same time there is a lot of compassion and a lot of love in the work. The compassion and the love are not overt. There is restraint and objectivity because he's a professional artist trying to make a statement and trying to make art that has a "presence." He is a traditional artist in terms of formal art. Bob mediates form and subject evenly. There is great compassion in the work whether the subject is animate or inanimate.

GB

The careful building of structure in his painting is what keeps you looking.

FM

Yes. No question about it. I mean you want the painting to have that collective vital mentality or a compelling effect. I think that's very important to Robert.

GB

What were key criteria for you in looking at an artist's work?

FM

The artist has to be a trained artisan. He has to know his craft, his tools. That would be the first given. He's not a student learning how to paint. He has to be technically mature. Then, the second thing is what he has to say that will change the way we experience the world around us. We tended to look for artists who had their own vision of the world. They projected beauty, adventurousness, and challenge in their work. Robert has these qualities.

Early on, he was an artist who really understood what he was about and was very confident about what he wanted to express. He was gifted in knowing art history and his antecedents, and when we talked he knew he wanted to create a work of art that had presence. He understood the challenge of creating. For example, when he deals with a figure in a portrait, he's thinking primarily about the entire painting. He does touch on the human being and sets up certain tensions in the painting, whether it's the device of some object that the subject is holding or the hat they're wearing or other objects that inform the work.

GB

I think that describes the essence of Robert in a very particular way.

GB

How did Robert's view of art and yours coincide?

FM

Oh, I think that we have the same values when it comes to art.

GB
Were you aware of that immediately?

FM
Yes. Robert has really never changed. He's very consistent. He is his own person. We can discuss something even though we may not agree totally. He'll do his own thing. He has a confidence and security in himself.

GB
When you selected Robert and David Barr, both local Michigan artists, for the gallery, how did you balance that against what you had as a world view of the art market?

FM
Well, I felt that they were artists who would be able to hold their own with anyone internationally.

GB
What a compliment.

FM
I didn't feel that we had to be patrons of local art. I do believe in being supportive. However, working with an artist is a marriage, and it's a long-term marriage. You are not only committed to exhibitions and catalogues but to bringing the work to the attention of critics, professional colleagues, and other artists. I think that the role of the dealer is to do all of that, but if the artist's work doesn't justify it, nothing's going to work.

GB
The gallery is the first step, but there has to be a consensus built around the artist's work as the second step, right?

FM
Absolutely. I do believe that.

GB
What's the dealer's role in consensus building?

FM
The dealer doesn't make the artist. I don't believe in that. My dear friend, Pierre Matisse, once made a very important and succinct statement. He said, "I did not make my gallery. The artists made my gallery."

GB
You have been a dealer for over fifty years and made a difference in artists' lives and definitely enriched the cultural life in this particular city in many ways. As you continue in your profession what thoughts predominate in your thinking?

FM
We wanted to make a difference and a contribution to the cultural climate in Detroit. It was very exciting, and we had the time of our life! We loved going to work. Our profession became all-consuming. I still become emotional when I look at a great work of art, it moves me. I believe that art changes human beings. It makes them better human beings and enriches their lives. We would be uncivilized if we didn't have art, music, literature, dance, and theater. The arts produce a better world and a better human being.

Notes

Florence and Donald opened the Park Gallery in 1958 and in 1960 formed the Donald Morris Gallery, Inc. Although Donald has passed away, Florence and sons Mark and Steven have carried on the family passion for the arts. Mark and Steven have received art and art history degrees from University of Michigan and Oakland University, respectively. In 1987 a satellite office was added in New York. Currently, they are continuing their work by placing major works of art in museums around the world and advising and educating clients in connoisseurship

Donald Morris Gallery has been a member of the Art Dealers Association of America, Inc., since 1963 and has also served on the board of the ADAA. The gallery has membership in CINOA (La Confederation Internationale des Negociants en Oeuvres d'art), an organization comprising the leading art and antique dealer associations in twenty-six countries. Donald Morris was an original member and adviser in the formation of the Michigan Council of the Arts. Florence Morris received the Women in the Arts Award for her lifetime achievement in the arts from the Jewish Community Center of Metropolitan Detroit.

Ellen Phelan **Mr. Wilbert and Robert**

From *Wilbert 1956–1995: The Wayne Years, Community Arts Gallery*, Wayne State University, 1995

The first painting class I ever took was in 1963 or thereabouts, and it was at Wayne State with Robert Wilbert and David Mitchell. I was clueless. I felt some confidence (perhaps unwarranted) in my ability to draw—but paint? I was floundering and more concerned, as most students certainly are, with the image rather than the means of its making.

Robert stood behind me one day, watching what I was doing. I remember very well; I was painting a piece of blueberry pie. And then he kind of casually remarked, "Well, in the final analysis, every brush stroke 'is a form.'" This had the effect of inducing in me a kind of catatonia of self-consciousness, brush frozen in mid-approach and an overload of, at that moment, unassimilable information. But I've never forgotten it and, of course, its perfectly true: every brush stroke is a form.

I never doubted that Mr. Wilbert knew a lot of stuff that I very much wanted to know. Finally, that's all that a really good teacher can teach; what he knows. And if what he knows is complex, humane, deeply felt and very serious, then a student is lucky indeed.

Mr. Wilbert's actual teaching/critical method was quite indirect, perhaps a mild suggestion here or there; a thought about color. More important to me, by far, than any technical information, was the revelation of his extremely fluent and flexible way of thinking about painting and its options. From him, I slowly began to be able to identify and articulate for myself an expanding vocabulary of formal elements and to feel that I had "some choice in the matter," particularly when it came to changing something or finishing something, which are hard things to do in painting.

Perhaps it's a little like dream work in psychoanalysis. You must access and remember the dream via language; the language you use to tell it and sometimes the language embedded in the dream itself. Finally, what becomes subject to analysis is that choice of words and their associations. The actual images of the dream, however vivid, remain elusive and incommunicable. However, to quote J.M. Coetzee, "Words are coin. Words alienate. Language is no medium for desire. Desire is rapture, not exchange. It is only by alienating the desired that language masters it." There's the conflict—the distance between image and language makes writing about pictures and teaching painting into the difficult things that they are.

Mr. Wilbert gave great slide talks, eagerly awaited by all. At this time, one of my jobs was being the slide projectionist in art history classes, so I was particularly struck by the differences between Robert's talks and those of the art historians. Gone, of course, were the periods and dates. One grazed around happily on themes and sub-themes, ways of painting hands (perhaps) and of handling pictorial space (always). Art historians, it's true, never do seem to acknowledge how contingent and conditional paintings actually are; how precarious and, in fact, the opposite of inevitable. Robert (Mr. Wilbert) would always notice the oddness of choices, for instance, the funniness of corners—if they were funny. He'd think of other things the artist might have done, judge what was achieved and what was left dangling. This was beyond exhilarating; it opened a world.

We became friends, Mr. Wilbert and I, and I would often wander by to see him in his office, just to chat. Mr. Wilbert was very good at chatting. I think he developed this to some extent to help put students at their ease. Since, at this time, I was really very shy, I was extremely grateful.

Over time I feel that I've come to know Robert

very well. In large part I think this is due to his quite singular openness, honesty (a quality which he values very highly in the general scheme of things), and great transparency as an individual (which I can't help but equate with his very real goodness). I've come to know Robert—the night-owl, the smoker (who doesn't inhale), the terrible driver (who insists on looking at you when he speaks). Robert (whom I think of as the quintessential Libra)—who must see every argument from both sides and moreover, wants to see the good in everyone. Robert—loyal generous and very kind (unless, God help you, you wind up on his bad side. I know of only one or two that have). Robert—the bemused, the proud and completely devoted husband of Gretchen (the Redoubtable), who had assumed mythic grandeur in my eyes before we had ever met and whom I was delighted to find to be mythic indeed. Robert—the always good, proud and sometimes anguished father of Matthew and Laura and Ben. Robert—the worrier, the fusspot, the producer of the annual, ever-expanding family portrait Christmas card which now might arrive by August if we're lucky, or more likely, by October. Robert—the serious Catholic. Robert—the collector, the inveterate haunter of flea markets and junk stores who, periodically conscience stricken, begins an attempt to clean out the attic, the garage, or the shelves, only to bog down in interesting newspaper clippings. And perhaps most strikingly, the Robert—who has always been fascinated by the daily, the ordinary, the absolutely mundane. (He muses for hours on chance remarks overheard in line at the supermarket; personally, I flee.) And, finally, Robert—with his very high standards and trenchant intelligence about painting—"Mr. Wilbert."

Once, when I was older, maybe I was twenty-seven or twenty-eight, I must have asked Mr. Wilbert something like "what was the point of it all; why would one go on doing this difficult thing?" He said that he thought "that artists could be spiritual examples." What a noble and ennobling ideal and one that I've pondered a good bit in the intervening years! Do I agree? Well, I know plenty of artists who are pretty miserable human beings, but then their best part often appears only in their work. And I know some artists who seem to me to be Olympian in every way. It is an odd and for the most part a very lonely occupation, one that requires quite a bit of philosophical stamina over the long haul. These general perceptions would seem to apply historically as well; at least as far as we are aware of individual biography.

Painting, on the other hand, seems to have an amazing transparency, where one reads through the work of art into the artist's personality and character. Any falseness is certainly easy to spot; any vainglory or pretension, any timidity or hesitation. But honesty, originality, the authenticity of an inner vision: these are blazingly apparent.

In Robert's work there is a fundamental allegiance to the seen and to the concentrated act of seeing clearly. This allegiance, although it may seem to be so basic and so obvious—stated simply, after all, he is a "realist"—has a much larger philosophical, even a metaphysical, dimension. (Structure is always metaphor and synecdoche.) It is as though the paintings tell us that the act of seeing clearly and inclusively will reveal a mysterious and unexpected perfection that is there in the world if we only take the time to "see."

The complex organization of the large figure paintings and still-life compositions have a sense of the improvisatory and arrested. (One gets the feeling that Robert doesn't so much plan these things as that he lets them sneak up on him.) There is a built-in paradox, a tension between the glimpsed and the momentary, and that which is apprehended, captured, and by slow observation/analysis and intelligent description, held.

It's almost a photographic impulse—that decision to include all that exists in the framing field. Robert however does eschew the automatic mediation of photography and always paints from direct observation. Strange pieces of things enter at the edges, sometimes these shapes are all but inexplicable, but all are given their due, their proper weight, their just attention. As though by this dissection, this peeling away of the layers of vision and focus, one can contain and hold and, by the act of attention, imbue with meaning the essential strangeness of any seemingly random juxtaposition—a broken chair, a tipped tricycle, a stuffed dog, a man in whiteface, a battered drum, a bunch of bananas.

His accumulation of silent objects (triumphant loot of all those flea market excavations) are things chosen, I think mainly, or at least, first, for their "paintability." They must not be too little: not too fussy. (One of Robert's favorite words in painting is "broad." He likes things that have "broadness." He also often says "described" instead of "drawn" or "painted"—an interesting distinction.) These are things that then take on their own strange, associative life. These silent objects, more and more now coupled with the model, simultaneously suggest/imply yet defy/disdain narrative possibilities. They are the furniture of a complex and, in its own way, an austere sensibility.

Ultimately, color is the key. As Robert continues to be increasingly involved in a project which conflates the figure and still life—two genres that both lend themselves to endless layerings of spatial complexity and composition—color still holds sway. It is an art of edge and juxtaposition (shape to shape), rather than outline, and all the variety of surface and texture are employed: matte things, shiny things, transparent and opaque, things in front of and things behind, highlights, half-lights, shadows. All the array and panoply of things in the world as they are acted upon by light are given their own right color. There is real mastery here and the simultaneous pleasure and deep unease of verisimilitude.

I begin to understand, perhaps, how these powerful works elevate Robert's interest in the "daily, the ordinary, the absolutely mundane" into a kind of metaphysics. I am deeply moved by his disciplined willingness to search out and value a hidden beauty and order in the apparently random and to allow the detritus of the studio, the odds and the ends of the commonplace, to share the stage and be webbed and linked inextricably with the more obvious "subject"—with the more apparent actor.

Marsha Miro

Interview with Robert Wilbert, 1977

The following is an edited excerpt from an interview with Robert Wilbert that Marsha Miro conducted for the Archives of American Art.[1]

You were born on October 9, 1929, in Chicago. Can you tell us a little about your childhood and how it relates to your development as an artist?

We lived on the South Side of Chicago. It was a very stable neighborhood, mixed national origins, a lot of Germans, Polish, and Irish. I just remember a kind of freedom and the neighborhood activities that I think all children are involved in. I have a sister who is seven years older than I...Until I went to school, I didn't know anybody beyond the confines of one small block. Life was easy. My mother was at home—she didn't work. My father always had a job. It was during the Depression but I don't think we felt we were suffering...When I was six I started attending a Catholic school where the teachers were Dominican nuns. It was a very disciplined kind of situation. I went there for the eight years of grade school...There was really no training in art. Of course if you were interested in art there were things you could do after school...In 1939, when I was nine, my family became members of the Art Institute of Chicago, for ten dollars a year. Membership included Saturday classes for children and also adult classes in life drawing. They were held once a week, sketch classes from the model. I went to those classes with my sister, and by the time I was ten I was going by myself on the bus. Those experiences were useful because they were unusual and nobody else I knew did that, and it was a kind of identification with art in a special way, which pleased me. The instructors used to give an assignment to the students. You would go home and make some kind of reference to this assignment. I remember the instructor holding one student's work up and there was a murmur in the hall and everybody started to shout that it was" a copy." The teacher cast it aside. This was the first clue that I had that you should not copy. I had never had any idea of what making your own thing meant.

I attended those classes right through high school. I went to life drawing classes where they had models in bathing suits. I had experiences in drawing the figure at ten, eleven, twelve through seventeen, that most young people probably would not have had. And these were in the nature of very quick kinds of poses. I still have most of those drawings. It's always been kind of interesting to me to know where I was or when I learned something. They don't look remarkable at all. But they do get better, just because one does get better as one goes along.

Once I got into [public] high school I enrolled immediately in the art class that they had. I had a teacher who, I'm sure, couldn't have been more inept, but I was just thrilled to be there. I think it was in my senior year that a young woman came who was full of ideas. Her name was Mary Cole. She was very good for me—had lively things for us to do. She really wasn't caught up with any kind of idea of modernity. She would bring flowers to class and we would make a composition with them. She would talk about composing, you know, more serious kinds of ideas than we had known before. But it had nothing to do with free expression. Mary Cole had studied with a nun in Chicago who was quite a good portrait painter and did portraits of wealthy families. Curiously enough, I got to know this nun very well myself, and I painted some in her studio. But that was Mary Cole's background, and somehow that traditional concern came to me, maybe in a secondhand way. That year I also went to regular adult classes at the Art Institute on Saturdays. The class was taught by Charlie Schrader. He had a method of teaching that was very strange. It was something about the figure having a great number, some thousands, of planes in it. We did frontal views of the head breaking things into planes. Actually they looked a little like Giacometti.

Was it cubist?

No. It was a peculiar goofy idea of anatomy. It had to do with analyzing the figure in planes and breaking it down.

At the same time I went to classes at the American Academy of Art. We were taught by a man I think was named Mosby. He taught portrait painting and I did learn something from him about color. It was the first time I had ever used real canvas. He told us how to make a dark that was darker than black. I can remember his insisting that hair never got as light as skin no matter how blond the model was.

Did you ever question him when he would say those things?

Well, the evidence on the stand was there. That might be true if you were talking about the light in the skin and not the dark in the skin. Who knows under what kind of lighting conditions. I remember there was a Chagall exhibit at the Art Institute at that time. I was surprised this man had no interest in modernism. He did think that Chagall was a marvelous colorist, but he didn't think there was any other value to his work.

I worked at home all the time. I did little still lifes. I did portraits. I did a standing portrait of my sister in 1946 or 1947, when I would have been sixteen or seventeen. She still has it hanging in her home. It doesn't look bad at all. I was very committed to art as my expression, not with any notion of it ever being a life work. When I got out of high school they gave me an award for art that they had never given before. I did all the stage design things, I did pictures for the school, pictures for myself, for the yearbook, cartoons for the newspaper. You know, everything that a young guy with a talent for drawing could do. There was a young fellow who was clearly the champ of us. I don't think he was really so talented, but he was extraordinarily skillful. We both competed for a scholarship [to the American Academy of Art] on graduation. And he won it. He never took the scholarship because he died that summer from a brain tumor. His names was Chavannes, like Puvis de Chavannes. I always wondered if there was some relationship. He had come from somewhere like British Honduras.

Were you conscious of being different from the rest of the children because of your interest in art?

No. I did most things that other people do...I did get used to going downtown by myself. I started by finding out about all the stores. And then, as I got older, I found out that there were art galleries. There was a gallery called the AAA Gallery, the Associated American Artists. They showed a lot of American scene people. They were the gallery that had those five-dollar prints that they sold. I think they were the first ones to make large editions of prints by people like Thomas Hart Benton and John Steuart Curry. That was an experience with paint and with paint handling of the day. I suppose this would have been 1943–46. I felt very free and quite special in being able to enter the art world that way and to see things that other people weren't seeing.

What about modernism?

I remember that I didn't particularly know what to make of a Chagall show at the Art Institute. Modern art? The Art Institute had all those Impressionists, and I can remember a big de Chirico—the one that has artichokes in it—a Lehmbruck bust. I think the stylization of Thomas Hart Benton might have been something for a minute. But you really taught yourself. I think that is what an artist does. You read books. You pick up a little of this. You pick up a little of that. You don't even know what you're doing. But my real exposure to national things and to more modern things came in college.

How did you decide on where to go to college?

I began to wonder if I should or could go to college. It wasn't clear to me if my family could afford to send me. I had a good friend who was at the University of Illinois at Champaign. She really urged me to come down and apply and be interviewed. When I was a senior I did go down. The only artist I knew who earned a living at it was a man at the Art Institute who did little watercolors and gave travel lectures. It seemed to me to be a kind of interesting life. The fact that I didn't get that scholarship turned out to be a marvelous break. The American Academy of Art was a terrible school, and I didn't know that...So, I asked Mary Cole if she thought I should study art. She said something like, "You always do things thoroughly, you always achieve whatever you want to do. On that basis I think you should do it if you want to." My family did not discourage me. Obviously, they had always encouraged me. I think I just announced that I was going to college, and they were agreeable.

The possibility of going to the Art Institute was very real...But I remember I saw all kinds of bohemian behavior in people, that I really didn't think was so terrific. I love books, so sometimes I would stop in bookshops in the University of Chicago area. There, too, I would see a kind of university type, which seemed to me to be very studied and kind of mannered and sort of overly intellectual. So maybe it was very natural to go to a place like the University of Illinois, where all kinds of farm people came, as well as a lot of people from Chicago, because it was a super school for many things other than art. I really wanted to get away from home too.

You enrolled there in 1947. You were a painting major?

Yes. Right away I was an art major. In your first year exactly half of the credit hours were in the studio arts. I did work for the newspaper right away. So when they had a preview for the press I went and got photographs for the newspaper. That spring they had a national art exhibition. The word "contemporary" was fashionable then and that was what it was called. It was an invitational and for the first year or two it was a competitive show. Later I think it became an invitational. The first year it was budgeted at $15,000. Half was for prizes and half for expenses. They planned to buy ten paintings from the show each year. I still remember some of the paintings that were in the show and some they bought [over the years]. They bought a Bradley Walker Tomlin...a Joseph de Martini...a large painting called *The Third Hand* by Hans Hofmann... So this show became something that I gave publicity to and then actually wrote a kind of criticism of it. My criticism was pretty limited. It was kind of smart and quick and judgmental. I think that show had a John Marin painting in it. If there wasn't a [Max] Beckmann in that show, there was one not long after...They published a great catalogue and all the artists wrote a statement that was printed in the back. The staff had certain favorites. Abraham Rattner was a great favorite. Later I reviewed faculty shows. I wasn't that courageous when it came to saying something about my own faculty. Later I wrote other kinds of stories, for example, what it meant to be a life model. I wrote feature stories. I was a real newspaper person.

How advanced were the art school staff?

The staff were not of that moment. They were open, but they didn't know what they were open to, or closed to. I think art teaching was not very good anywhere, except if you were at the Brooklyn Museum School with Beckmann or at Black Mountain. Maybe it would have been different there. The professors [at Illinois] were all gentlemen, and they worked at their art. Morris Graves would have been in their shows in those days. I don't think Mark Tobey is anyone they would have looked at. If there was craftsmanship in the work, people kind of understood it. From that very first [invitational] show they bought an early Philip Guston, when he was a figurative artist, with a very indirect way of painting. The only way I knew that you could paint was by putting a color down and dragging another on it. That's what everybody did. That gave it a quality and a richness, and it was really a European way of painting. I didn't know about the Germans. I knew about Klee. It was really the tail end of American scene painting. Maybe in New York there were other kinds of adventuresome painting at the Art of This Century Gallery, or something. There was a whole school called magic realism that had a sort of surrealist tack to it. There were a lot paintings of storefronts—people doing kind of sad-looking things. Loren MacIver, I think, was somebody you might have thought of at that time. The university might bring in a Pollock, because they meant for the show to be encompassing, but I don't think that's where their taste was.

What did the curriculum consist of?

I had one course in sculpture, or maybe a year of it, the whole time I was there. And it was terrible. It was the only thing I wasn't any good in. The classes were very big and there were a lot of GI's—it was just a giant operation—There was a great emphasis on drawing which served me, I think. And there was a great emphasis on a kind of craft of painting, which I'm sure influences me. There was a year of still-life painting. Life drawing was a continual activity there. The training in drawing had a kind of funny effect, in that it became quite difficult to move into a more modernist mode, because of that training. I can remember moments when it seemed as if... Well, I would look at Ben Shahn or at Max Weber, or maybe at Picasso—Picasso seemed very remote as a model—but I would look at how he did a hand, like a kind of stylization of a hand. You wondered if you could invent a stylization of a hand that would be your own. The hand seemed to be one part of the body that didn't stylize, or couldn't be abstracted very easily. So that kind of process of overcoming drawing and getting into a kind of more abstract, more modernist notion was somehow in your mind. But there was no pressure to do it. The life training was very academic. It was taught by a portrait painter. In our senior year he went on leave and we were going to have a more modernist teacher. We were all looking forward to that term because then we could do what we wanted to do. And then it was very hard to know what you wanted to do or what you were going to do, because we really weren't prepared for it and it wasn't part of our life.

What about painting technique and the relationship to design?

At the time we were being trained to paint more like Frans Hals or William Merritt Chase or anybody who paints directly. That's what made it so hard to accept or understand a Pollock with the oneness of form and paint. Or accept a de Kooning. For me it was not de Kooning's form as much as the paint handling that seemed raw. I mean you just couldn't do that. You just simply could not do that. It was not a beautiful surface. There was a lot of talk about the beauty of the surface.

In freshman design class I didn't know what design meant. They gave us all kinds of rules. I tried to apply them. The Bauhaus techniques, which went through all the universities in the country I think, hadn't reached us yet... I think also from my background, from my own nature perhaps, I was a very practical, pragmatic person and even really anti-intellectual in a certain sense. I mean, it [Bauhaus methods] seemed fancy. It seemed indulgent. I didn't want to see myself that way at that time. I can really understand it now and the value of it. But as it turns out that kind of flat-footed straightforwardness seems to be something that has served me. I would have been uncomfortable with anything that seemed, what we might have called arty, that seemed strained in any way.

There was just something about open-ended research that maybe would have been hard for me to understand, unless someone explained it. I must say that no one explained anything. No one suggested the value of an activity. When I think back on it, I'm just dazzled by the innocence with which people went through that school, and I think many art schools. Now, I understand that students don't hear half of what their instructors say and they misinterpret the other half. I say this in fairness to Illinois because I have some respect for them. So maybe marvelous things were being said to me and I didn't hear them.

By the time I was a senior I was doing paintings that were a little more sophisticated. Some of them I can still look at. They would look not so different from some of the paintings in those [annual] shows. But the quarrel I would have would be that maybe someone could have suggested a bigger vision—the reasons we were all there, what art was about. I really didn't know what it meant to those men I studied with.

You were searching for the answer to why people paint?

Yes. You went to school because you were talented, because you had certain kinds of skills. It's the most marvelous thing that very often young people go to school to be artists because they have skills, which then the art schools sort of discount. And then they find that art is about something else, and they may or may not have the mind for it.

Did you receive any art education outside of Illinois?

When I finished my junior year, I went to Colorado and studied with Julio de Diego. He was in a number of the annual shows at Illinois. I was a little interested in his work. He was a kind of Spanish gypsy. It was a very small class. We were all very close—Julio taught what he was doing at that time. Not so much the form of it but the technique. We did paintings on true gesso. We painted with casein paint and then glazed on this with oil. I went down to Boulder to the college there and saw an art exhibit. I saw Marsden Hartley. So I painted some things with sort of lumpy clouds. These seemed like a strong form. It was an interpretation of a cloud, the way you were searching for that design of a hand. It was finding a symbol for the thing or finding some way that transformed it from being what it really was, into art. So a lump in the sky for a cloud meant that it was closer to art than the cloud would be. That summer I painted a house, and I remember seeing shapes in a way I hadn't seen them before. I felt I had made some small discovery. I felt very much an artist that summer, maybe because the work had a kind of consistent vision. Most of the things were simplified, flattish, and I was working with this strange glazing technique.

The other important thing was to see this guy who was living as an artist and that was interesting. He was married to Gypsy Rose Lee and that seemed quite exotic. He lived fairly simply...I visited de Diego in New York where he had a studio full of magical things. He made little things that hung from the ceiling. He would pick up bones and scraps and webs of fabric. And I think he was a serious artist.

Your senior year brought two other commitments: the air force and marriage.

The Korean War started the summer I was in Colorado. I went back to Illinois. There was a real clear indication that people would be drafted. Seniors had the opportunity of going into accelerated R.O.T.C. classes where you could become an officer, and I did that. On graduation in 1951 I went into the air force with a two-year obligation. Curiously, I was assigned to an air base seventeen miles down the road from the University of Illinois. I didn't even leave campus.

I got married shortly after, in February of 1952. I met my wife Gretchen when I was nineteen and working in a large outdoor pageant in Chicago. It was on the lake shore and called the Railroad Fair...a celebration of a hundred years of the invention or the establishment of railroads. She was a singer in this pageant. In one scene I was a Chinaman, when they drove the Golden Spike for the meeting of the transcontinental railroads. She was a graduate of a music school in Chicago and had gone to New York to try her hand at theater, mostly at musical comedy.

We were married and lived in Champaign. I worked eight hours a day in the air force as an administrative officer.

How did you pursue your art?

During that time I enrolled as a graduate student at Illinois. It seemed kind of fancy, you, know, further study. I mean they used to say that in four years you were prepared to be a professional painter. I don't know if many people in art school went more than four years.

So whoever was teaching you might not have had more experience than you?

Maybe not too much. But in graduate school they were the older faculty. But I had the same people all over again except for the occasional visiting artist. I painted at night. No one was there. I worked, saw some of the other students. That final year I taught drawing to architectural students. I was a graduate assistant...I learned a lot. I didn't realize how much you learn when you're teaching. I found ways to indicate kinds of relationships between objects so they could be put down. I saw things increasingly in terms of relationships. And that is something that has never left me. And this led to an appreciation of Cézanne...and certain relationships in form. It was also a moment when I saw de Kooning and worked quite a bit like him, too much like him. But I felt that I really understood what the works were about spatially and how they were ordered.

Did you feel like you knew a lot? Or did you feel like you needed to know a lot more?

I thought I knew everything at that moment. Maybe it was just the fact that I really knew what I was seeing in a painting. In my final year I had some difficulty with the faculty because my work looked different from all the things they had anticipated. I can remember their urging me to put a very nice frame on my thesis painting, and I felt I was sort of being slipped underneath the door to my degree. Later they sent the painting around the country. Apparently they were prouder of it by then...In the painting there were two seated women, more abstract than de Kooning's women, more like {Jack} Tworkov maybe...But I didn't feel real supported by people on the faculty. It was just that they're trying to guide you and you're doing something that they don't think is good for you.

From there you went to Flint, Michigan?

I was married now. I wrote to many museums to see if they needed anybody to work in them, little museums anywhere. There weren't very many teaching jobs then. Abraham Rattner came to Illinois in the last year and a half I was there. He talked to me about working with him on a mural project that he might have. And his wife talked to me about working in a gallery she had in Greenwich Village in New York. On graduating I went to New York, but the mural project wasn't in the offing. I went to Washington, D.C., to the Smithsonian, where I had a friend who had just started working. I applied for exhibit preparation. He had taught at a little museum in Saginaw so maybe that was one of the reasons why I thought that was the route to go. He sent me a list of all the museums in the country, and I wrote to all of them. There was this position in Flint that was not generally known about. As it turned out, the man I applied to I had met when he taught at the University of Denver the summer I was there. I think Flint needed somebody in a hurry. I flew to Flint and got the job, which meant teaching adult classes at the Flint Institute of Arts. It also involved putting up shows and doing a certain amount of administrative work. Part of the job was teaching a class for Flint Junior College. The students came down from their campus to the Art Institute to take the class once or twice a week. The very next day after accepting the job in Flint I got a telegram offering me a job at Ohio State University. Of all the jobs in the country I had known about, the Ohio State job seemed to be the best one. I was really just crazy, heartbroken. I wrote to them and told them that I couldn't take the job, but that I certainly would be available the next year. I heard later that it wasn't such a marvelous place to teach. So I was really happy to go up to Flint. I was paid more. It was an eleven-month job instead of the nine-month jobs that were usually available in universities. I had friends in Saginaw…I was just so glad to get a job.

I had been in Michigan. I knew the work of Zoltan Sepeshy [at Cranbrook Academy of Art]. I knew the work of John Carroll. The man I knew from Colorado was Clarence Van Duzer. He was director of the museum in Flint. He was an artist. The important thing he told me was that you should always put your investment in your work, not in your position.

Chicago was never an alternative for you?

At one point, I applied to the University of Illinois in Chicago to teach architects to draw and got an interview. I tried for a job with the Art Institute of Chicago. It seems preposterous to me now—presumably the city was full of artists, of people who had been at it longer than I had. But I didn't get any job there. I guess I was in a traffic jam when I was thinking Chicago wasn't any place to live. It didn't seem attractive to me then. Now it looks terrific to me. I love the feeling of that city. I like their sort of uppityness and always the effort to be some kind of a center.

How was the art scene in the Flint area?

Steve Davidek [a painter] was our closest friend. We knew no one in Detroit except former roommates and fraternity brothers. The architects we did know were all in Detroit so we would come down to see them. They worked for Saarinen or Smith, Hinchman and Grylls. It was kind of exciting. We'd go to the General Motors Tech Center and to Saarinen's office and see the planning for that. [At work] I was sort of off on my own. One of the people who came to Flint to teach was Svea Kline. She was a fixture around Cranbrook. She always said she was [Carl] Milles's assistant. She taught ceramic sculpture classes in Flint. And it was in that way, that eventually I got to Wayne State University. Svea was at a dinner at the old Stockholm Restaurant and some Wayne State University people were there. Wayne Claxton, who was head of the department, said they were looking for a teacher to take Louise Nobili's place, while she was on sabbatical. It was to teach watercolor. Svea told Claxton that she knew this "nice boy" in Flint. I had been doing watercolors there…So it was reasonable for me to apply for this job. I think Bill Woolfenden [then a curator at the Detroit Institute of Arts] and David Mitchell [teacher at Wayne] were coming in the spring of 1956 to jury the Flint Annual Show. I had paintings in the show and they were to see what the paintings were like. I did get a chance to come down to Wayne for an interview. That is how, eventually, we got from Flint to Wayne State...Also, some lady in Flint had a daughter at Kingswood School [Cranbrook] in Bloomfield Hills, and there was a moment when it looked as if I might go there to teach. They'd give me a little money, and I'd live in a tower or something. And maybe the opening at Wayne came about the same time.

But what about your work in Flint?

We were in Flint for two years. That was a most marvelous moment with my painting. I was out of school. There were no teachers watching you. You were a free man. I've mentioned that de Kooning had been such an emphasis in my final year or two in graduate school, and I continued that kind of work in Flint. I painted and I did these watercolors. I did some drawings, curious drawings in ink that were very severe and in some ways I think look a little like Graham Sutherland, in that the space was all divided and very tightly formed.

How did you feel moving from Flint to Detroit?

The Flint people wrote us letters when we were leaving. I had won a prize in some state competition, and it seems to me that the Flint newspaper referred to it, you know, like on the editorial page and said it was sad they were losing us. When we came to Detroit I was excited about being in a city again. I loved it—the buildings, the oldness, the signs, the expressways. It was a job and it was a city and the possibilities seemed great.

What was the art department at Wayne about? Where was the curriculum? Who taught what?

At that time Wayne was not yet a state school. It was under the Detroit Board of Education. The art department was in what had been a large private home—a small building for an art building. I met the faculty. David Mitchell, who was teaching painting, had been in Europe on a Fulbright. Pete Gilleran's teaching load consisted of some painting and some advertising design. So he and David were teaching oil painting. Louise Nobili was teaching watercolor painting. Mary Jane Bigler was teaching watercolor part-time, as well as some course to home economics students. They had a design course for home ec students. It was less professional than the design course for artists. Now so many of the staff take leaves and have more time for painting, but that was not the case at that time. I think Louise was the first member of the staff after Wayne Claxton to get one. In any case, I was hired for a year to take Louise's place. I explained that I wouldn't leave the job I had, if I didn't think I could stay. Claxton, who was head of the department, said that that was not impossible. I would be teaching painting. My experience was that you didn't teach painting unless you had been around a place for many years and other people had died and then you could teach painting because that was really the desired thing. Most of the artists and the faculty wanted to do that. So it seemed marvelous luck to be able to do that only two years out of school. There was a show of Wayne students work up when I came for the second interview. There was a great emphasis on "craftsmanship," or finish. A lot of the work was influenced by [Otto] Feininger...It seemed to me that his was a kind of traditional space with simply a kind of geometry applied to it. It wasn't something I thought very much of. It was a cubist kind of emphasis. Claxton was very much influenced in his own work by Feininger. I think the students were given little balsa sticks to print those lines on the paper with. It had its greatest effect in watercolor. I think Louise's paintings of those days and Mary Jane Bigler's had that cubist emphasis. The people at Wayne put great store in the Moholy-Nagy book *Vision in Motion* and the *Language of Vision* book by [Gyorgy] Kepes. And I think because they did that, I just chose another route. I wanted to be my own man.

The whole thing was so different. I mean we wore suit coats to class in the early days. I don't know who it was that first didn't. When you were in class you wore a lab coat over it. We bought these mechanics coats at a used-clothing store. Every student wore one.

How did you separate yourself out as a teacher?

My memory is that still lifes were set up with a great kind of precision and clarity and a kind of built-in sense of the designing—handsomeness. So my alternative to it was really an older one. I think from some experiences I had at Illinois of really cluttering up space with lots of stuff. I would have still lifes that had hundreds of things in them, and the students could choose to paint all or part of it. In that period I did a lot of watercolor. I didn't have studio space outside of my dining room, so every night I just did watercolors.

The department had fifteen full-time staff members and a few graduates and people from the community who taught. It was a very congenial and close group. This may have been because many people were trained at Wayne, and if they weren't trained at Wayne they were students of Wayne Claxton. There was a lot of talk about kinesthetics and that came, I think, from Claxton, whose wife, Margaret Dolber, was a professor of dance at the University of Wisconsin. Some of this carried over into life drawing, for instance. They did very quick drawings. There was a lot of emphasis on doing them. There wasn't so much probing of the forms. I think this also carried over into watercolor. We would have called this empathy in some ways, that somehow your activity in producing the reflection of, say, a figure that was posing in front of you had something to do with how you felt in terms of reacting to the muscle strain, and so that was there. There was a good deal of Bauhaus influence. That, I think, was everywhere. This notion of the kinesthetic response to some kind of factual subject and its effect on your drawings or on your painting was something that was in the air. I wasn't interested in dealing with it, but I was interested that somebody else was.

I was used to a more informal approach to subject matter…I think that there was a kind of anemia in the use of color and in the application of paint, not a whole lot of vigor—it was more aesthetic. There was great emphasis on a firm kind of cubistic designing, and I thought the watercolors tended to be quite pale and not very juicy. What people associated with me was a much more cluttered, less arranged kind of stimulus, that is the subject or still life or whatever, and then very quickly with a much fuller use of color.

In the drawing class they made a lot of use of [Kimon] Nicolaides's book *The Natural Way to Draw.* There were things in it that I absolutely disagreed with. It was a drawing book that emphasized dealing with the human figure as an object. And it never seemed to me to deal with environments or relationships. It dealt more with volumes and wholes. Still-life drawing didn't deal with the situation. It wasn't pictorial. There was a great object emphasis. When you study drawing that way it doesn't have great carryover into painting. I emphasized things like perspective and the construction of objects, and I think other people did too. So it was a very academic kind of beginning, comparatively. There wasn't a lot of notion of free expression. There were some good students. But I think there was a certain kind of timidity of expression in watercolor. I don't remember very much collage being done then. There's more now… [in 1977]. I think it was a good school.

When did you move into the current building?

When I came to Detroit to be interviewed, I remember the building the department is now in at Wayne didn't exist. It was one of the first buildings that any college had put up after the war to house an art department. It was sort of a fluke. The city had its 250th birthday, and this building was a gift to the city and that's why it's called the Community Arts building. Wayne University originally was a city school and the city gave this Community Arts Center to itself as a birthday present. Up to that time they had existed in a lot of small buildings all over campus, generally large, old private houses and in some of the classroom buildings.

Juried competitive shows were very important in those days.

In 1952 the Metropolitan Museum had a big national competition, including watercolor, drawings, and prints. I sent a painting to it, which was accepted. I felt terrific. I was going to be an artist, because I had a painting in a big show like that, with other names that you had heard of. I don't think there are more than two a year now. But they happened all the time then, regionally and nationally. The Corcoran Gallery and the Museum of Modern Art had them. The Brooklyn Museum had them, the Print Club of the Pennsylvania Academy [of the Fine Arts]. I've sent work to the Denver Art Museum. My friend in Flint, Van Duzer won first prize at the Butler Institute show the year he was fired. And it was such an eye-opener to me that it didn't make a bit of difference in his life. Now that doesn't mean that we all didn't continue to send to shows. It was hard for that system to die down, until suddenly you realized that there was nothing to it…I think there was a little more attention paid to people in the regions in those days. It seems like New York is even more of a focus now for all the activity. There was a notion that the way you became successful as an artist was to enter these competitive shows and slowly you because famous or recognized, or something of that sort. It was very common for all the artists I knew to send to exhibitions. This system became unworkable after a while because they were too expensive because of shipping and handling both for the artist who sent work and particularly for the institution putting on the show. It was costly, the crating of stuff, the energy that went into it, the broken glass on watercolors, the traveling down to Railway Express at night to deliver things at the last minute so that they'd go to some show in a town where no one cared. It was like some kind of poetry.

When did the style and curriculum begin to change from the traditional approach to a more contemporary one?

When Wayne Claxton retired we did a search for a new chairman for the department. Somehow the search disintegrated and Alden Smith was made acting chairman and eventually was appointed full chairman. Alden was much less of an authority figure. So there got to be quite a decentralization of what was happening in the department. Alden created an area of painting and sculpture, so these little separate disciplines were emphasized in a way, so you could move a little bit if you wanted to. In the early and middle sixties we had an especially good group of students. It seems to me that for the first time a couple of students went on to Yale. I don't know that anybody had ever applied to Yale earlier.

We would assign a specific kind of problem to a class. It might be such a simple thing as doing a landscape where there would be a common figure experience. Or do a painting which had an emphasis on color with some limitation or a painting which used some kind of stimulus. Maybe things were done in very large scale. I can remember giving a problem which had students produce an interior space that you really couldn't inhabit, so that would be a thing to stretch their imaginations...Then you would grade them in terms of whether they were really intuitive, whether they came up with something unusual or with something ordinary or did something ordinary in a very special way or not. There was a lot of emphasis on grading.

One day we came into the classroom and there was a gigantic painting. I think it was six panels, each one four by eight feet hanging on the wall, with a note...telling us about some arbitrariness of grading. I think we loosened up a little after that, but not that much.

I suppose the notion of the student's own development, searching out their own thing, was somehow in the air. I think a big influence in changing that was John Egner, when he came. He was not of that [old] mold. I don't know if he had those experiences or didn't like them. But there was a lot less emphasis on them in John's teaching. And I think that it affected everybody in the department. It was what we would perhaps call, "the student facing his own void." It became very clear that this other method was valuable. It didn't always provide the student with direction. We all began to realize that it was important for the student to search that out. I think I'd have to credit John with that. And I think it affected a lot of the department. This also was the time of student unrest, and there were a whole million reasons for it, and maybe John was a product of that in some way.

John Egner represented the freedom and individual emphasis of the sixties?

Right. But that was a real big change. I've never been convinced that it necessarily made for better work. But I thought it was better philosophically. And the work was easily as good, and it just made more sense. So now we care less about grading. We grade only once during the term, at the end. There is a lot less emphasis on students being in class because we have so many more students with studios.

Nowadays [in 1977] we might have a student who never touches the representational idiom, or one who hasn't touched the nonobjective consideration. In the old days that wouldn't have been possible. Everything would have been insisted on, as if the student really didn't have any mind. Now what we try to do in terms of presenting other ideas is to lecture, show slides, talk about it, but not insist on the students doing it. If someone comes in as a sophomore and starts painting apples and continues to do that until he is a senior, no one would ever really tell him not to. We wouldn't think it was appropriate, and perhaps we would see the possible value in doing that.

The difference between 1956 and 1976 is enormous. It has to do with the student being given charge of his own direction. The instructor is not operating out of their own premise. But they are operating out of the student's. So it's a whole different kind of relating. You are confronting something that you didn't anticipate. In the old days you couldn't anticipate everything the student would do, but it was within a range that you had set up. If you said to the student, "Here's the problem. Walk from there to here." And if he walked on one foot or two feet or three feet or dripped paint as he did it, that was his expression. But now you wouldn't tell him to walk from there to here at all.

The students seem to be into the real world much earlier as exhibitors, as studio maintainers, and in thinking of themselves as artists.

Has Wayne produced many nationally significant artists?

A person who was at Wayne in those years and had a lot of attention and still does is Lee Byars, James Lee Byars. Well, he was really out of place in a remarkable way. I think he had been a business school student and came into the art department and would not work within the system. I'm fairly sure he graduated as an art major. I don't even know what kind of work he did, maybe a very early kind of conceptual. He's really unclassifiable. He went to New York early and got in the hands of Dorothy Miller at the Museum of Modern Art. He was the fellow who one time closed off one of the main streets of Manhattan and put down a great big piece of water-soluble paper in the shape of a person and after people frolicked on it, and rolled on it, and so on, the fire department came and rolled it away. He always does big projects like that...He was a student when Wayne Claxton was still there and then somewhat afterward. He was no one that I understood at all. But he has had a real effect. I saw something of his at the Museum of Modern Art last year. He's a little quieter now, but he was a real early force in that sort of thing in New York. Olga Constantine and Phil Fike had a lot to do with him in terms of talking to him and reacting to him. David Mitchell did also. I did not. I was really much too conservative to deal with somebody like that. I just thought it was all theater and didn't trust it much. But I've learned that there was something. But anyway he was a student who didn't come out of the system but was certainly there. There other people like Walter Hamady of Private Press Books...Ellen Phelan is in New York and doing well. Nancy Mitchnick, too. We've had good visiting artists like Elizabeth Murray and Jennifer Bartlett.

What made Wayne a successful art school in the seventies?

It is a center, in the sense that it is in the center of the city. It's where artists live. There is a community around it. There's a lot of interaction between the Wayne staff and artists who have graduated, too. The student who is working while he is going to school establishes a total kind of lifestyle as he's learning art and becoming an artist. The student finds a way to support his art. I think that's different from what you might find in an art school connected to a university in a typical college town, where at the end of four or six years they must find another kind of job. In a way our students learn to sustain themselves as artists. An interesting example might be a guy like Doug James. He was a graduate artist in Detroit. He went to Yale and came back to Detroit afterward with a family, with a child or two. He taught at Wayne and the Lawrence Institute of Technology. That's typical of what you might expect a graduate of Wayne to do in this city—working, being an artist, showing in local galleries. Now, of course, he has gone back to New York.

Let's go back to your professional development. What kind of gallery scene existed here in 1956 when you came to Detroit, and how did it evolve?

In the city I think there were three professional galleries, Garelick's, the Anna Werbe Gallery, the new Gallery Four, and the nonprofit Detroit Artists Market. Bob Garelick on Livernois didn't have the kind of art I felt very close to. I don't think he showed many Detroiters. Anna Werbe showed Sarkis Sarkisian and Walter Midener and there would be some of David Fredenthal's work around. I became quite friendly with Anna in those two or three years before I went to the Donald Morris Gallery when it opened. Peggy DeSalle in Birmingham was selling jewelry and some paintings, but it didn't seem to me to be a place for young contemporary artists at that moment. Gallery Four opened on Livernois and had Mary Jane Bigler in their opening show. And I did show some drawings there and sold one or two things. But I didn't have a real exhibit there. It was the first gallery that had openings and champagne and everybody thought that was really fancy and very big time. They showed lots of crafts also. In 1958 I had my first exhibit in Detroit...at the Rackham Building, in the lounge. It was a show of watercolors. In the process of preparing for that show I went to a framer on Grand River Avenue—John Germaine at the AAA Frame Shop and purchased stock and glass. We liked him and suggested that we might ask really good artists to show there. We repainted the whole place and hung pegboard all over the walls and got basket furniture. We made it look better. Galleries now are so fancy here that one doesn't know what the norm was then. But by the time we had finished it was a lot nicer-looking than Bob Garelick's gallery. I became known as the director of the thing. I organized all the shows that it had for two years, from the spring of 1958 through maybe 1960. One of the very first shows was of Peter Gilleran's drawings. Peter taught painting at Wayne before I came and also taught advertising design. In that first year we showed the paintings of Gerry Kamrowski. Some years before he had won the Founders Prize at the Michigan Artists Show at the Detroit Institute of Arts. We had a show of Len Zemiska from the University of Michigan—mostly watercolors. We showed Steve Davidek, a good friend of mine from Flint. We showed some people I went to school with at Illinois—Billy Jackson and Lee Chesney.

One of the very first things we did was to have this exhibit of work by Charles Van Duzer. We coupled that with a slide show that Milton Cohen put on. That would have been in 1958 or 59—a very early avant garde experience. Cohen taught at the University of Michigan. They hung big sheets in the gallery and ...there were art marks of sorts on these long strips that were like slides and they could feed the slides through the projector. There were two projectionists: Milt was one of them and Luis Tavelli, a painter at the University of Michigan, was the other. They would slide these things through, and they would superimpose them one on another. And then they had color wheels in front of them so they could change the color. There was also music, with the notion that they would interact with the music. They would react to what the other fellow was doing and would just somehow create a thing.

We had a show almost every three weeks. I think the reason we did it was because it was a place to show that felt good. It was like your choice, your surroundings. We also had shows of Al Mullen from the University of Michigan and Irving Kaufman. I think the next year Kaufman showed at Frank Rehn Gallery in New York. He did tapestries. Edgar Richardson [then director of the Detroit Institute of Arts] came in one day and bought a Zamiska drawing. I can remember Florence Barron [a major art collector who lived in Detroit] having framing done there. She bought a few Peter Gilleran drawings. Mr. Germaine didn't care if he made any money on the gallery. We hoped we could cover expenses.

The show I had there had watercolors in it... and a lot of absolutely new oil paintings. It was a big show. There were lots of still lifes. They were somewhat abstracted—bottles and tin cans. Some of the paintings of expressways were in it...A big painting, say a three-by-four-foot painting would have been $350. We got reviews of every show by the critics of both newspapers. I thought that the public would come. I thought that if paintings were hung, no matter where, the public would come. I just thought people would come and look at art. I made all the artists come to every opening so that there would be people there. And we got a little clientele. People from Wayne would come, other artists, and then a few curious people. It was no big success.

I think one of the reasons I stopped doing it was I didn't like to tell people I didn't want to show them. I wasn't into judging that way. Then I realized we just couldn't sustain it anymore. We had a baby. We dragged the baby down there in a car-bed. We'd hang pictures at night. It was just crazy. So we stopped it.

Then Lester Arwin opened a gallery. The Donald Morris Gallery must have opened around the same time.

Did you begin showing at Donald Morris then?

Not immediately. Anna Werbe was my friend and had suggested that I might show there. In 1960 or 1961 Florence Morris asked, "What was I doing about a gallery?" So Don and Florence came to the house and looked at paintings and I went to them. They've been very supportive. They've never really interfered in any of my work. There was a moment, one moment, when they weren't completely happy with the progress of the work, when they felt it was just a little dusty and didn't seem to be as spirited or as personal as they wanted it...You can't underestimate what it means to have someone who is just always there, sticking by you. In a very early show they sold a few things. That was terrific. The early work that was shown there, I think, was figurative. I don't think any work they showed ever had very much of the look of de Kooning in it, or the cubistic sense about it. The work was more frankly figural in 1962 and without as much sense of abstracting planes. The paintings looked more like German Expressionist work. It was still all-over, active painting. The brushstrokes were active. The surface was agitated everywhere. They were quite figurative, with a very free use of color, patches of color, gestural, quite graphic, a lot of drawing in them. The cover of the catalogue for the first show had a little dancing girl on it and looked like a Manet. The abstractness came from the individualized brushstrokes that were in it, rather than any kind of planes or geometry. At that time, I was doing a lot of drawing with Jens Plum and Jim Rosen and Dick Kinney. We drew once or twice a week from the model.

I wanted the work to have a sense of something about reality in it. The notion of touching some kind of reality. There might be a bird in the sky or a dandelion in the grass, and it would be put down as a kind of symbol—the yellow of the dandelion and a little shape of it, but not a real exploration of it, a kind of graphic, notative, almost comic indication. I wanted the thing I was looking at to nourish me, to stimulate what I would do, even how I would treat it. Later I began to realize that a certain kind of yellow could mean dandelion, and it wouldn't have to be described hardly in any other terms. That all-overness that came from abstract expressionist work would be the reason that you would put a big red blob on a woman's cheek. It was to break up the unity of the face. You were trying to keep everything active and everything of equal intensity. That was a form of abstracting. A big blotch on someone's face makes you see the face less quickly as a whole. That was the work that I first showed there.

Over the years the work has moved around a lot. There have been moments when there has been an emphasis on extraordinary flatness that really left illusion. There were moments when I thought that I was more caught up with a kind of classical, academic drawing that would purposely distort. I would let the movement of the brush dictate the drawing of a finger so it was a case of the paint being the finger rather than sort of coloring within a finger outline, you know, whatever kind of adjustment a painter might make. The work has moved a lot. It's been figural ever since 1956 and there were figure references earlier. Clearly still life, figure, landscape—those themes have been through it all. But the degree of simplification, the emphasis, has changed a lot. The work from my show in 1972 really looked a lot broader than the work in 1977.

What do you mean "broader?"

Somewhat flatter, much simpler, less incident. Maybe a shell painting in 1972 looks almost like a "paint by numbers" show. There may be twenty colored areas in it. Now maybe more of them slide together to be blended a little bit more. There's still a sense of the same distinction, but it's a little more complex, a little more illusionistic. I was much more worried about illusionism in painting. I didn't want the things to look like they had much shine.

Why do you think you felt that way? Was it the tone of the times?

I was so interested in the color, and color has just a clear kind of intensity if it isn't modeled. So the flatter a thing is…[the better]. Unmodulated color, color that doesn't go through light and shade, has a kind of colorfulness that it doesn't have when it does other things. So the emphasis was not on strong highlights or strong darks. Painting in the sixties—1965—would have much richer shadows than the work has now. I simplified the color of the work so that the thing I thought was so important—the precarious location of things—was emphasized. I did that in a series of paintings, which got very lean in terms of the amount of incident. And it helped me to see a shadow as a shadow. I mean to see it as a dark or to see it as a shape. And that, I have retained. But it took a period of very simplified painting to do it. And I think I've just been able to add more incident and still be able to control it…I guess you asked why did I want to avoid illusion in them. I did a painting that turned out to be much less simple. It was a head of my wife, a painting that I call "Gretchen." I painted the painting as best I could and I didn't quite manage what I intended. It was maybe a year later that the painting seemed to me to be very strong, and it seemed to give me some allowance to move into something that was more illusionistic. I found I could control a highlight and still see it as a discrete white or light in the painting, or as a discrete shape. For a while I thought that if I put the shininess on someone's leg that I was painting that I wanted to really be sure I was seeing the shine, not as part of the leg, but somehow as a light strip in the painting, which is hard to do. You get lost a little bit.

How real are your still lifes, figurative works, and landscapes. Were they meant to look exactly like something you saw in front of you? Or were the subjects meant to be the sources of abstractions?

I don't think the kind of reality that I would have been after was ever totally an illusionistic one, or in many instances, hardly involved with appearances at all, being so mimetic. When I say "reality," I only meant that there would be a way in which the subject would speak back to the painting, inform the painting. I meant that one would ignore the "pimples" of the subject matter. And of course I would never be interested in exploring vagaries. I never wanted to clean up, so much, the reality that was in front of me, or want it to be predetermined too much, or restructured so that it lost its identity. That's one way of talking about reality. How real would they [the subjects] be? I can't remember when I've been excited about reproducing them. I just presume it's possible to do it and I don't find that a challenge. The subject is—at least reality is—a vehicle for me to react against…So a color could inform another thing. That would have been the way I would have seen that in 1960. Now a lot of the paintings since, I guess, 1970 have had extremely flat backgrounds, extraordinarily simple backgrounds. I'm sure it was a reaction to the agitated environments of much earlier paintings.

But it also is a reminder, because one thing does inform another. That flatness and that simplicity has to be matched by the object that is in front of it, so it's a way of holding your hand against an excessive kind of exploration of the things, and it means that then the picture and that background, which we decided will be painted flatly, will have a similarity of some sort. Painting a flower so that it has the quality and wholeness and even implied volume of a flower and still somehow making it refer to something that you have already announced is flat is a challenge, and it's interesting. It gives the painting a certain kind of focus. In memory people always think they (the painting and the object) look alike, but when they're next to each other, they don't at all. The paintings of 1970–72 were those where I really wanted to remind myself always of the structure of the painting, and that meant that every tonal change and every wrinkle and every dent had to be seen as a dot, a slash, a mark in the painting. And I think that I do that now without the reminding. And maybe it just isn't as important to me anymore. Something else is taking its place.

When you're putting all these things into your structure, or your colors, your tones, the flat background versus the illusionistic foreground, the play of all these forces; are you seeking what you would consider a moderate order, a synthesis rather than something that would have extremes in it?

I'm always nervous about something seeming to be too clearly intelligent or smart or clever. There's always a way of moderating between something which is limp and something that is too firm. The idea of quality in painting anything is one that seems to me to be hard to be sure of. There is such a thing as too much color, or color that is too good or too unusual. For instance, [there is also] a relatedness of forms which is too overt, too compositional in a sense. I want it to be extraordinarily tight, but I don't want it to look that way. I want it to feel that way. I'm not interested in somebody seeing the links and the geometry that I might see. But I just want them to feel that the painting is right, and when that's done I think there gets to be a kind of permanence about it. And I think that's a mark of quality.

That's your overall approach too, isn't it?

Yes. Right. I do think that it's in the smallest touches that the art is sometimes revealed. For example, if you're painting an apple and you see that it's dappled, that means that you're going to put some red and green areas in it. The moment of painting those, there is a judgment about putting that red into the green. How much? How little? It doesn't just have to do with what it looks like, although that might be something that one would pay attention to. I mean it's hard enough to make it seem to be as right as it seems in the apple itself. But it's just the feathering of the edges of the stroke, or not feathering it, or it's too blended, it's not blended enough. Those are judgments that you only make moment by moment. With some kind of experience your idea of what's good enough expands...Let's say that you're doing a still life which has a subtle relationship of colors. Now the degree of that subtlety is something we still have to experience. At a certain point it's unexciting. At a certain point it announces its subtlety. For instance, I would not be so sure that I would want to do a painting which had a lot of white on whites in it. I certainly would put a white thing against a white form sometimes. But for the painting to say, "I am a subtle painting," I think I wouldn't feel comfortable with that. Any of these things that interest me, I don't want to be communicated to a person looking at the painting. It's more a total quality of the painting. People might think that I use a rare choice of colors. If the painting announced its rarity of color as almost the idea of the painting, I would not be very happy. I would want it to be the inevitable result of what was there and not to seem in any way to be too conscious a choice. So it's really a case of art covering up art—not revealing itself as art. That interests me very much. I think that then leads sometimes to a subject which might not seem to be as useful as a subject for a painting because perhaps it's a little corny, or a little overused, or a little banal. Well, that interests me because that's a challenge.

Is that why you do flower paintings?

Yes. Well, I love them anyway. I mean I think that they're not so commonly done. First of all, they're just delectable and gorgeous. But to take them and make them into something that's like clockwork, that really interests me—to have them belong where they are. I know that flowers turn to the sun. I know a lot about them. I recognize those things. I might even allow them in the painting. I don't go and cramp them into position. But if one has eyes for it, you find the clockwork there. The order is there. And that clockwork means the relationship of flower to flower, of leaf to leaf, of mass to mass, of flowers to background—the fitting together of all those forms. That's a constant, that's an absolute constant. Sometimes it seems a little old. I mean I think anybody who is a kind of composer or arranger or designer [knows] that there is something mechanical about it. Let's put it this way: I think any job, I don't care what the artist wants to do—if he approaches it with a full range of understanding it can be a route to expression. I don't think there are any really cheap ideas. It's the magnification of the idea and the insight into it that makes it meaningful. So I don't necessarily search for a remarkable idea. As you work with an idea you get more and more insight into it. Simple ideas. I mean the idea of correspondence between figure and ground is a permanent one. It's just that de Kooning did it differently than Raphael, and I don't know any more successfully, just differently. So I don't mind at all dealing with those old problems. And I do landscape, still life, the figure. They're traditional, and my deviation from the traditional, slight as it may be, is the thing that reveals me. That is what you want to see in a painting. You want to see the artist. I would really want it to be a Wilbert rather than a still life. [Wilbert's] level of expectation in painting one is what you should begin to see. And that also includes his limitations and his everything. So if you find the mind that does [the painting] kind of interesting then maybe it's an interesting painting. And if you find that mind, if you really know the painting, or the painter, or what he is about, you see him at certain moments surmounting personal problems and informing it with a kind of human presence in that way. So I think that explains in some way the choice of subject. I think it's kind of silly to claim any real radicalism for what I do. I mean there have been moments when other people haven't done it. But other people have. My influences are enormous.

Do you think it's beyond painting; the other things that influence you—like the day to day?

Well, I don't know. Nothing in world events particularly. I suppose the lesson of the American scene painters and the protest painters—their paintings seem to be so unimportant now in terms of their ideas—that I shy away from that. Incidentally, I think one could do a good painting of that sort. I wouldn't even deny that as an avenue. Just in dealing with everyday life, I know that I never see a thing without complications. I always find it difficult to understand how anyone can be sure of an attitude toward the Russians or the Cubans or the Republicans or the anything. It always seems to me to be very complex. And a real balance—this guy is right, but so is that one. And that extends to my notions in painting. In that way I'm influenced by everyday existence. I would never insist on the primacy of any specific idea in the painting, except that it has quality. So I always do see what I do as a kind of balancing of efforts. I've always thought that it would be great to make a painting that no one would think was good art until later. I guess, in a way, that is what good art is supposed to be about. But is has always interested me that it would look better later [rather] than it would look good first and terrible later. And so if it had those hidden qualities...I mean I think it's marvelous to think that, and I think this has sometimes happened for me, I feel some support among artists who don't work like I do. And I think it's terrific that maybe they would look at paintings that are as traditional as mine are and then think that they begin to see in them things that they are doing in their work—to make links to make it clear how much all art can be alike. But that notion of its having a hidden quality interests me very much—and of its not announcing a specific quality in an overt a way, I think it terrific.

Is that why you pick things like still lifes and landscapes for subjects? You could have done abstractions, pure abstractions, just as easily. But then you would have lost touch with reality that touches with tradition...

Sometimes I think I would be a terrific nonobjective painter now. I really know so much more than I knew when I did it. But probably I'm not going to do it because I have more to do here. But it interests me, a bit. I have made my investment. Did I choose them because they don't announce their quality? Yes, I think so. I mean I think that's part of it. I know the first flower paintings that I did, I've certainly done them as early as 1959, the early sixties, and did watercolors of them earlier. It seems to me that Donald Morris never sold a flower painting. I think they never showed one, truth to say. It always seemed to be terribly tough to sell one. The man in the street would think they would be very easy to sell if you were just talking about selling. There are two ways of looking at it: they are going to be bought either by people who don't' know what they are looking at, they just like flowers, or else you're going to convince people who never thought a flower could exist in a serious contemporary painting—but indeed it could. I like to think it's the latter, but I recognize that obviously people who like flowers buy paintings, too, and I'm pleased that they get something more with it. But that was the notion. Don said no one ever sold a flower painting. And I don't know—who did they ever show who painted flowers? But the idea of painting something and ennobling them, making them important, I mean an important artistic effort, I think that's great. And I think that maybe in the things I do there are fewer people doing that specific motif who do them well. I think that's probably absolutely true. I can hardly think of anybody that does that kind of painting. [Giorgio] Morandi has done a few lonely tulips. You see, now that's an interesting thing. A guy like Morandi has informed me a great deal. He had a great deal of courage—painting small painterly paintings when he did them. It turns out that he was a real provincial. I mean he was part of a big metaphysical art movement, but I remember reading an interview with him where he said that he had never been abroad, except once when he went to Switzerland. And that would hardly seem like abroad to us. So obviously Morandi would have been an influence. But there's an aspect of Morandi, the lonely, mysterious severity of him, that I've never enjoyed. I mean I've enjoyed him, but it always seemed to me to be a little—it announced itself in some way as a design too quickly. And I never enjoy working with a still-life object which has too clear or clean or neutral an appearance.

It's too obvious?

Yes. The other day I packed away some crocks that were cylindrical. But I'll never paint those because they are already geometry, and I like the thing to be more resistant, so I would rather it was a pitcher or something with a flower on it that one had to paint. The job of making figure and ground correspond is perhaps more pronounced in figure paintings. The figure is this terrifically interesting thing, which is so unlike everything else, so if you're painting a still life and you have an object which meets in personality, then that's a little tougher job. And it's also a more interesting object—it has all kinds of connotations. I obviously choose with a very limited range of objects that I want to paint. They happen to be thing that kind of look light, sometimes they have a certain kind of personality, some decoration on them, or they might be a folk object, a dime-store object. In the end, the objects I choose for a still-life painting are very limited in range, and they often look like things that I would have been familiar with when I was growing up—1930s kind of objects. They often are mass-produced and not very expensive. They're dime store jars and things that are a little fancier than the cheapest, and to me they seem to have a lot of personality. I often think that those things have some kind of verve about the making of them that interests me, that there's a human behind them. But I've never painted things just like Chardin, you know, the copper pots. That would be very hard for me.

Or a silver pot?

Right. A good one, maybe. But it isn't something I quickly move to. Or kitchen things. I don't think I've ever painted a real guitar. I've painted toy, junk guitars. Those things that Picasso and Braque might have used as a subject matter never seemed quite right for me. But I don't think it has great meaning. I can't imagine why. I mean there might be a challenge for me to use something else. But there is a range of things that I choose. I don't really like to have to buy flowers at a florist. They're maybe a little more exotic than I would want to paint—so [I choose] kind of banal flowers. We grow garden flowers—tulips and marigolds and zinnias. I don't mind at all painting gladiolas, which a lot of people hate. I think they are vigorous and they're one of the biggest, showiest, cheapest flowers you can buy. I've hardly ever painted roses. They're a little too refined. If they were from the garden I would. I don't know what that means. It's a choice within a humble range, but it's not one that announces its humility, as, say, eggbeaters and mixing bowls would. Maybe I use the thirties and forties things just because that's what is available in junk stores now.

But you could take things from your own home that are thirties and forties things, if you wanted to, couldn't you?

Yes. Sure you could.

I think that there is a personality in the objects that you pick and that they are part of the conflict, part of the interest in them. And a lot of machine-made things these days have lost that.

That sort of humanity that's behind them, yes...I'll buy an object, never with the notion of painting it. And I may never paint it, but just because it does express some—it's mass-produced, but it's folk. I mean there's a sense that some crazy man decided to make a milk pitcher that looks like the Eiffel Tower. I wouldn't buy anything that extreme, but that has some peculiar humanity about it, or that is expressive of a very bad idea, but is still expressive.

You get most of your things in junk stores?

Yes. I'll pay a little bit more for them in an antique store if I see something. But generally those things don't get used so much. But there is a real range. If something gets broken, I'll patch it together again so that I can use it some more. In some cases many pieces have been put back together. I get kind of fond of them.

Do you ever feel that you know that object so well that you keep repeating it?

I do see them as painted objects and know there are other possibilities—that they just have a configuration that is going to be interesting to me, and then even though I've painted them in a new situation, it's kind of a new thing. You don't paint them just the same way. So who knows? A lot of them are patterned. What does that mean? A patterned base means that it's broken up. It's made more all-over. It's like the rouge spot on a cheek. It has that same possibility for abstractness. And I am interested in the things not being seen just as the object they are—but as part of a bigger whole. And that does mean, in some way, that you're going to abstract them. But with what subtlety is the issue. So part of the job is to take that object and make it belong to its neighbor, to its whole. And what I would really want is for the painting not be read in terms of its pieces, but that it be read whole. Everybody wants that. But I don't think everybody gets it or works hard enough at it. I did a painting a couple years ago that I can't really describe because it won't make any sense in words. But it had a passage in it that was explainable in terms of the situation. It was a little square area that was on the wall behind the still life, and it had a real strong compositional function in the painting. It was the only way to solve something that seemed to bother me. I thought it was appropriately there. A lot of my students referred to it. They all wondered about it. They all asked about it. They thought it was clever—or, I don't know. And that really bothered me. I never want anything to announce itself. I mean I wouldn't want them to think it was somewhere in the painting because it was serving a specific function. That would be the thing that you might notice much later. That would interest me. But that it was filling in an edge, propping up something, completing a movement—if that's a word we can use—that isn't something that I would relish, that someone would see those devices. I don't think any playwright wants you to know that what happens in scene, [that] there is a device. It's supposed to seem to be an inevitable result of everything that happened before and after it. That kind of correspondence between art is very clear. I guess we're talking about still lifes, but what I say about them would apply to everything I do. They're meant to look arranged. They're not meant to look as if someone just came upon that informal situation. In that way, they announce that they are devices, or they are an art situation, that they are extra reality in that way, and in that way are interesting. You see, that's not real, but the objects are real, and there's all that kind of balancing. But I would hope that the specifics of their arrangement would never look too clever. And then that would extend really to every choice of color. I wouldn't want any of it to look other than that it just happened to be in that position, but appropriately so, not cleverly so. The idea of cleverness, the idea of—well, that's a wish for some kind of mystery—I don't think a painting should look like it tries too hard. But I think it should try very hard. All that trying should be hidden. That's absolutely the way I feel and that all goes along with the painting looking like it's not so important. It's like finding out that the guy you're talking to is the vice-president of the United States. You see the painting and you don't know how marvelously important it is, but really everything is there. That may sound perverse. Why would anybody want that? But I think that's kind of the working situation to painting—to have an unassuming quality.

I think you work in reverse too. They're very unassuming objects, but you're finding what's very special about them.

I think that's true. Whatever is in one of these paintings is more than I can know. You remember a moment that is in the soup of the painting. I try to be tidy about it. I try to tally up everything I'm doing, but I allow something. I don't know I'm painting. I don't object to someone looking at the paintings and reading something that isn't hard in my mind. That's fine as long as it doesn't destroy something that I really intend. You have to be intelligent about it. You can't put together disassociated objects as things, without knowing they're dissociated and they're going to bring up connotations. If they're kind of open and not specific and not corny and not overly literary, that's fine, and I would often recognize a few of them, as I'm painting, or many of them, or the possibilities of them. But that's not the message of the painting. My point is, you can't do that and be dumb and not know that's going to happen. If you put things together obviously that's going to be part of it…And I think I would edit an object that announced too strongly a literary connotation or a position or poetic reference. When you're working representational art this way, you're working toward a sort of neutrality, but with objects that have a great absence of that. They are things and yet you want them to go away as things. But if you want things to really go away, you paint boxes. You don't paint goldfish bowls. What you're doing is quieting the power of all the objects. There are a couple ways of doing it. Let's imagine that you have a still life of extraordinarily interesting objects and you want a neutrality or kind of calmness. You have two choices: You can make the things that are most important less so. Or you can make everything vary. My tendency is to think that you never weaken, you always strengthen. So I would work toward emphasizing peculiarity and the presence of everything as much as I can. In some cases that's why a cloth in the background is seen as a cloth, rather than an area of color, so that its presence is there and that makes the presence of the wall that supports it more real. That's a kind of working arrangement that I endorse.

Do you ever think about the future of your work? Or do you think it just happens as you're working?

I know I'll do some larger paintings now because I just enjoyed doing the last one and it was an unusual format for me. The last painting was *Still Life with Chair and Bobcat* [see pp. 86-87]. I think it was seven and a half feet long by four feet. I've never worked in that proportion—maybe a standing figure might have had that proportion but not a still life. Stretching something out like that is a kind of spatial problem. It's a challenge. I imagine a way of painting where there is less…My paintings are quite consistent, so that the way one form is seen is the way another thing is seen quite a bit. So that the chair is no more realized than the floor and so on. I keep imagining a painting where that might not be the case, where there might be more realization in one form than another. That means that this apple may not be resolved in the way that pear is. It may be thoroughly considered, but not be as illusionistic. I'm really not interested in the things being seen as anything but paintings. And I'm not interested in them having deep space. And that's an obvious way of working against that… Since the objects are worked a little bit larger than life size, now the whole problem of that being illusion and a window you look through seems to me to be dispensed with, and that's a very efficient way to do that. So it sort of solves that. Let's imagine a painting which has a pear in it that is painted as a yellow pear shape, and then you have an apple which looks much more illusionistic. It would make the factor of illusionism an ingredient rather than the consistency of the painting.

I had thought of doing a painting that would indicate a passage of time. Some people do things like painting rotting fruit—something of that sort. I haven't done much of that. I've changed bananas from their greenness to ripeness through the process of painting. But I've never made an emphasis of that. Anything can be fine. It's just a way to get started, and then you begin to test your ideas. Would I paint a bouquet that was alive and paint the same bouquet next to it when it was dead? That's like Degas painting a ballet dancer in two positions. It has some richness. It doesn't mean so much to me, but it might mean something. Or would I paint a compote of fruit, and then three days later in its new position? It interests me a little bit to see what that would mean. But it's nothing heavy with all those things. If you start doing it, you get into richer thinking from the thing you first think of, or it looks so trashy, or it is so trashy you just realize there isn't much there. I would entertain ideas of that sort all the time.

What do you do now if you're painting flowers or a still life and it takes five days? Obviously, the flowers fade.

I paint them very fast, stay up all night. Or there have been instances where I have replaced the flower and then I repaint it completely, but I've known it was going to be there. It's amazing, if you really look you can get a gladiola that's almost a duplicate of one you have. Then you wait for it to grow up to that point, or decay to the point of the other flowers. Or you honestly say, I can't say anything more about it because it's gone now. That's a funny way of reflecting—that it stops at that point because the flowers are dead.

Isn't that a statement about time?

Right. The painting reflects, in terms of its look, what the situation was. But there have been cases where I have just replaced things. I'm looking at a painting of some fruit and I might just set up that bowl with new fruit and begin painting right on top of the old one, having known better what it was about. So that's what I do with flowers. But generally I just paint very quickly, or I paint long hours and hope they don't change too drastically. And then you get smart and you work on the ones first, that go first.

That time restriction on you is probably exciting. Certain flowers and certain colors probably change faster than others?

Tulips get greasy and shiny when they're old. That idea would interest me. But I've never painted a greasy tulip—it always seems unattractive—or a shiny one. It's like it has cold cream on it, when it gets older. They lose the bloom.

Have you found it difficult to see your own ideas and seek your own identity in a place like Detroit?

I don't think so. I don't have any experience to compare it with. I've always been here. I think if anything it's probably easier. I don't have a lot of dialogue with other painters. I teach, so that's a great big dialogue. But people don't talk to me much and tell me they do or don't like my work. So it's my own judgment and I have not been pressured or influenced. I haven't had such importance that I worry about losing it. So I've been able to do pretty much what I think I want to do. So I suppose it's been easier.

You are planning on leaving Detroit for a couple of years to live in New York. Why did you decide to do this at your stage of life and what do you hope to find there?

I've never felt any need to go anywhere for a motif, and I don't need New York for any motif. I don't have to go there to see a mountain that I want to paint, or anything. It's something that I can do right now financially, with an ease that I've never known before, and I can bring my family. I can afford it and I think we can benefit from it as group. I know I would like the pictures to have some effect beyond this area, and it's very hard to do that here. So I think there is a sense of audience or someone seeing the work. In New York there is just simply a bigger audience for things. I've felt that the work could have been shown outside of this area. There were certain kinds of museum exhibitions that traveled that touch on areas that I touch on but no one knew my work. So I'd rather that people knew of it, so that they could make a more informed choice...Dialogue with other painters in New York: I know some of those people and there will be some of that. I do like New York. One of the reasons I most want to go is just to do something different. The possibilities of being in Detroit for the next twenty years—and that may well be the case—I think it's good to take a break. It's an experience I've never had, so you want to know what that means...And I do want to look at a lot of art. I always do that when I'm in New York...I'm not going necessarily to seek something but to find out what it might offer.

Note

1. Interview conducted between August 9 and August 19, 1977. Microfilm reel, Box Number OH114, Archives of American Art, Smithsonian Institution, Washington, D.C.

Interview with Robert Wilbert, 2009

Conducted by Marsha Miro in four sessions, February 19, March 18, July 10, and July 21, 2009

Why write about me? asks Mr. Wilbert.

What is usual or unusual or interesting about me? I've had a conservative position [implying he is not part of what he calls "the up to the moment set"]. I was not always at the peak of the interest in some style. I've always liked teaching, though I don't think of myself primarily as a teacher. I've always been interested in a lot of things. I'd like to think the paintings are beautiful, which is why people wanted to do this book. Let's hope what is interesting for people is the work, which could lead people to an interest in a person's life. My life is about how an artist has managed in Detroit, working for fifty-three years.

Realism. What does that mean to you?

The work comes out of realism. The truth is not necessarily about the realism of the image, but the purpose. Realism is not a word I deal with. Being fancy and entertaining is not what I like. I'm not interested in Picasso's representational figure work. I like the circus paintings of Walt Kuhn because they were no nonsense, no fanciness, and no falsehood, not cranked into some shape to become a picture...I'm not a representational painter. And I'm not insane about being radical.

Why the figure?

The business of figure work is distressing to me because a lot of people get trained for that and don't know what to do with it. They find strange ways to hook meaning into it. Some artists use it for sexual content, others as social protest or to record history. What to do with the figure? Why use it at all? Why not? If there is something in my work that could be interesting, it's using the figure in a formal and not a cold way. Too many people believe that if you want to work with the figure you have to learn how to draw it. But then they don't take time to learn about color value and other things that control a painting. They never think about locating a figure on the paper, what is going on around it. There is a lack of thinking about it as a pictorial depiction.

I could always draw the figure. When I was in grammar school I went to a figure drawing class with over one hundred people at the Art Institute of Chicago. I was this young person. I had some ability. My figures were credible. My figure drawings from college were graded A's. I was doing less literal Max Weber's. When I graduated from college in 1951 I was more affected by abstract expressionism. Slowly the abstract got to be more figurative. At that point I was doing coarse German expressionist figures. Then I was very taken by de Kooning. I began doing a kind of loose organic cubism, a figure where one form fits in with another.

I did [his wife] Gretchen's sister in a kind of abstract expressionist portrait. I painted Gretchen many times. She was great looking...big eyes. It's just a job, doing something as well as you can. It's about color, likeness, handling, composition, trying to make a perfect thing. I don't want anyone saying I wonder what she's thinking. I don't want them [the subject] to look better than they do in person. It is to be a good recording of them in artistic terms. I don't show people with their teeth showing. It's too active. It's part of my unexamined tradition not to show teeth. I'd stick a tongue out before that, because it would be more original. I wouldn't paint someone holding back a giggle.

What is the difference, for you, in painting the nude or a model clothed?

The nude is easier to paint because you don't have to think about what the costume means and the traditions of it. Painting the clothed figure is funny business. I use some models and some friends because I could sit there and talk to them. I've hardly ever paid anyone who wouldn't communicate. I painted the fencer because of the colors and shapes. Michael Mahoney [an artist and student of Wilbert's] had an interesting body. The male nude reclining on a bench from 1981 was because he was terrific looking and had a wonderful shape and was very bright, so you could talk to him. I painted my own kids, my wife, my mother, my dad. He had my hands. I always try to do a likeness. It's respect for the sitter. I would never change them. It would be like putting more shine on a vase than was there. But you can do a million things with what you place and how they are painted.

I put my wife in a band hat. It was a costume, but I'd put someone in that before. The hat is a prop. I never pretended she was a drum majorette. It is an interesting thing to paint and refer to the usefulness of such things—previous things the world has known which are different from common going-to-the-store clothing. I like mixing things up.

What interests you with the landscape?

There is something to measure against. Something to avoid. I'm most worried about doing something with them that is too exciting or showy. I did not want a narrative that was too insistent or too surreal. All that would be interesting to the layman, I would avoid. So much history painting can be measured against them. I don't repeat the past, but it is a measurement for what you do. If someone can recognize a painting as yours there is something in it that is yours. I don't like to be too clever or too interesting. I don't paint the landscape from memory, so I don't do that many of them, mostly watercolors and some oils in the summer. It is probably something I could still do even though I can't see it very well. I did a big landscape of Palmer Park [in northern Detroit] in the sixties. A lot of it is notative, what you can do in twenty minutes as it changes in front of you. I don't like stuff to not be with some rightness and together.

How do you approach the still life?

I'm surest about the still life, I think. But I like it all. I would never do a painting that looked like someone's breakfast table, or their clothes. The justification for doing them is to work with form, color, and making things belong together; that is what is interesting, belonging together. I paint this edge, balancing between how much description should be used. You don't need a lot of detail to say enough. I paint things simply to make a separation between the thing and what is around it. The edges between things are critical. So is the right tone with placement, color, and groupings. The still lifes do not tell a story, they aren't a mystery or provocation. I've never used a ping-pong ball with an apple, but I painted a mime with a stuffed dog. The dog looked like he was guarding the figure. There were chairs that were destroyed. Much is the formal moment. How does that all add up: A reclining figure of a man who may be sleeping or may be dead. Things like rabbits or dogs suggest movement is just about to come or has happened. It's interesting to corrupt a quick meaning by mixing stuff up. When I use a child's chair it is taken out of the child's realm. But it carries questions. I have a birds' crèche. I like stuff. Maybe that's why I paint still lifes. I'm not happy with ships. I'd never paint them. I saw a folding table I would paint in a moment, but I wouldn't paint a Herman Miller chair. I like things that are peculiar, that make an out-of-placeness. I have a personal interest in this. I've never painted a TV set. I'm not drawn to it, only odd things. I've never painted an orchid or a gardenia or a bunch of store-bought roses, only roses from the garden. I never think of it as a rose. I think of it as a colored flower. Nothing too fancy interests me.

Matthew 1982, Oil on canvas
Figure 16 40 × 40 inches
Collection of the Artist

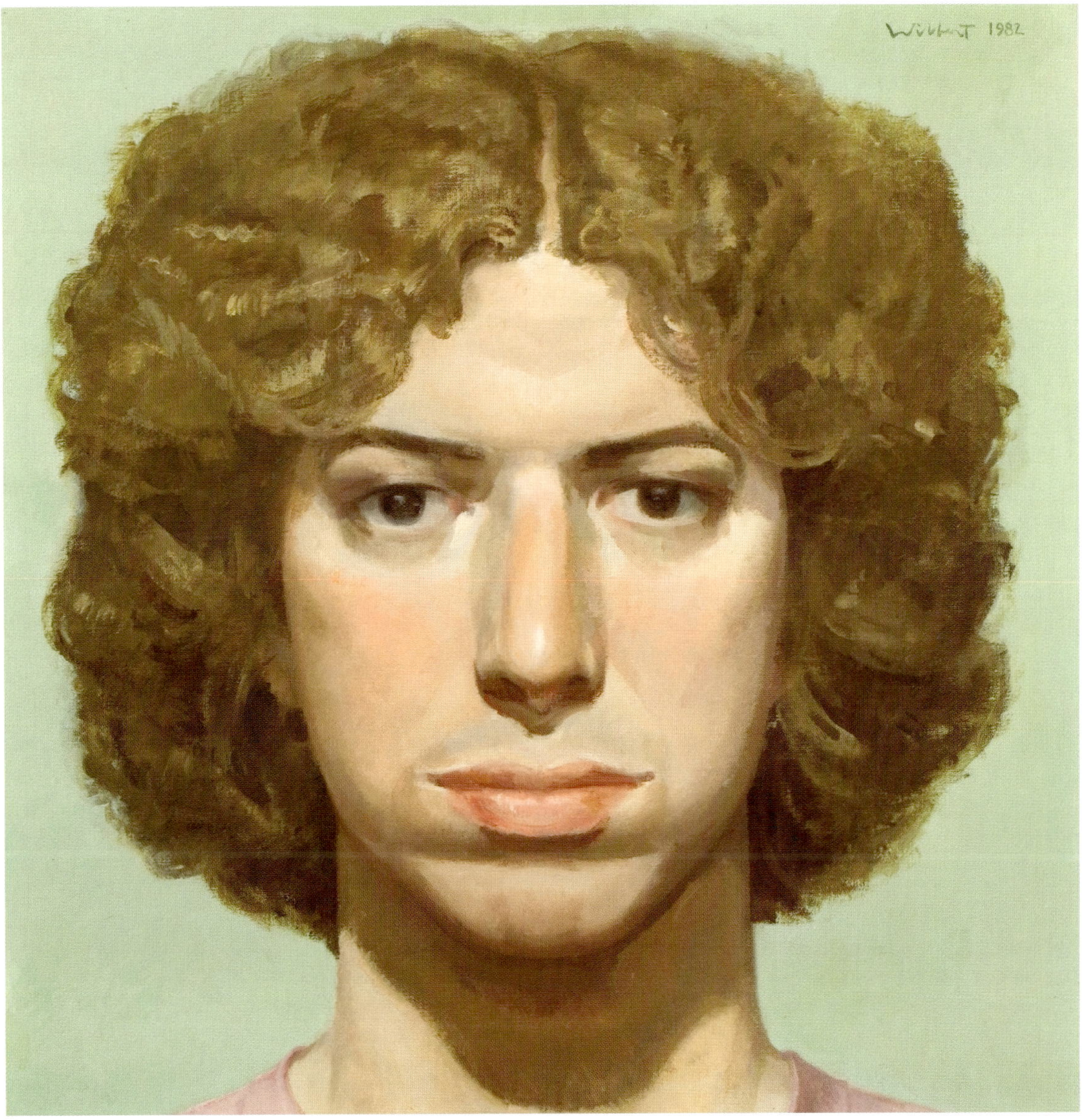

Color is a critical component of everything you paint.

Sometimes it's quite a mystery. You set it up. You play around and try this background and that, to get a symphony of color. Everything shifts when you change a color, which is interesting. I just never want any one thing to be the first thing you see. I did a portrait of Matthew [his son] that has a green ground. I thought it would be better hung on a purple wall than a white wall. The question is what color to read it like—a fresh drink or something old. If a color is there, it's often because it could be a local color. I'd more likely keep it local and light for objects and figures, but not the ground, which is a place where I have more freedom because it's not identified with anything in real life. I do it because I can. If I put color on a mouth, I don't put it anywhere else (on the facial features).

Tone is always a question. I don't want to get too dark. Grays in similar tones, things are like that in existence; the slight yellow of light. Colors have to get close before you can see something that is interesting to me, like dull wood versus dull dark orange. I like the business of things that are close and don't quite touch.

Given all this, what is content for you?

There is no narrative, or not a strong one. If there were a hint of one, I'd befuddle it, such as not having a person be too happy, or too hungry. I'd never paint anyone with an earache. I look for a kind of neutrality, holding back so you can't find quick meanings. I want a presentation that has a security, not being off in many pieces, solidity, an Egyptian wholeness.

There is a beauty in bringing together two things that are surprising. I tend not to paint things that are contemporary, but painting an old fan is romantic, or I may have a fondness for an old straw boater. The hat isn't as interesting as some of the memories from my life—a little romance, a little history, a little surprise—that would be okay. I would paint it on a model, a woman not a man because it would be more surprising. But I don't spend a lot of time thinking about this. I just do it. Somewhere here is a little airplane with wings that went up and down and a vase with light green leaves on it and I was inspired by the idea of the Bermuda Triangle. So I hung a cloth in the background with a grid on it and put it all together.

Who interests you?

Cézanne was the artist whose ideas had a real influence. And in my early watercolors I really did certainly look a little like Cézanne. There's a funny thing about watercolors. When you paint them you can't paint everything at once. You can't put color over the whole canvas, or sheet of paper, because it stays in watercolor, so you leave a lot of white spaces you begin to fill in and after a while those white areas begin to have presence and to function and it's easy to leave them. And the work can look Cézannesque, when it isn't. In the end I don't think it's about the space and Cézanne. It's just the integrity of his work and the permanence of his forms. They're really always nourishing to look at.

But Manet, in a lot of his work, is not strong enough structurally. But I can look at a foot and just marvel at how simply it's seen. For representational painters there is a Manet foot. There's just a way in which that paint configures and there are certain things he emphasizes that another foot painter doesn't emphasize. And that's a big statement for me as a painter. You search for that and perhaps that happens as your work moves along. I look a little bit at Chardin. There's a flatness. And with Ingres, there's a flatness and a clarity of color, an edge, that I like very much and that is wrapped into my work some place. And Picasso always. It isn't stylistic, it's just an example of openness. And I think those things are as important as the idiom that one might take. I never felt like I gained anything from a colorist like [Mark] Rothko...[Josef] Albers, I've thought of. I've never liked his work so much, but I have thought of the economy of those things and the single-purposeness of them. And I do often think of a still life that has a frontality and maybe a kind of centered form operating not so differently from an Albers, so that it would be as "groundless." When you paint a still life against a background, it can't be "groundless." It's just the effort that's important, not the success of it. It may be that it was only that I could like Albers in terms of what I was doing, rather than any influence. His color doesn't mean anything to me, because it doesn't come out of experience from things.

Corot means a good deal to me in terms of something in the paint. I have a real affinity for nineteenth-century French painting. That's just a beautiful touch. There's something that really excites the eye when you look at a passage in his paintings, and he's a marvelous figure painter at his best. Maybe I never painted a landscape at all like he did, but the figures would be inspired by him. But not Gauguin, not so much Van Gogh. I think of Puvis de Chavannes. Fantin la Tour is somebody: I like the clarity in his work.

Donald Morris [the Detroit art gallery] always handled Milton Avery's work. The color and flatness of those things have been influential. It's interesting that in the sixties there was such an emphasis on flatness. I've always liked Bonnard;

his choice of subject is very much like mine. {Max} Beckmann has a kind of structure, and he's a marvelously beautiful colorist. I find it fascinating that he is on the one hand so brutal, and on the other so sensitive. That balance interests me, and I'm sure I've learned from that. With {Giorgio} Morandi, it is that when you first saw those things they looked like art, and that kind of painting hadn't looked like art before that.

{Philip} Pearlstein's work is better before it was hiding behind a million objects. Every muscle was carved in paint and cut into space. There was plenty to look at: a modern flatness, simplicity. He does more than I'm capable of. There is something credible about keeping an idiom alive. The influence of the costumes was Walt Kuhn. I saw apples he painted just before he died. Cézanne was clearly where the apples came from. Kuhn was a good painter. I don't want to look at him too hard though. Alex Katz has not nourished me, though I find his cut-out canvases innovative. I respect the work, but he doesn't say anything to me.

One of my teachers, Forest Bailey, was important. He set up the figure with lots of stuff around it, made it contextual. I'd always look at {Lucien} Freud. I thought about {Hans} Hofmann in 1970. It's about something that grows from something outside, seeing things and how they join and combine.

Self-Portrait with Electric Fan
Figure 17

1984, Oil on canvas
30 × 36 inches
Collection of John D. Mellen

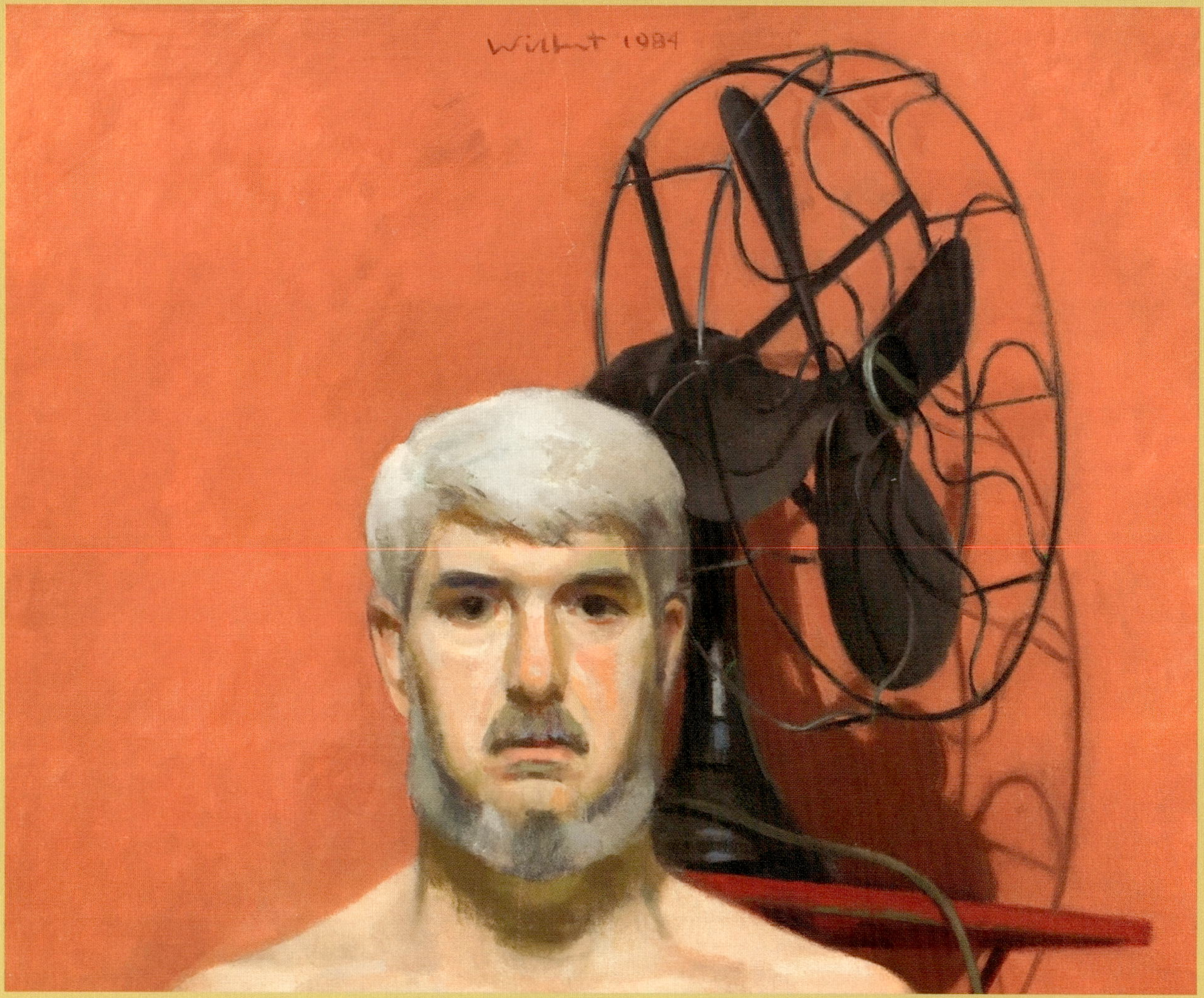

Peter Williams

The Real World of Robert Wilbert

Wilbert paints the world not as we see it, nor as we experience it, yet he brings us into contact with exacting, expressive, and familiar moments. The ideal and the classical, the balance between the thing that is seen and the practical application of its translation in paint begins the artist's colloquial journey. Desire is kept in check or is at the very least circumspect. The familiar is often achieved through his insightful handling of paint and subject. Each painting reveals the artist's ability to shape and layer the paint, molding it into something that has the feeling of substance, while at the same time making us aware of its location within the space of the painting and of its form. He gives us the grandeur of a performance under the guise of looking, or better yet, the subject as performative within a mise-en-scène.

We feel the ache of each dramatic moment, encapsulated in the unnamed interior spaces his figures occupy. Family members, friends, fellow artists, posers, models, even Wilbert himself, exist merely as fact. The figures also play a separate and major part in his work, sometimes without ever declaring exactly who they are or what role they play, leaving us to act as designators. We admire the ability of each portrait to devise a complex character study. Even characters that appear as sexless mannequins give us an easement toward the latent sensuality they possess, not by means of their physicality but through the expressiveness of their facial mask. Such figures can never take hold of anything or simply exit the narrative; they are forever held in place by their formal arrangement.

It is easy to see Wilbert's paintings as premier examples of the craft of making a work of art. The selection of a color, the drawing of a shape, the ability to transform, to make an idea about form into the subject—this is truly the work of the artist. The practical test of the capturing of a moment is in its timing and the suspension of our knowledge. It is a great wonder to lose oneself in Wilbert's world. All things have a purpose in his work—whether they support its meaning or simply have the ability to cast beauty in their wake.

It is in his self-portraits that we find Wilbert taking ownership of his task as an artist. In his self-portraits we can feel the moment in which the artist is caught and framed into the picture plane—no longer confined to simply crafting the work in itself but placing himself into the matrix. In *Self-Portrait with Statue* (1989; fig. 4) the artist seems caught in a candid moment inside of his own scene, the dynamic tension of this decisive moment being made evident in the simple parting of his lips as he gazes at the viewer. In *Self-Portrait with Electric Fan* (1984; fig. 17), as we look up into the space of the painting, a great light leans its weight against the fan, creating a strongly cast shadow that turns the artist into a ghost in the machine, a moment of darkness and enigmatic bliss. It is as if Wilbert is weighing in on the world and the dilemma of existence, presenting a separate narrative of Orwell's *1984* through this tangled web of man, machine, and shadow.

Wilbert's paintings are characterized by a perfect sense of order, whether within the space the figure occupies or in the space of the still-life arrangement. As viewers, we are led by Wilbert's successful process of making a painting to complete the fiction about what we see. We are caught in suspension, weightless and free from the exertion of gravity. Time slows as we embrace the logic of his choices. In this triumphant act of making beauty, beauty proves capable of revealing its sources and mechanics, pushing us back into the realm of an unknown world. The things the artist

Toy Chair with Birds
Figure 18

1999, Oil on canvas
28 × 24 inches
Collection of the Artist

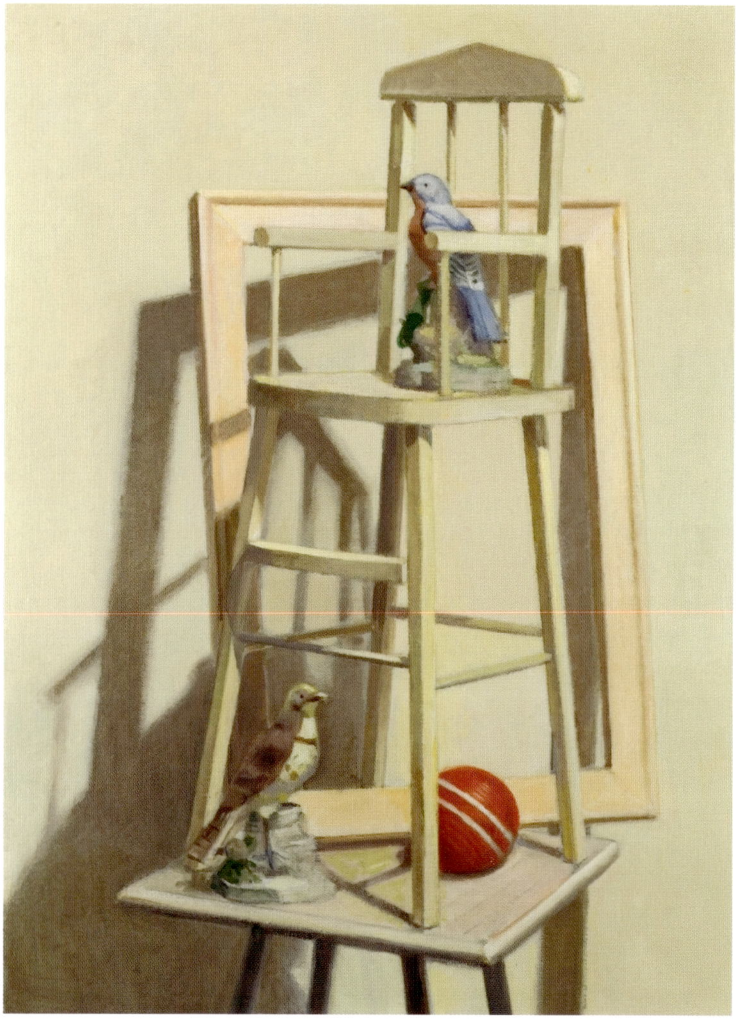

collects to complete the figurative arrangement have their own logic, and that logic is found in the condition of beauty and its ability to satisfy a multitude of demands. Wilbert's logic arises from decades spent intellectually honing skills that are never easily acquired or formed. Such sharply honed instincts are the result of a lifetime discourse on a variety of subjects and a wit manifested by his interests.

In his tautly conceived *Toy Chair with Birds* (1999; fig. 18) the arrangement of the subject matter is startlingly unexpected. What is this arrangement for or about? What role do the materials of this still life play? Entering the space of a Wilbert painting is like entering a darkened theater; the elements in the work are slow to reveal themselves as familiar objects. The objects cast themselves immediately as complex assemblages that exist as both large and small dramatic moments in the painting. In this arena the artist reveals his very real love of harmony, balance, and complex alignments.

While Wilbert's work has a strong formal face, it also displays subtle themes or arrangements that exist "off to the side." A small tableau or group of objects may serve to temper the scene. At times a veil of paint manufactures an atmosphere through which we view the components of the work. But always there is a firm arrangement of forms that intersects with the picture plane to hold the figure in its place. This template, or face of the painting, allows us to unlock the pleasures of a work like *Michael Mahoney* (1982; fig. 19), to take delight in the simple austerity of its arrangement and its ability to exist simply as portrait. But even in this portrait shadows exist as dark tonal intercalations, locked between the deep yellow ocher that highlights the background.

At other times, the presumed subject matter is multilayered and has multiple meanings. There is much to regale us in any of Wilbert's works, and it is the "made" space that the subject occupies, suggesting a potentially complex meaning, that is most satisfying. In his figurative tropes, we catch an almost candid moment, although thoroughly posed, or we find the subject in an introspective and therefore expressed mood. In *Marilyn in Rabbit Coat* (1984; fig. 20), notions of light, color, shape, and repetition capture a particular moment and are indicative of Wilbert's ability to shape the mood of the work. At the same time that Marilyn's gaze looks outward past the picture's edge, inviting us to speculate about our own placement within this space, everything in the picture is thrust forward into the foreground, each object reflecting a sense of responsibility to and for the other elements, creating a sense of focused intentionality. The arrangement of the objects allows us to grasp the

Michael Mahoney
Figure 19

1982, Oil on canvas
42 × 48 inches
Collection of Eugene and Ellen Rontel

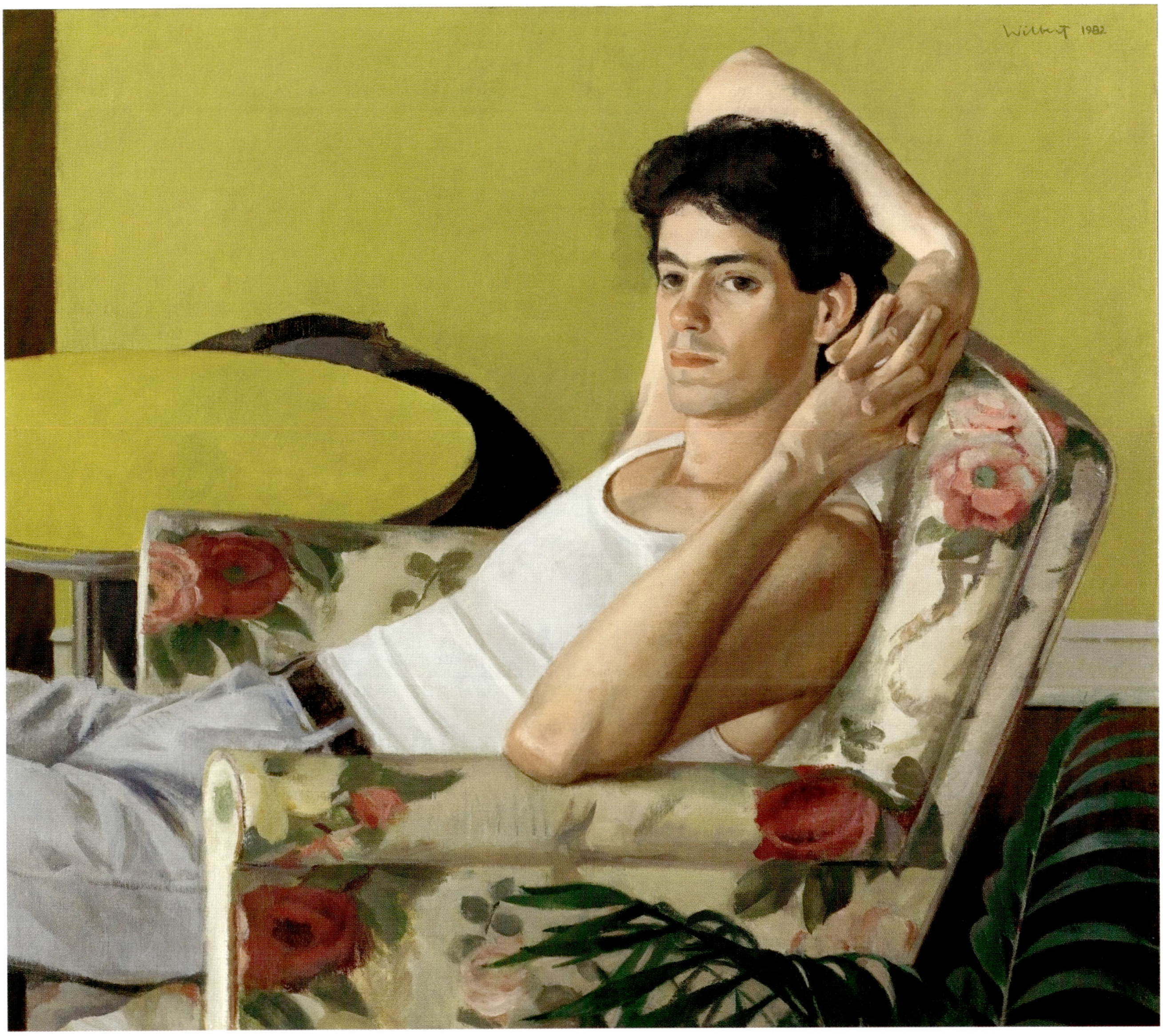

Marilyn in Rabbit Coat
Figure 20

1984, Oil on canvas
60 × 46 inches
Collection of Little Caesars Enterprises Inc.

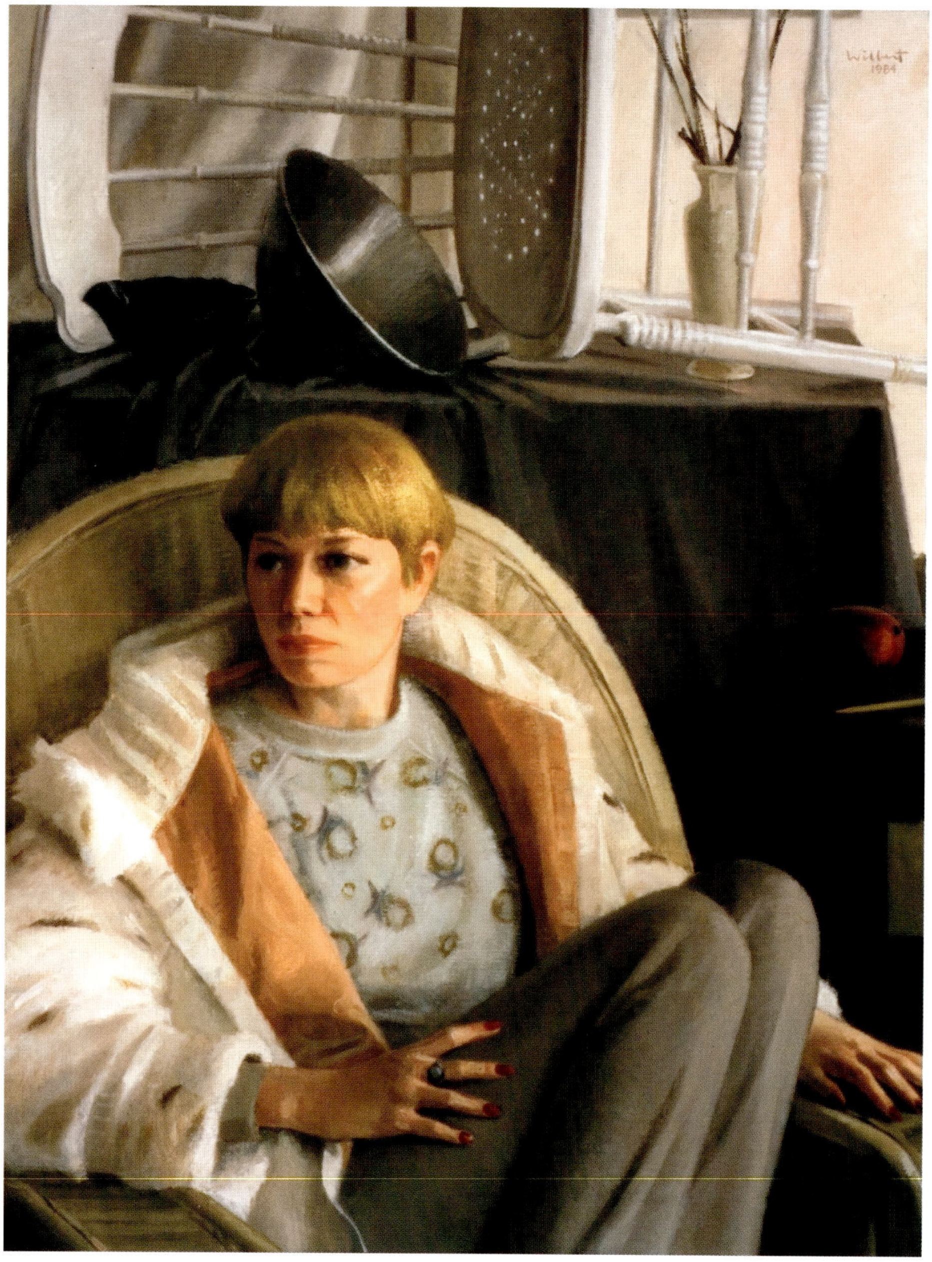

complex personality of the sitter.

A figure dwelling in this exacting space where everything is arranged, where even the floor plays its role with ample conviction, brings with it a sense of containment. And it is this container that reveals the veil of modernity in Wilbert's work. Modernity in his work is about reflection, about seeing himself and his ideals contained within a reflected truth. Truth thus understood negotiates the lineage of form and its cast shadows, finding in the performance of subject or the rendering of space its purpose or being. It is this sense of modern construction that holds the figure still, also creating and allowing for the possibility of newness. That sense of the new is captured in the feeling of timeliness in his work, which despite its formal means is thoroughly modern in manner and subject.

In *Male Nude with Glasses* (1981; see fig. 14), we return to a theater that is not rife with drama, but in which a drama unfolds nonetheless—in the design of the painting and the choice of subject matter. A lone male nude figure reclines upon an emerald green mattress on a silver chaise while holding a pair of glasses above his face. He is not erotically disposed, and while there exists the opportunity for a naked male to shock, in Western culture the nude is often used as a declaration of more complex ideals. Either as statement of desire or as fashionable icon, seen through Wilbert's eyes the figure represents a more modernist moment, lending itself to a more conceptual testament. The figure is invested with a framework of formal constraint, dwelling within a quiet landscape-like setting, more image than icon.

But perhaps most revealing is the thoughtful manner in which the painting does not shock. The anonymous figure holds a pair of glasses but does not yield to the necessity of wearing them. He, after all, will never need to see us, and his presumably unfocused gaze thus puts up a metaphoric veil that allows us to see him as nude as opposed to naked. We are spectators, not voyeurs. The spectacle of the painting can be found in its field-like formality. It possesses its modernity through the establishment of shape and form, not its sexual aspect. Motionless, the figure is as steady as any of Wilbert's mannequins, revealing itself as a device, material means serving methodical ends. The erotically charged subject gives way to the painting's mechanical means, serving the purpose of delineating the flatness of the surface and forming the space, with its application as visual escape.

It is equally remarkable that the painting is not simply a likeness but an expression of the tension existent in the subject's face and pose. Our sense of recognition is such that a story begins to occur between us and the subject. What appears simple and direct actually has a deeper level of meaning.

Benjamin with Gladiola Bouquet (1989; fig. 21) is not at all a candid picture. It is very posed and exacting in the relationships the artist sets forth. Each element begs for release, sliding between its form and its content. What appears to be a classical arrangement encompasses unspoken thoughts and appearances. The colors of the picture and the now-expected ball on the edge of the table are parables within which introspective meaning can exist. Germane to this story are the variables we bring to the viewing, a contested storyline or an unequivocal sense of placement.

Timing or its suspension is a quality that Wilbert brings into the painting's interior, into its space, onto its color, encompassing the temporal nature of the space he makes for the viewer—a space that fluctuates between its "thingness" and its poetry. In the suspension of time Wilbert opens us up to our thingness, our isolation, our sense of dissonance in ourselves. In Wilbert's portraits of Gerry as a harlequin, as a fool, or as a mime, the subject adopts the persona of a performer or actor. In the suspension of the subject's identity we can see perhaps Wilbert himself. In these spaces vignettes make up small scenes in the background to which the figure clings— a simple thought or grand design perhaps attaching itself to the conceptual framework of the painting.

In *Performer with Religious Figure* (1995; see fig. 5), Wilbert negotiates the meaning of the painting

Benjamin with Gladiola Bouquet
Figure 21

1989, Oil on canvas
46 × 44 inches
Collection of Linda and Leonard Sahn

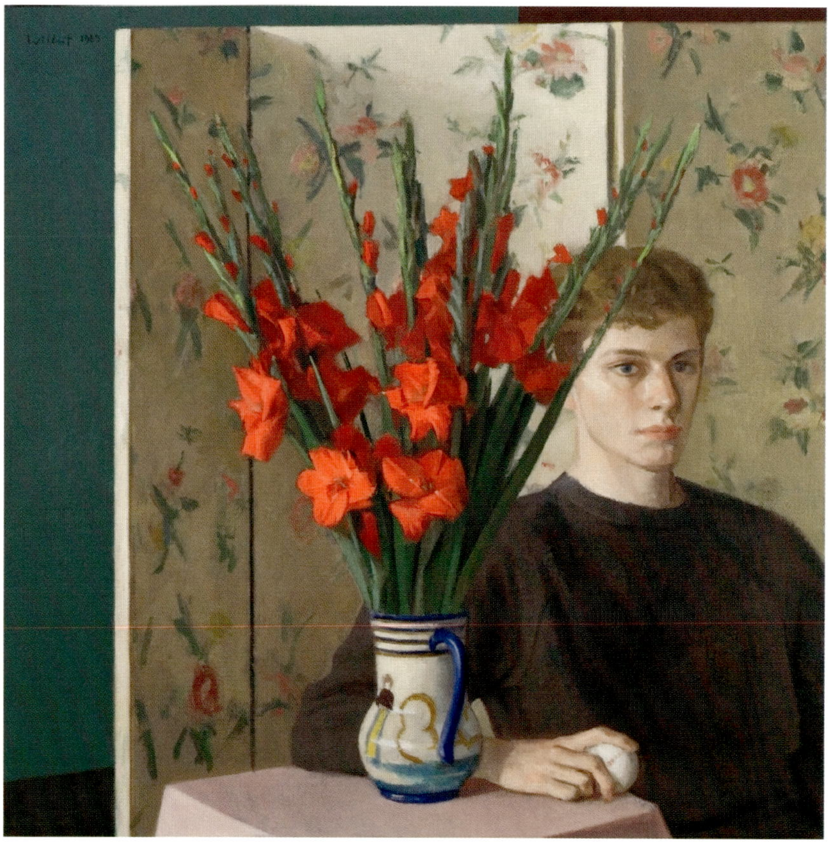

within a formal apparatus. This work is in essence a double portrait. The two figures, one a plaster statue of a Benedictine monk, stand beside each other, facing away from the viewer. The monk's cloak is worn, although his profile betrays no such deterioration. The other figure is a live performer in white tights, nude from the waist up. The monk is painted in a warm light reminiscent of the glow of footlights in a theater, and both figures face the vertical edges of the canvas, with its violet gray background. A small tableau of a simple white mask and a glass ball sitting on a wedge of blue table in the lower right-hand corner anchors both figures to the picture plane.

The overall sense of the picture is one of formal restraint, but its simple visual story invokes our curiosity about the many parts being played. The question becomes: who is the performer? Is it the Benedictine monk, lit as if facing an audience, his face enlightened, calm, and dispassionate? Equally demanding of our attention, the ostensible performer turns away, his face in deep shadow, ruddy and inward-looking. The painting functions on several levels: as a reflection on still life, on portraiture, on allegorical monasticism.

In Wilbert's work, every form, every action, achieves its own entry into the space of the picture plane. The space itself becomes transparent and oblique, dissolving under the weight of the subject's own content. The crush of paint weds the material aspect to the subject, imparting a sense of lusciousness that is contained within the stroke of the paint, inside of which is a bloom of color or light. In that stroke a million things can be described. The stroke can exist as itself or in its guise as a flower petal; it can even exist as understatement. The crush of paint seeds the possible reading of what's on the surface, of what the picture is made of. It creates a narrative under the pose of still life or the repose of an ideal figure.

Plates

Bathers at Sunset 1962, Oil on masonite
24 × 18 inches
Collection of the Flint Institute of Arts
Bequest of Mary Mallery Davis, 1990.28

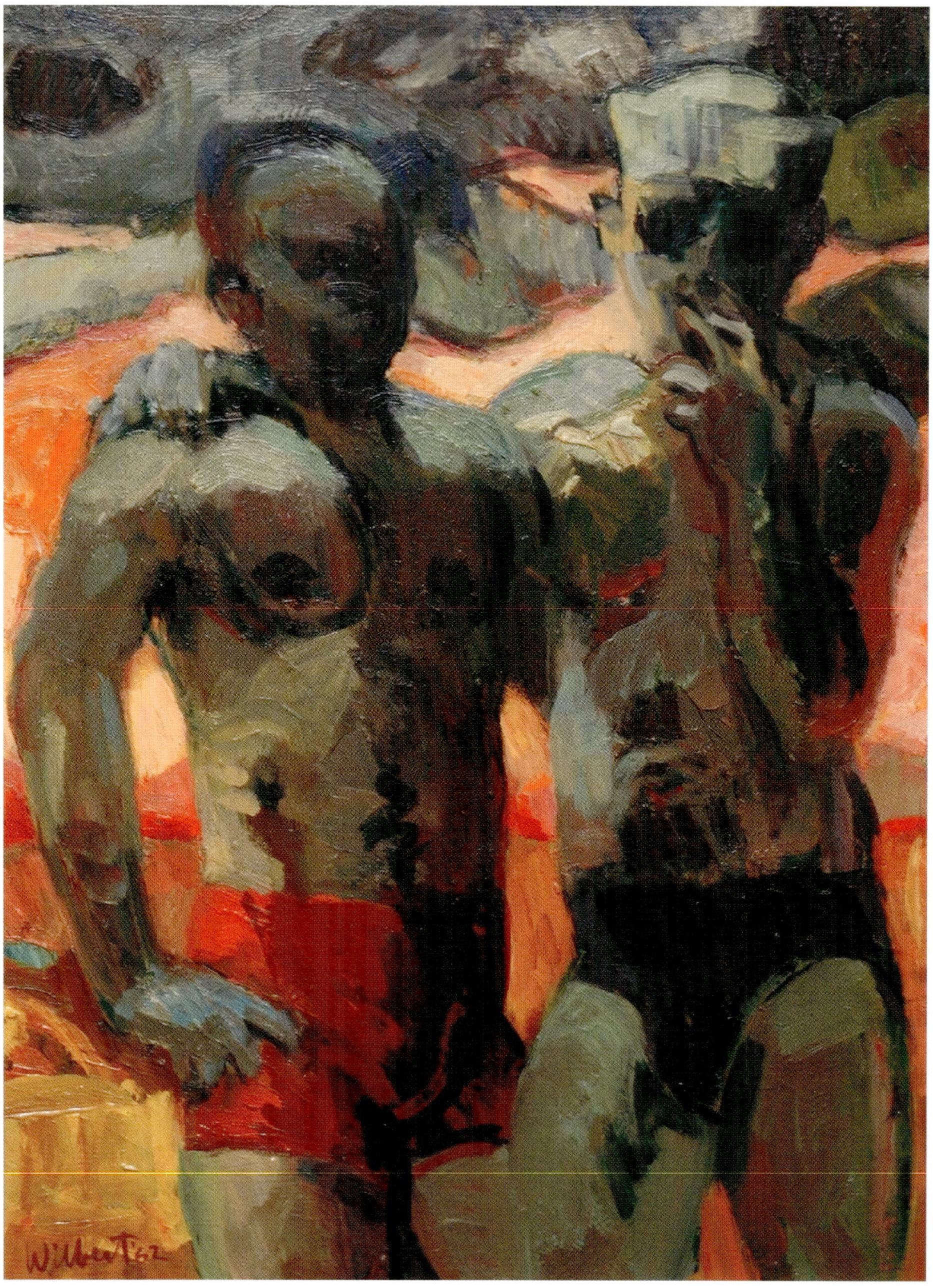

Still Life with Salvation Army Hat

1962, Oil on canvas
36 × 48 inches
Collection of W. E. Upjohn Institute for Employment Research

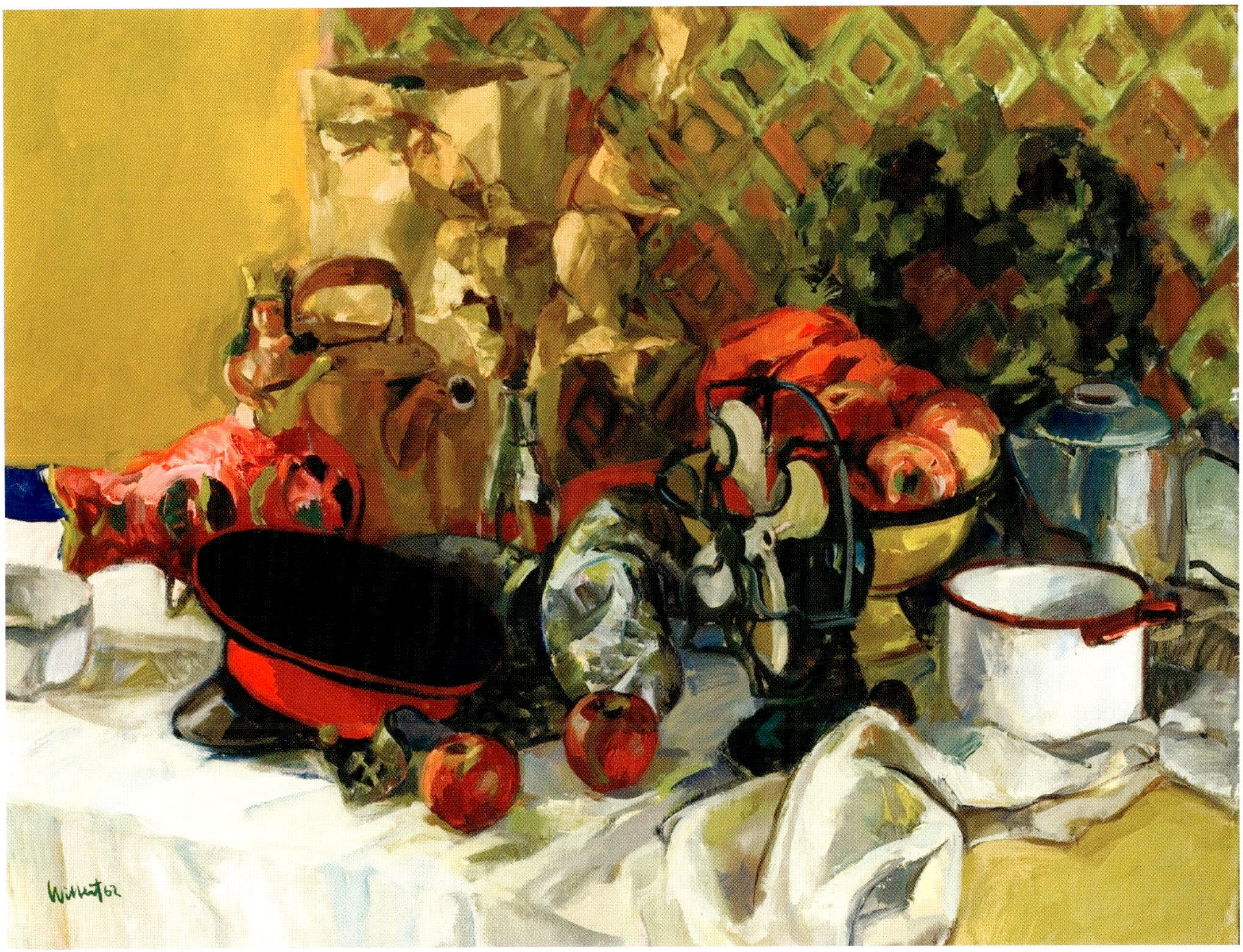

Matthew Doing Splits on Third Avenue

1962, Oil on canvas
36 × 48 inches
Collection of the Artist

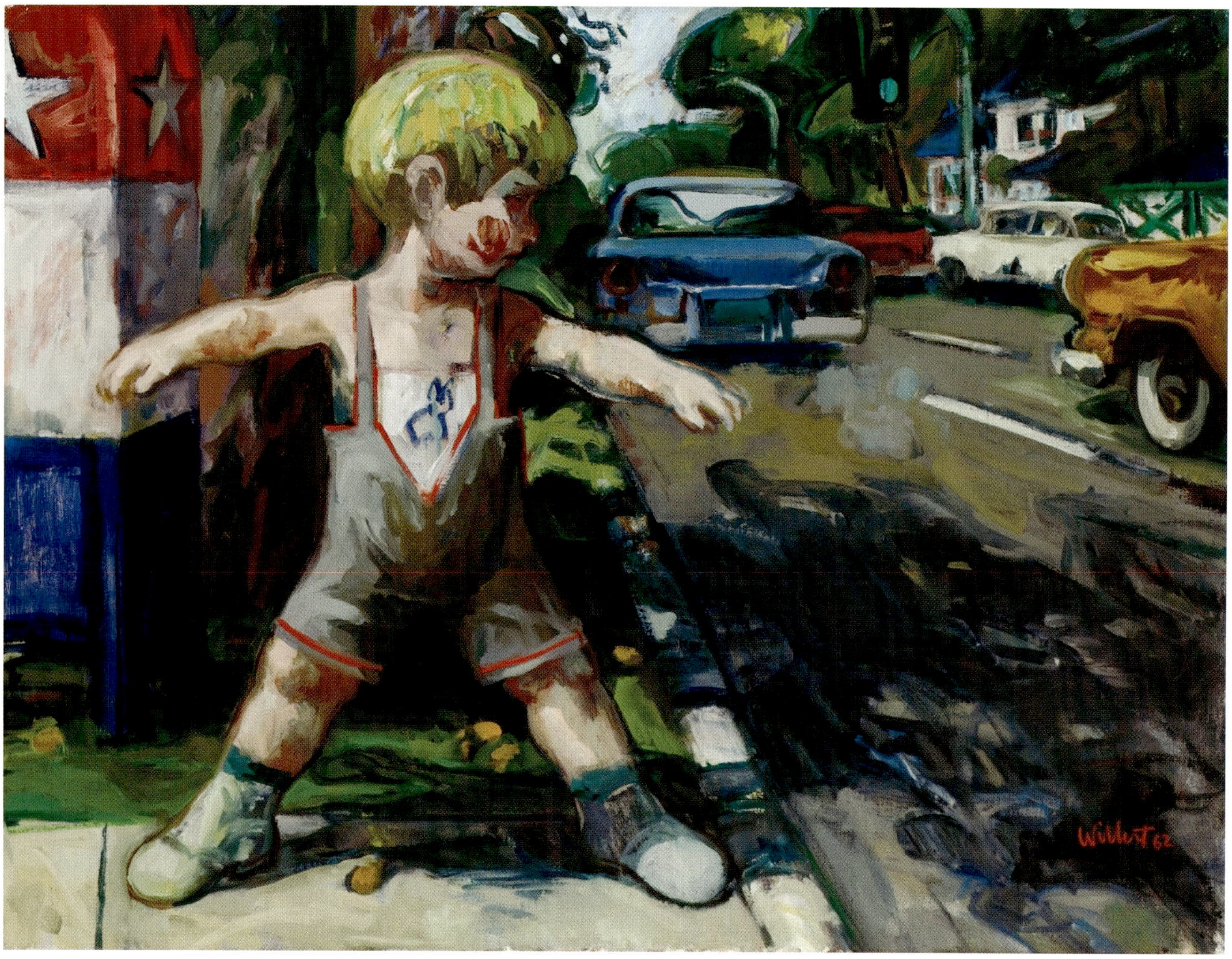

Dancer Waiting

1964, Oil on canvas
36 × 30 inches
Collection of Lillian and Norman Levy

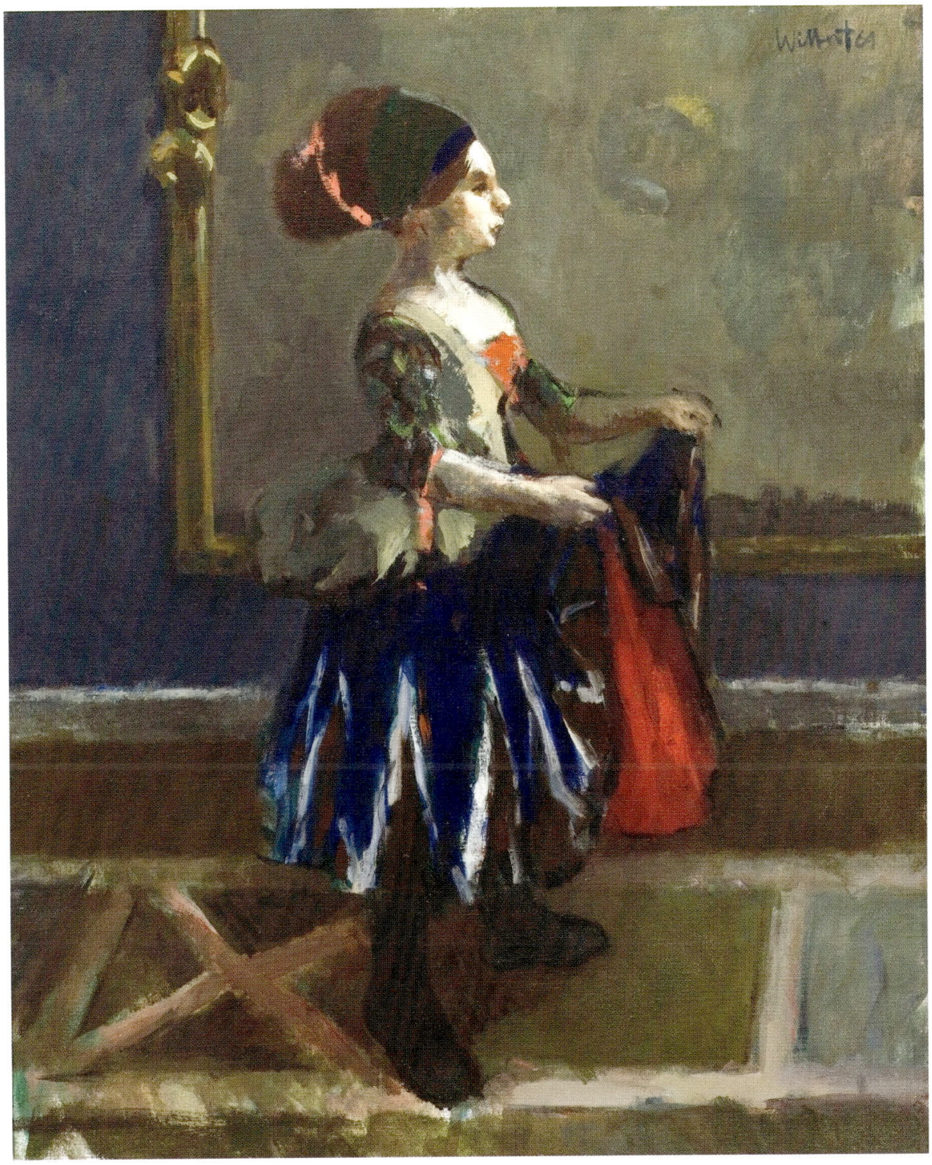

Dancers on Red 1966, Oil on canvas
36 × 30 inches
Collection of the Artist

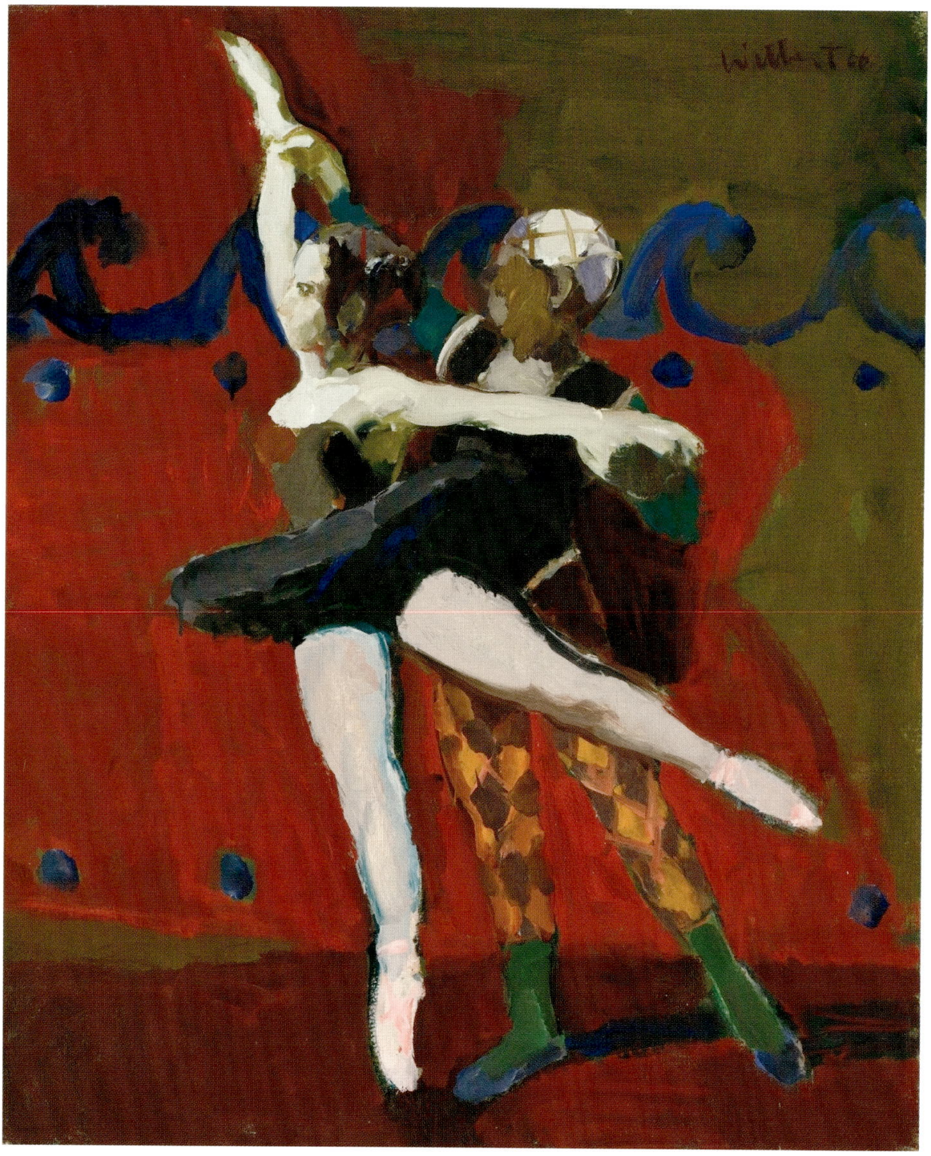

Bathers with Collies

1966, Oil on canvas
48 × 36 inches
Collection of the Artist

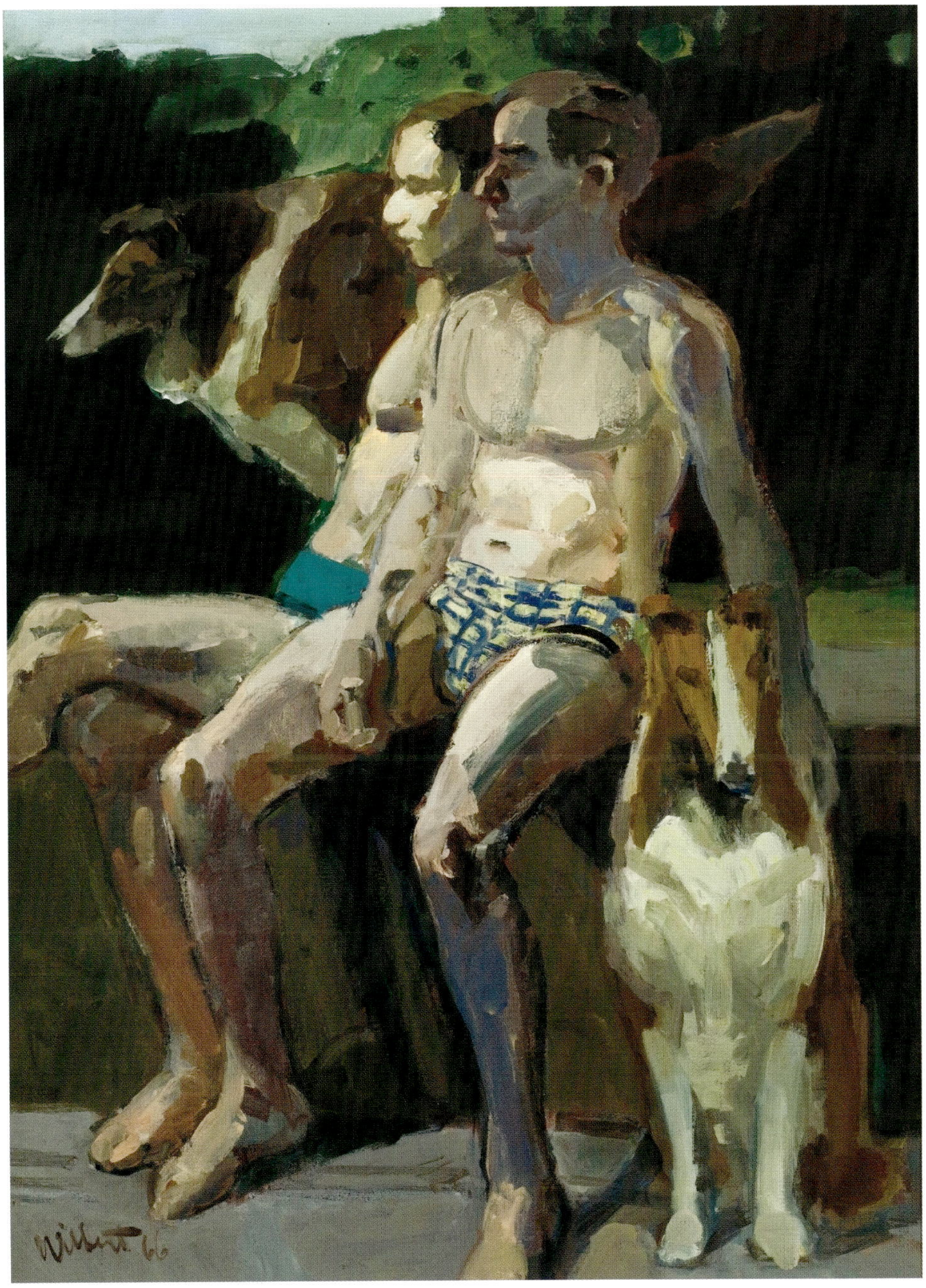

Ducks 1970, Oil on canvas
48 × 60 inches
Collection of Barbara and David R. Lucas

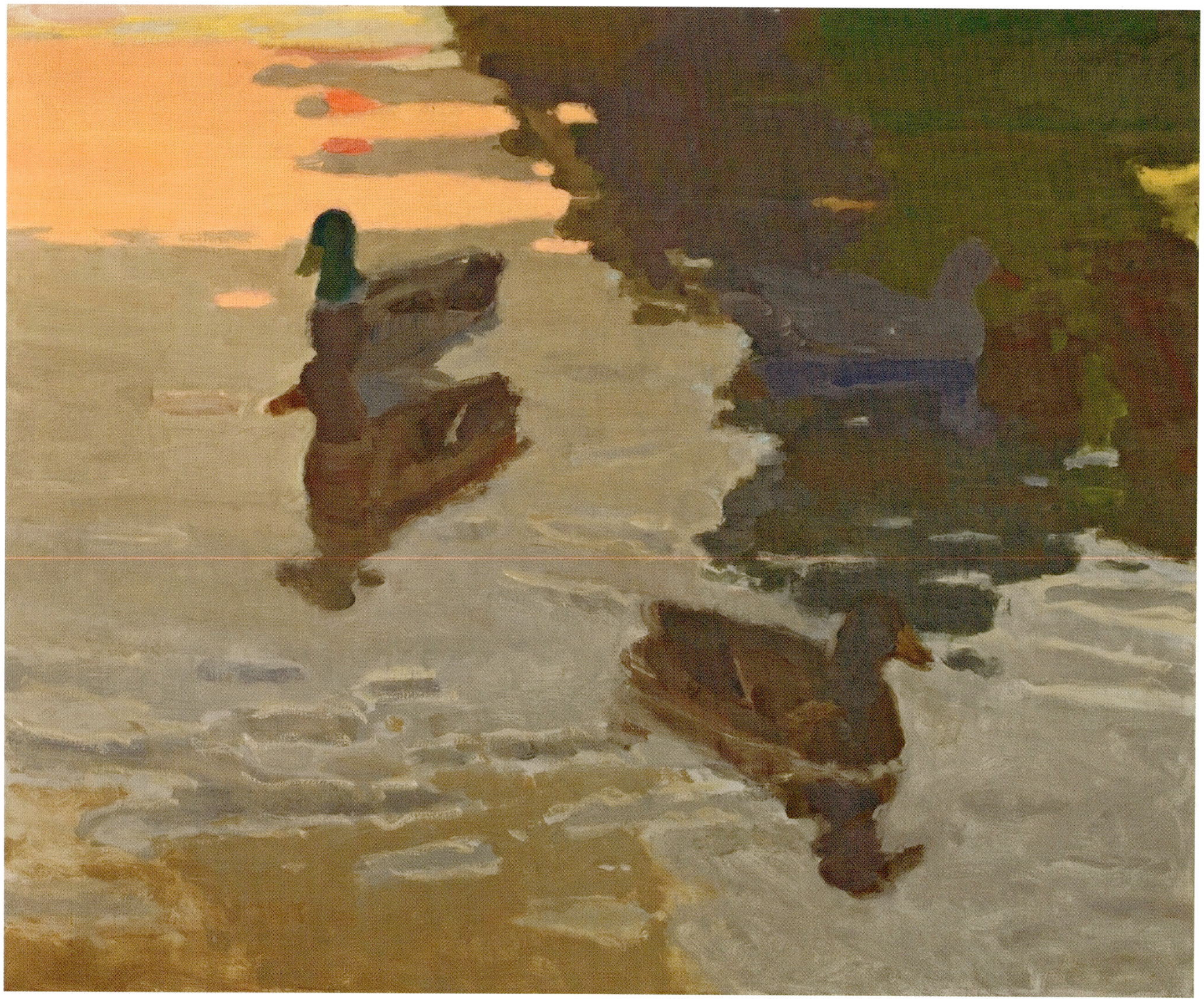

Tulips on Polka Dots

1971, Oil on canvas
36 × 48 inches
Collection of Gary Saretsky

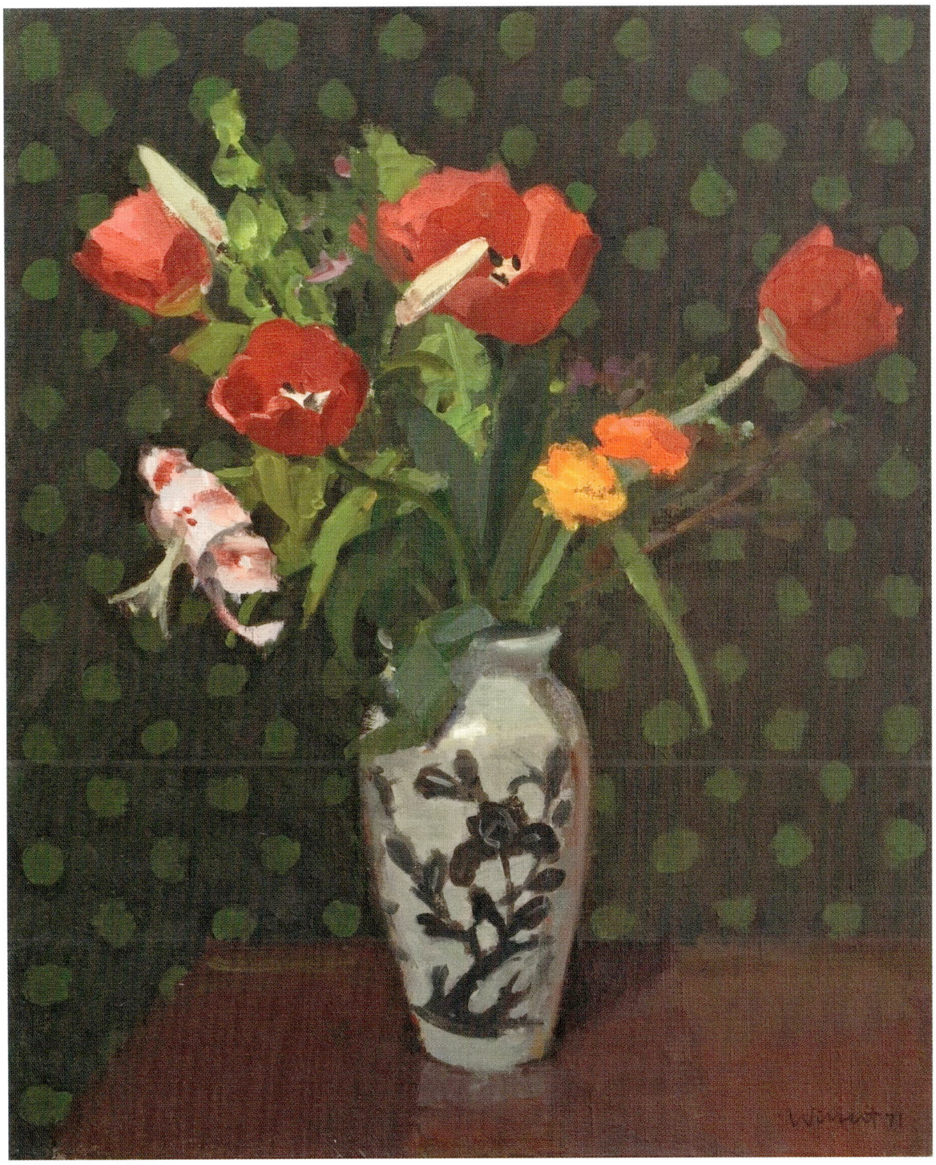

Gretchen Reclining

1972, Oil on canvas
60 × 72 inches
Collection of Pauline and Harvey Lewis

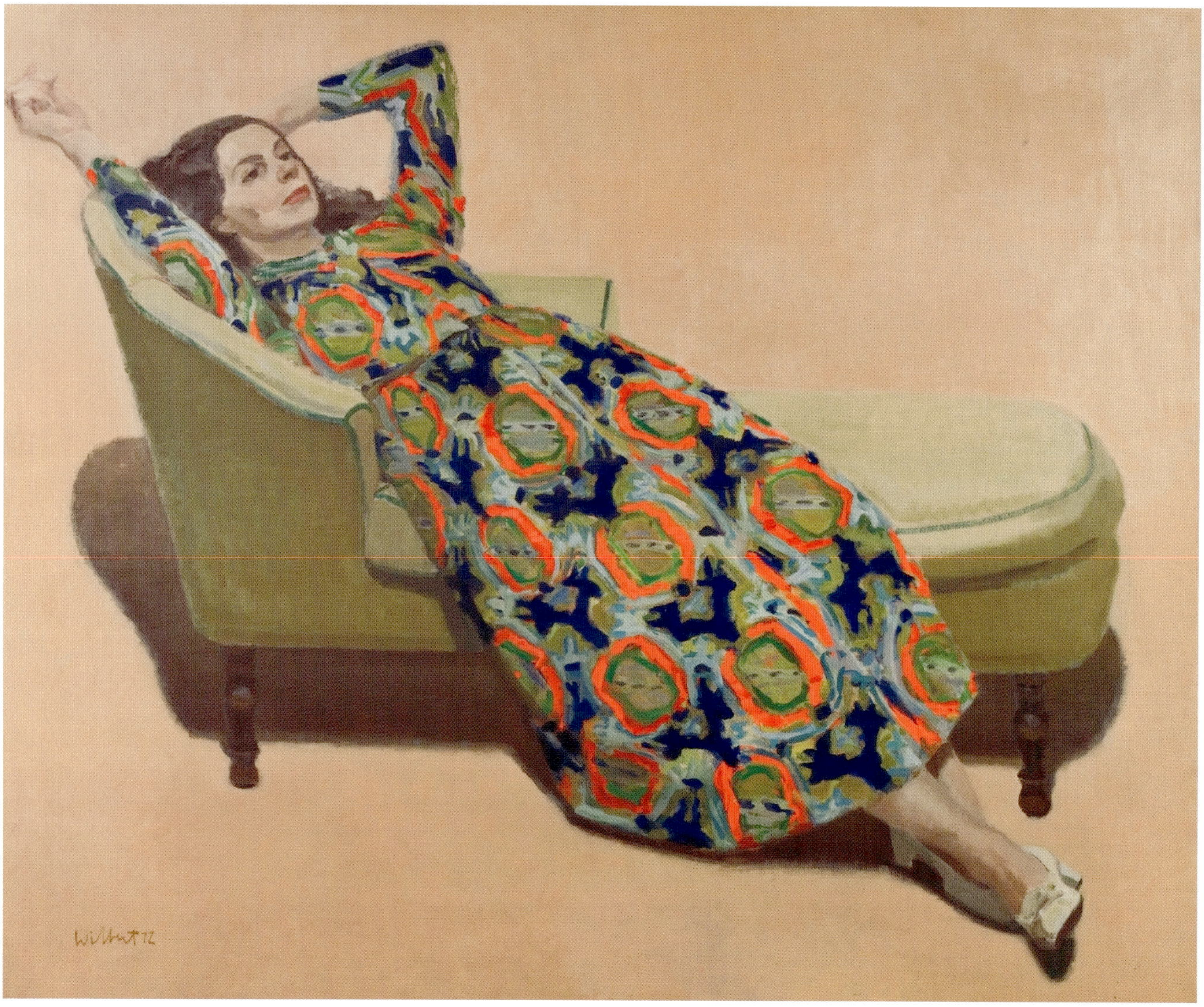

Mary 1972, Oil on canvas
48 × 36 inches
Collection of Eliot and Elizabeth Bank

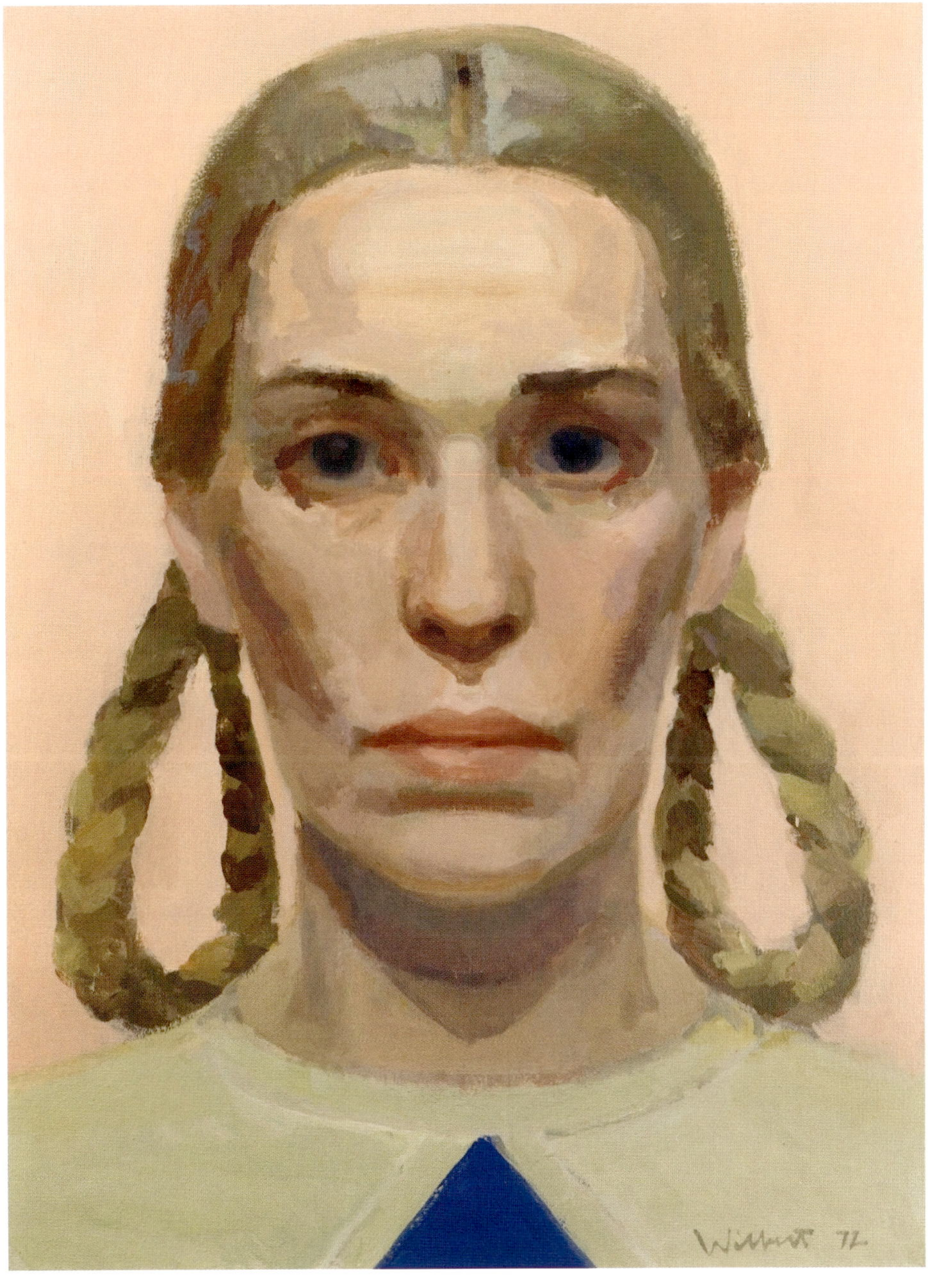

Banana Cluster 1973, Watercolor on paper
11⅜ × 19 inches
Collection of Pauline and Harvey Lewis

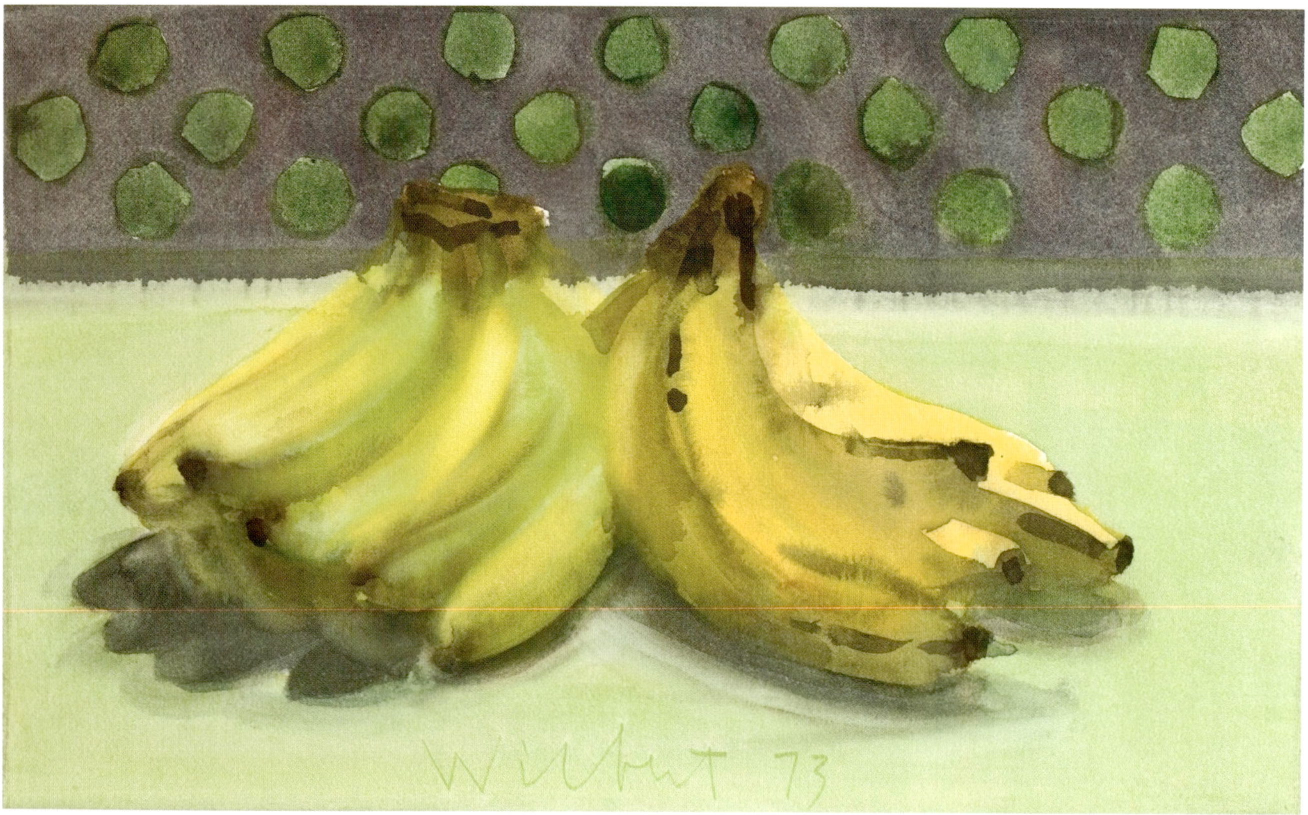

Still Life with Toy Guitar and Billiard Rack

1976, Oil on canvas
36 × 48 inches
Collection of Linda Golden

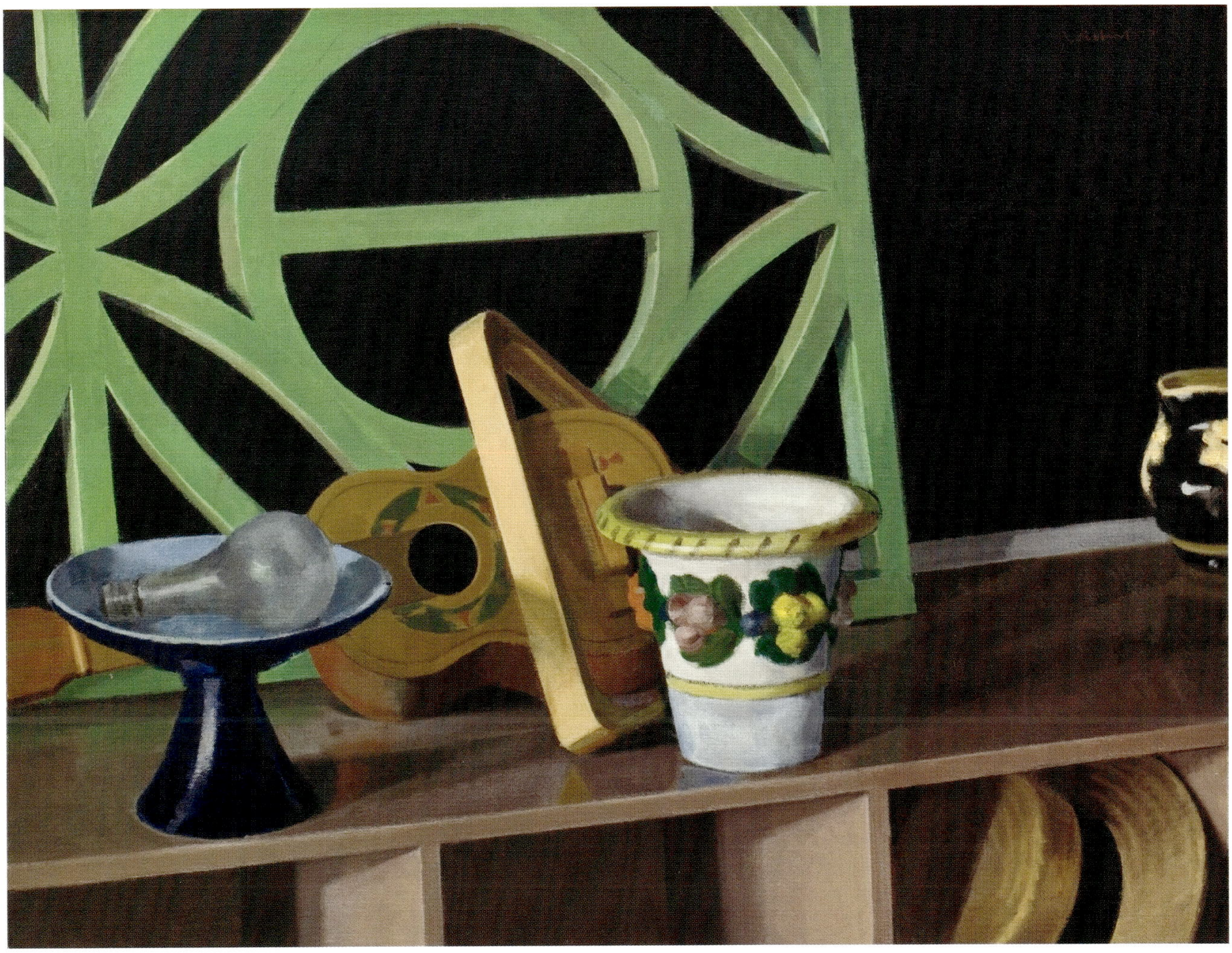

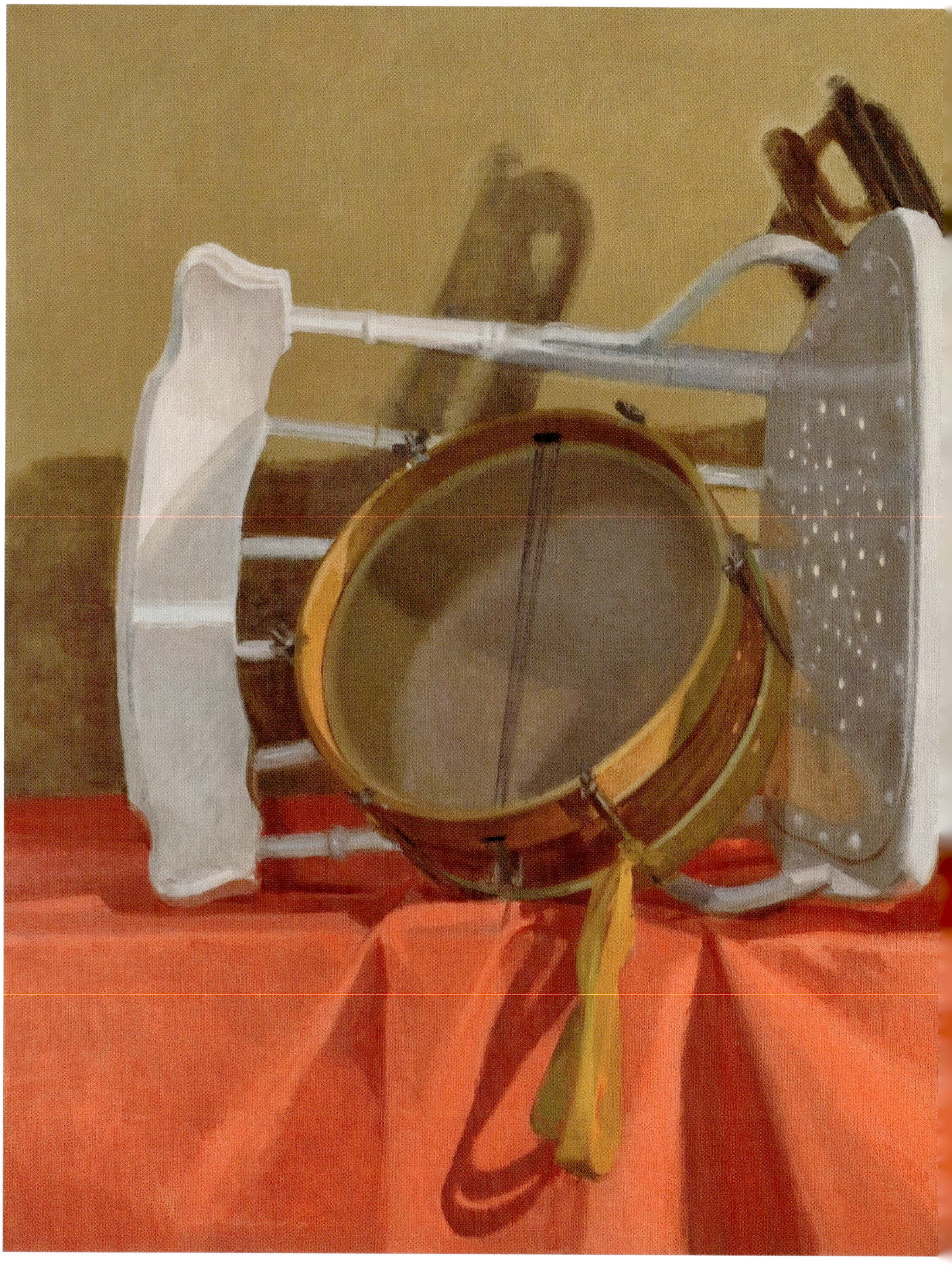

Still Life with Chair and Bobcat

1977, Oil on canvas
48 × 90 inches
Collection of Leet E. and Patsy Denton

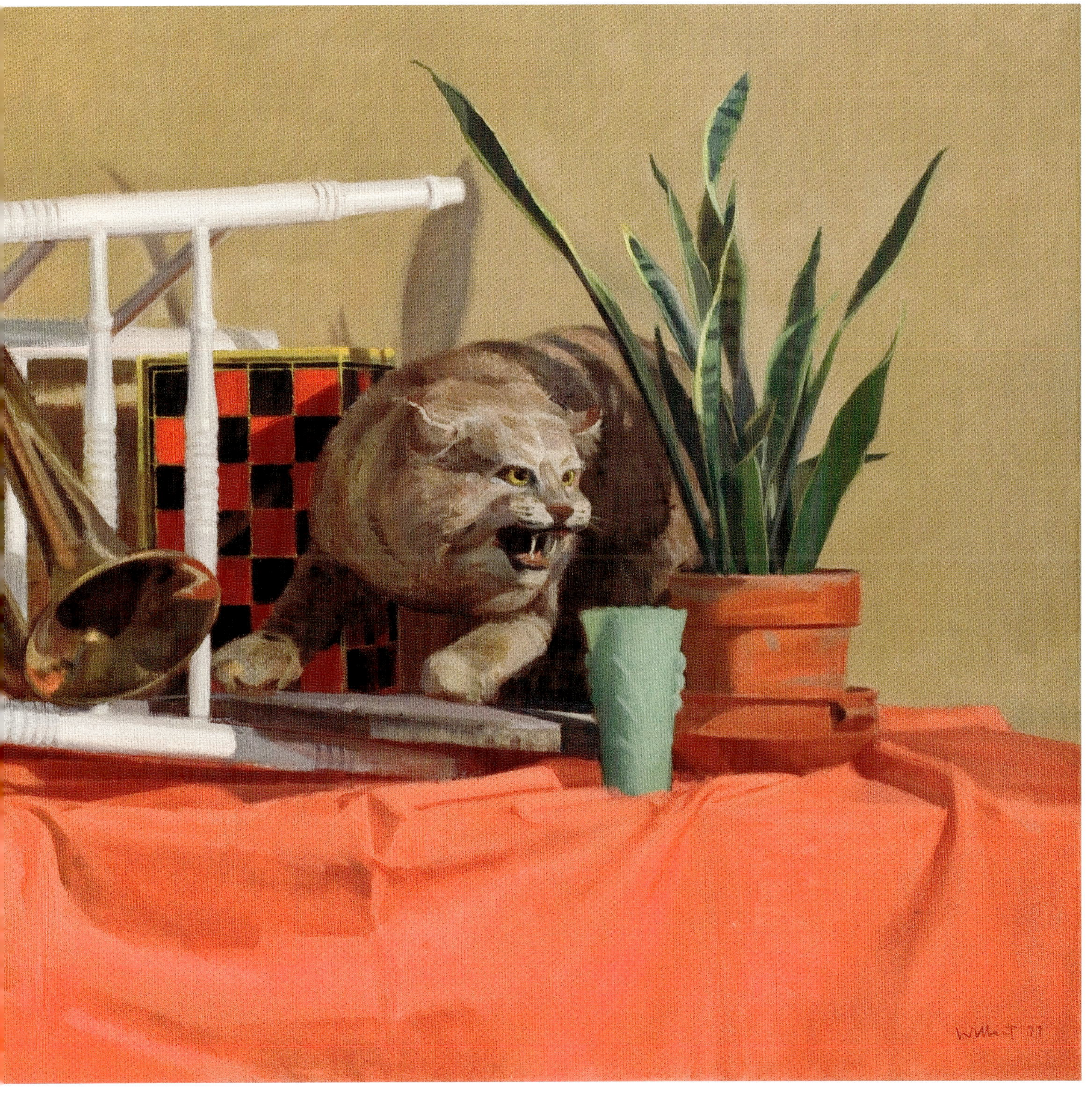

Lilacs and Carnations in Green Vase

1978, Oil on canvas
36 × 30 inches
Collection of the Artist

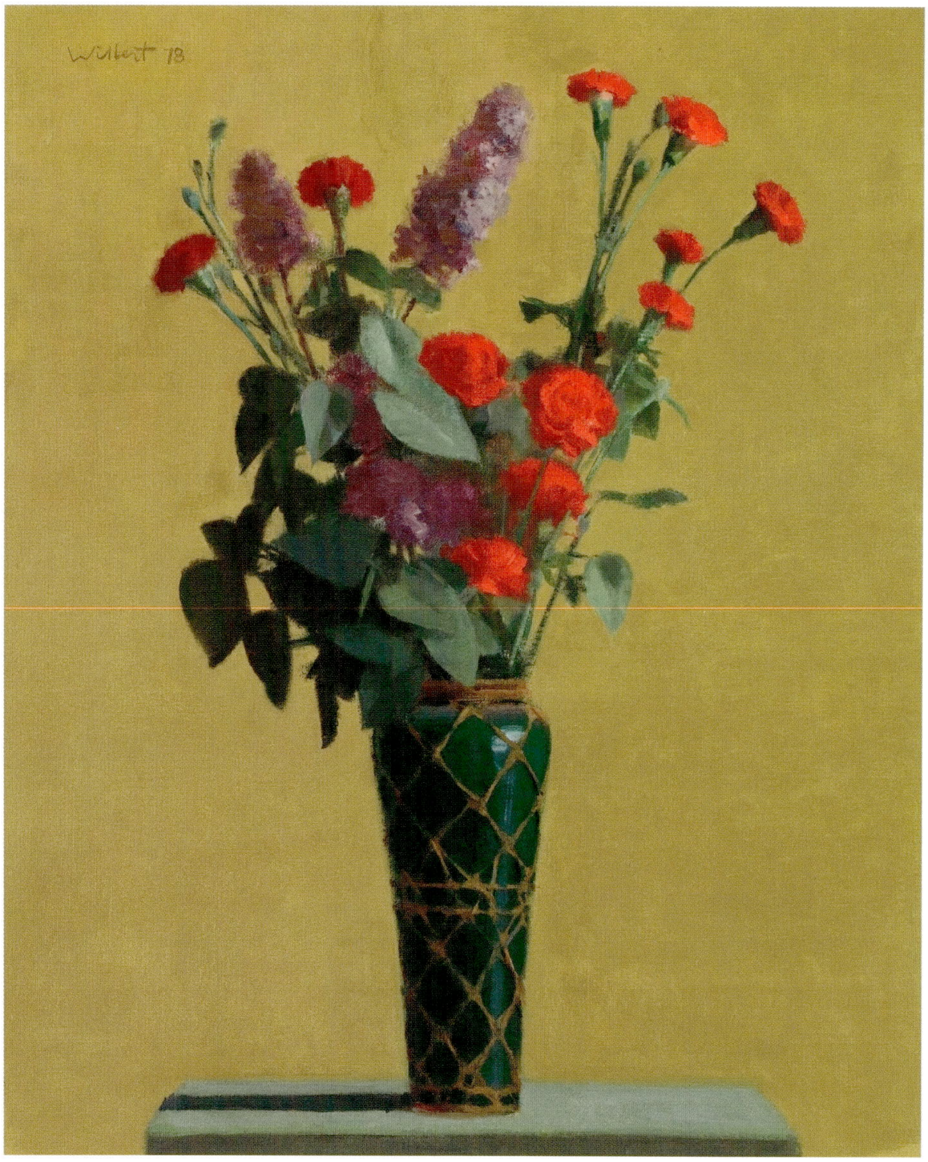

Still Life with Shoes and Horn

1979, Oil on canvas
60 × 48 inches
The JPMorgan Chase
Art Collection

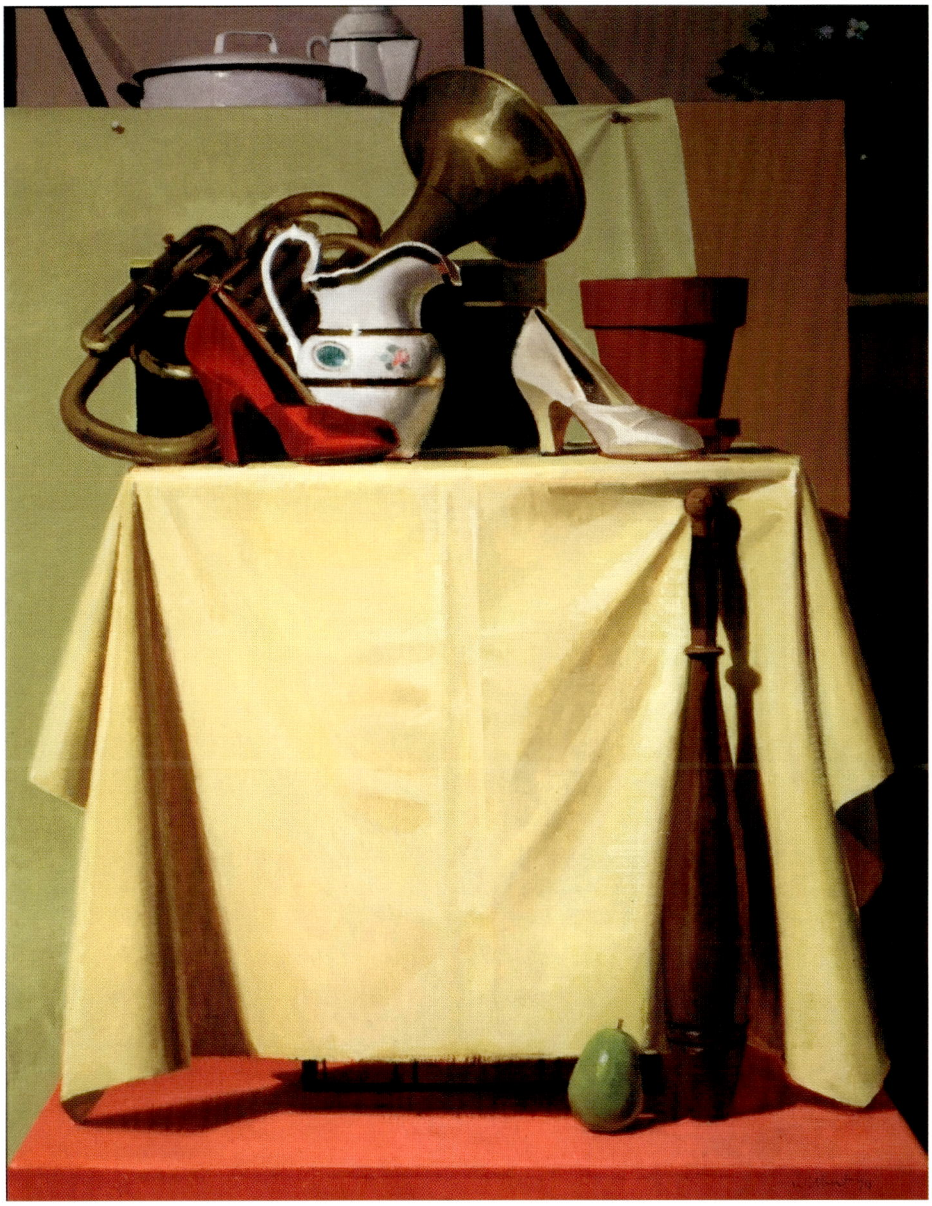

Still Life at Night 1983, Oil on canvas
36 × 32 inches
The JPMorgan Chase Art Collection

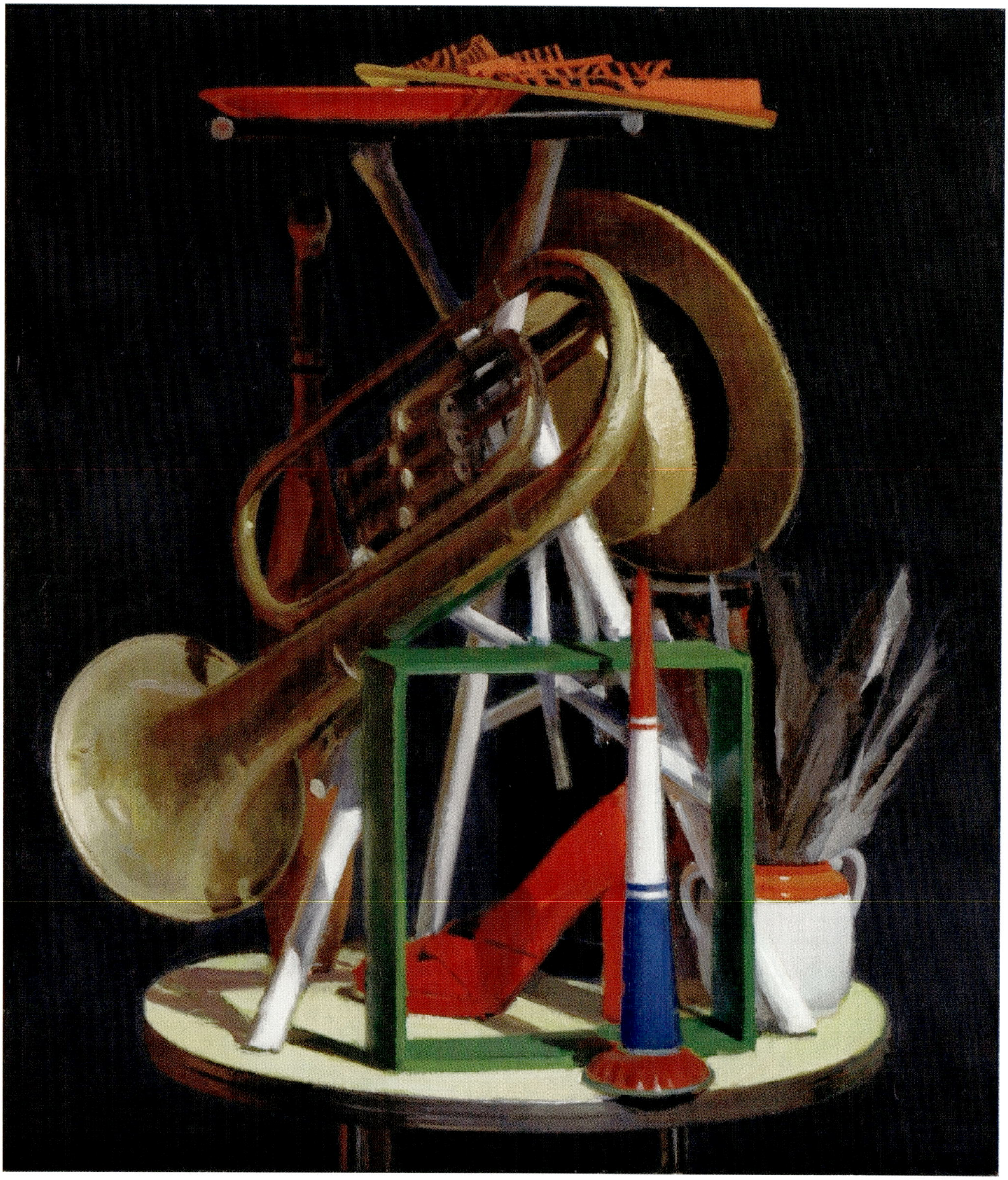

Tulips with Indian Club and Blue Dish

1984, Oil on canvas
30 × 30 inches
Private Collection, Chicago, Illinois

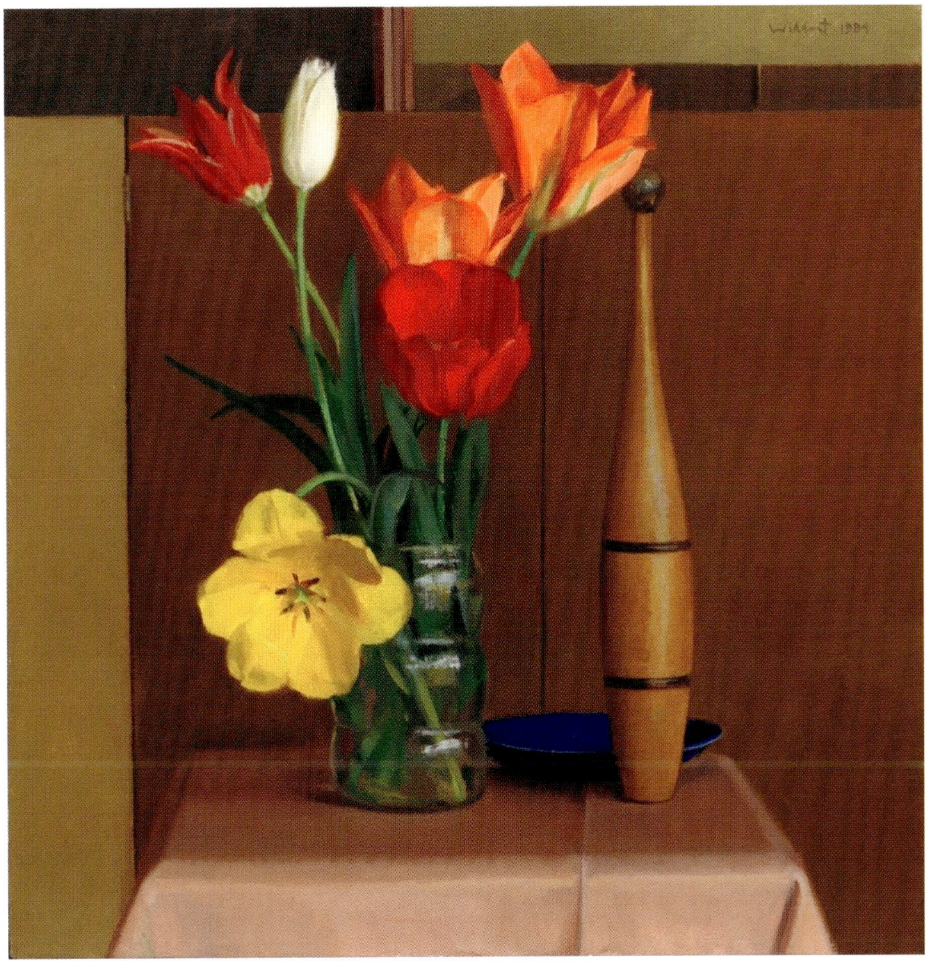

Laura Seated 1984, Oil on canvas
60 × 40 inches
Collection of Gretchen Wilbert

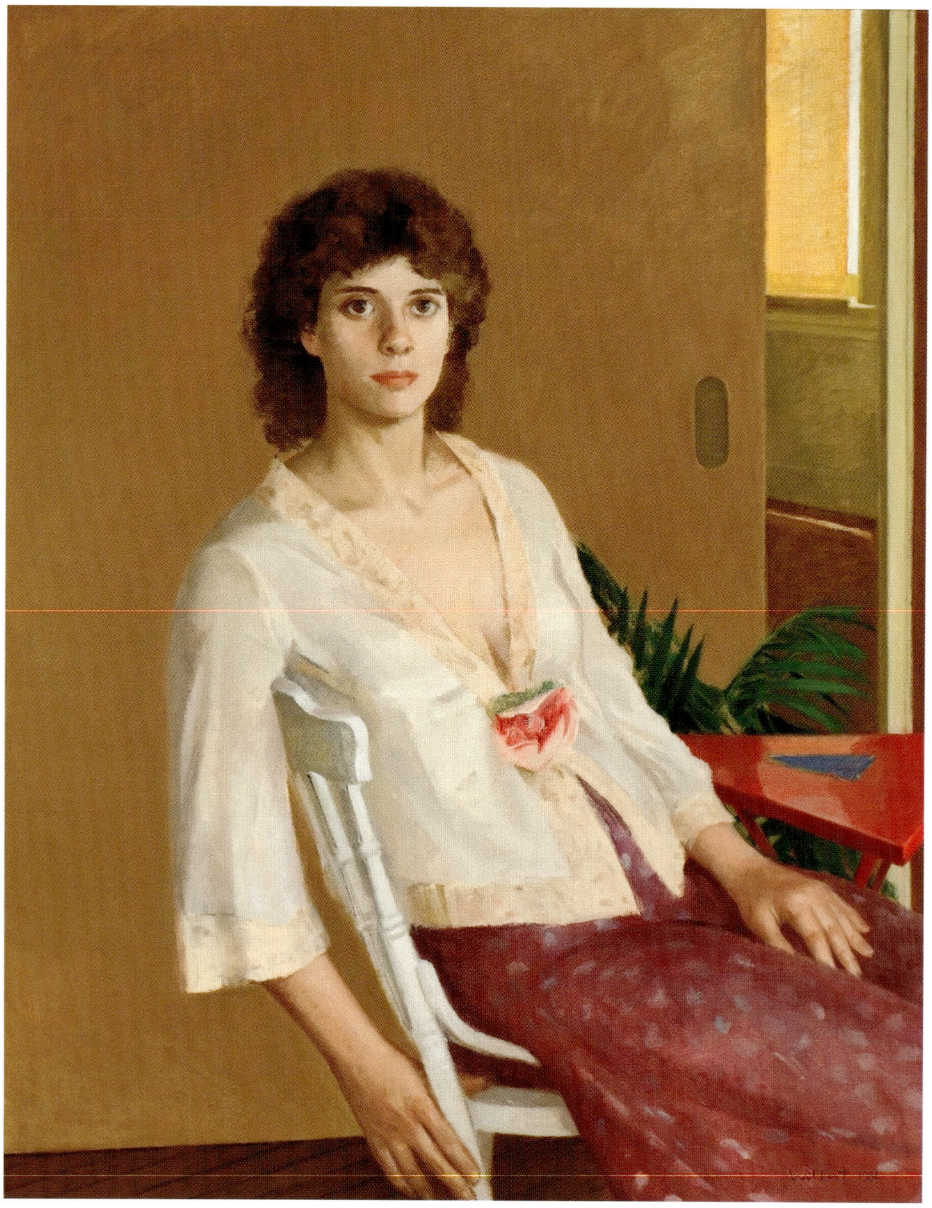

Mary with Wicker Chair

1984, Oil on canvas
72 × 84 inches
Collection of Adrienne and
Herschel Fink

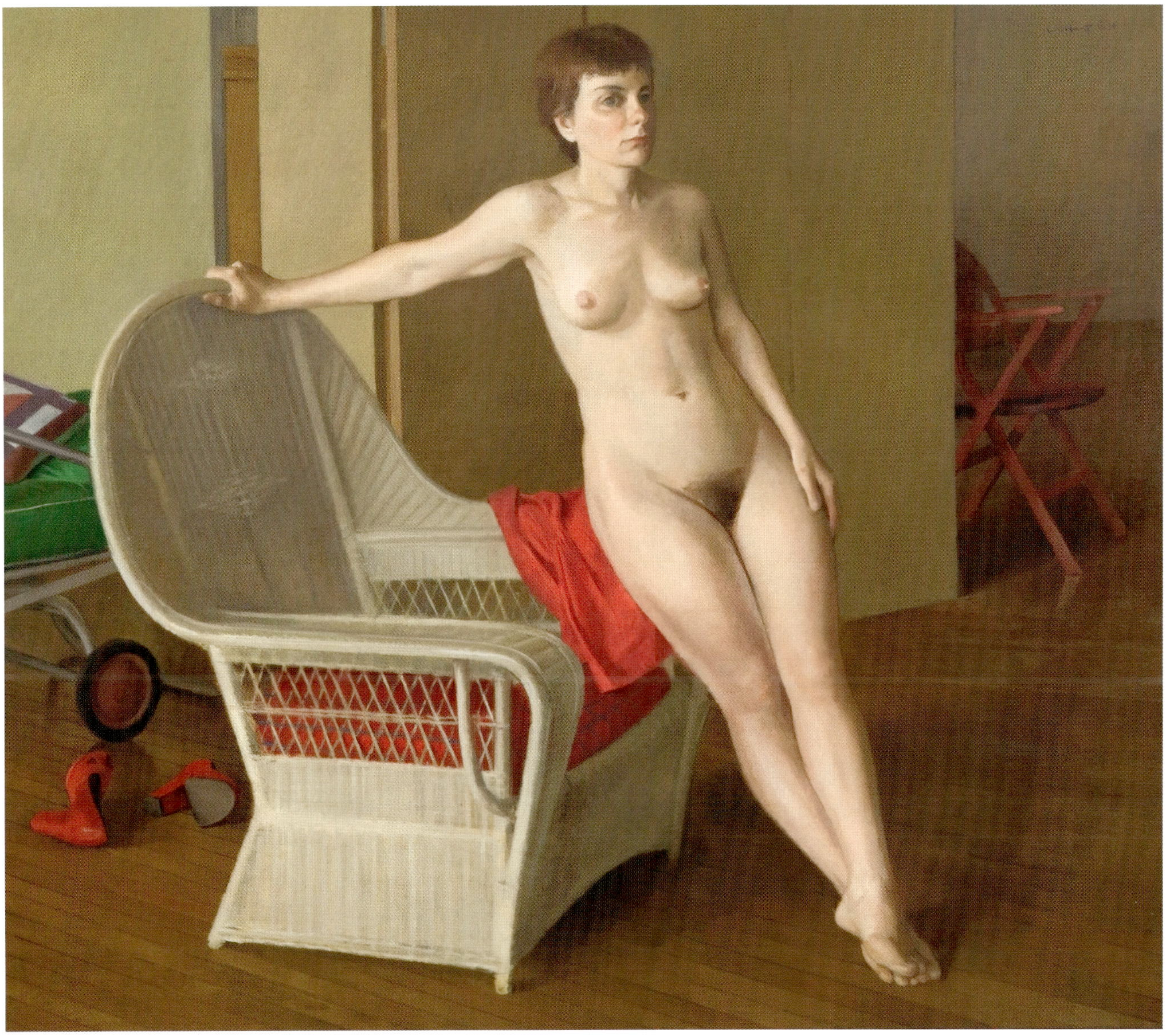

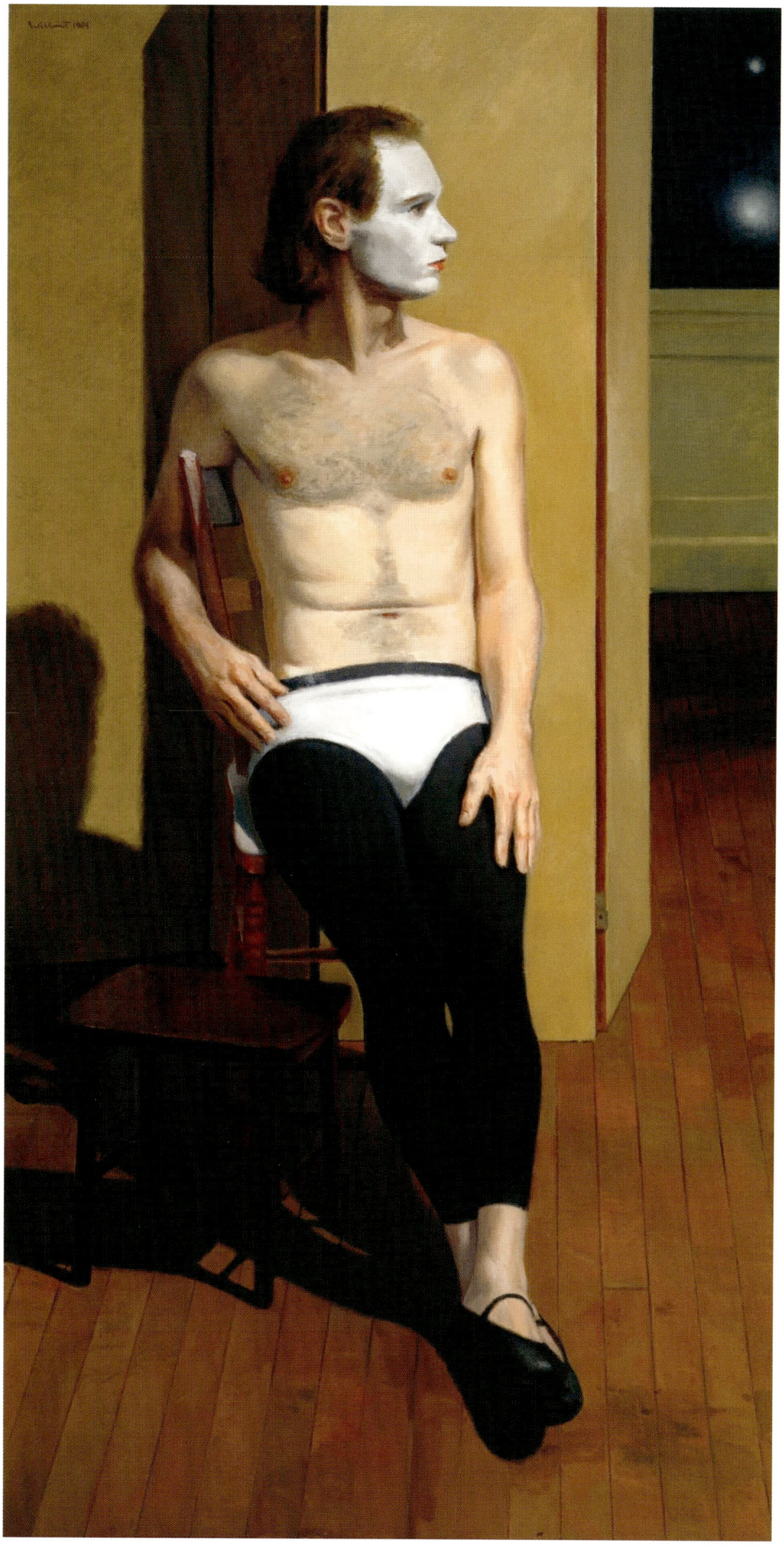

Gerry in Whiteface

1984, Oil on canvas
92 × 46 inches
Collection of the Detroit Institute of Arts, Founders Society Purchase with funds from Mr. and Mrs. Maurice Cohen, F82.27

Mime with Drum

1986, Oil on canvas
42 × 48 inches
Collection of Sonnenschein Nath and Rosenthal LLP

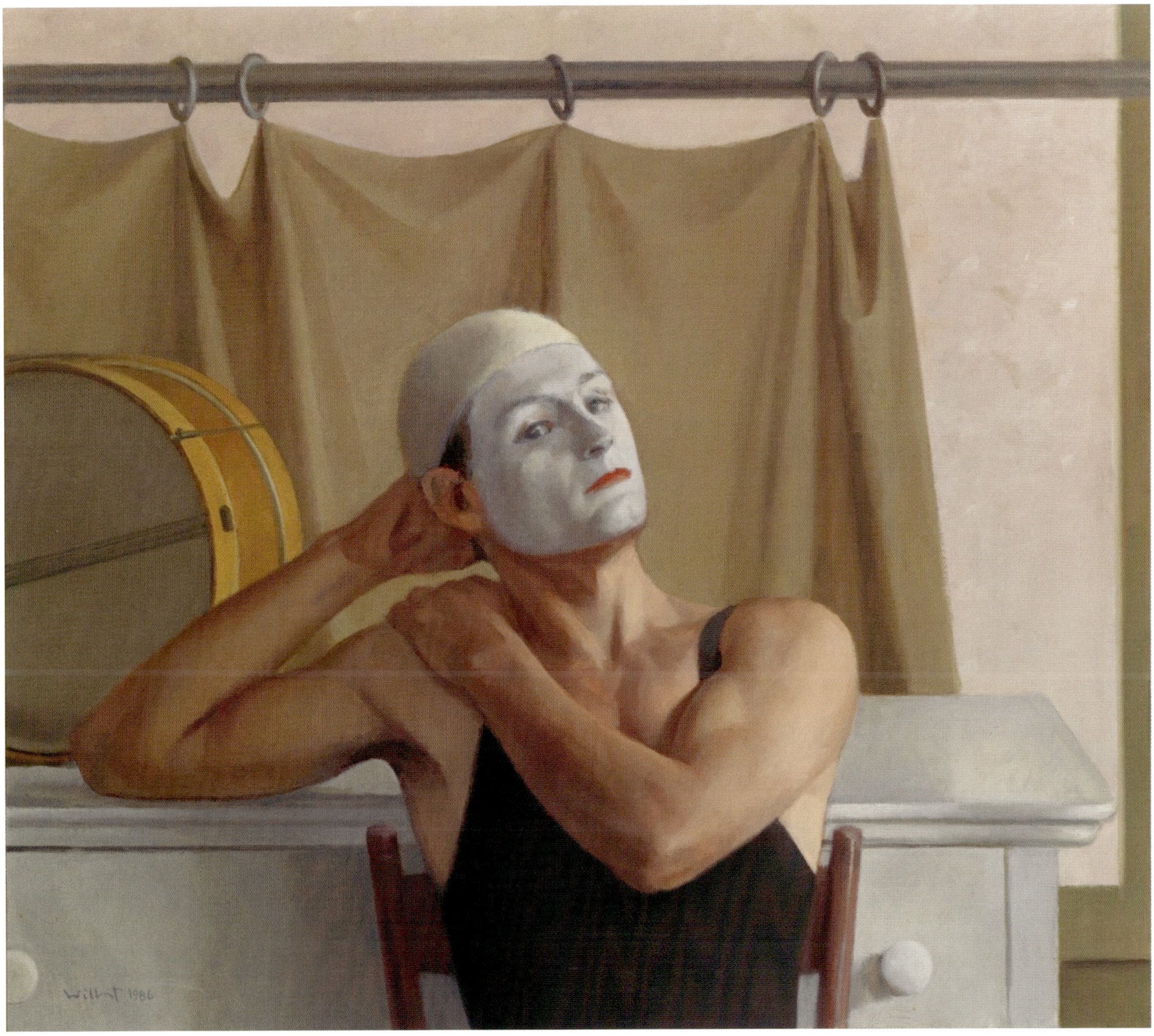

Mary with Spider Plant

1987, Oil on canvas
46 × 38 inches
Collection of Marilyn and Steven Victor

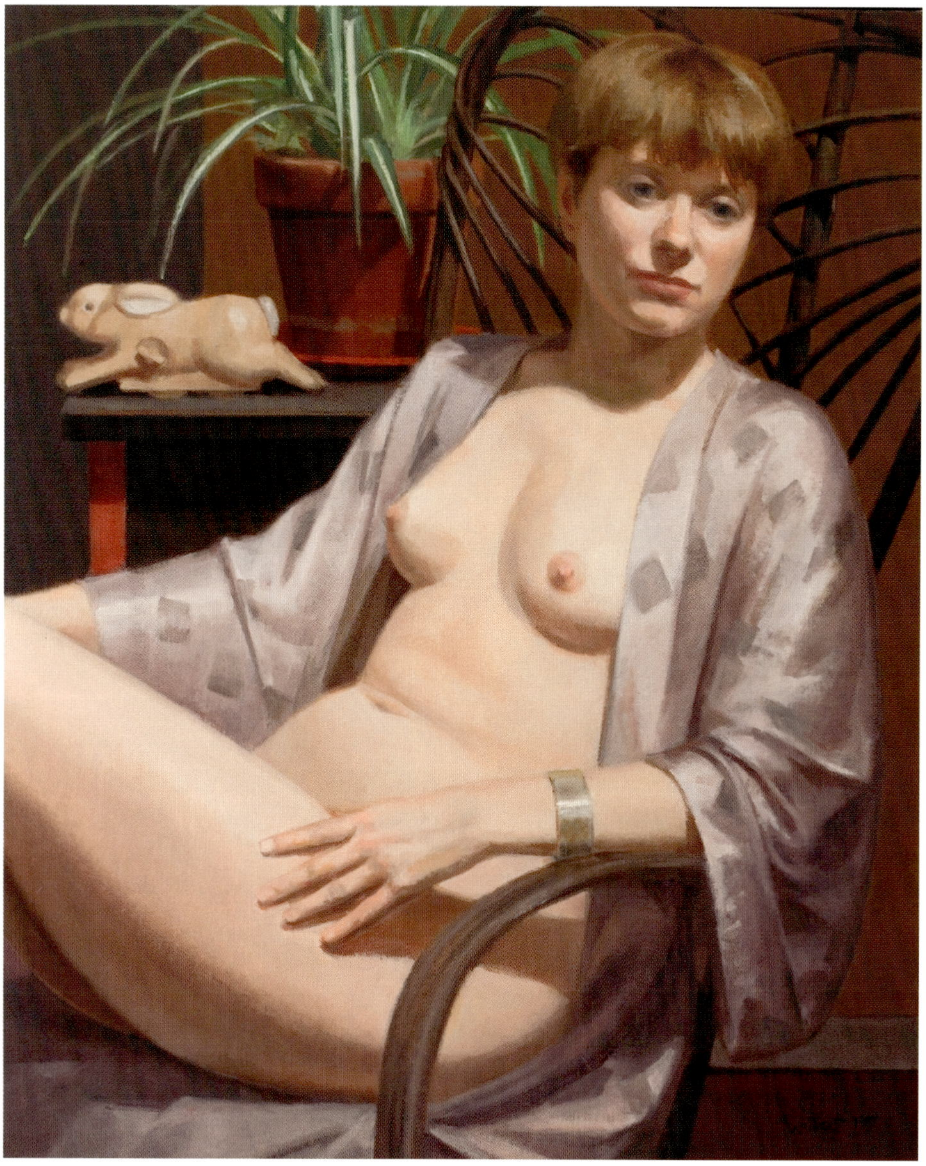

Bouquet 1987, Watercolor on paper
30 × 22 3/8 inches
Collection of the Artist

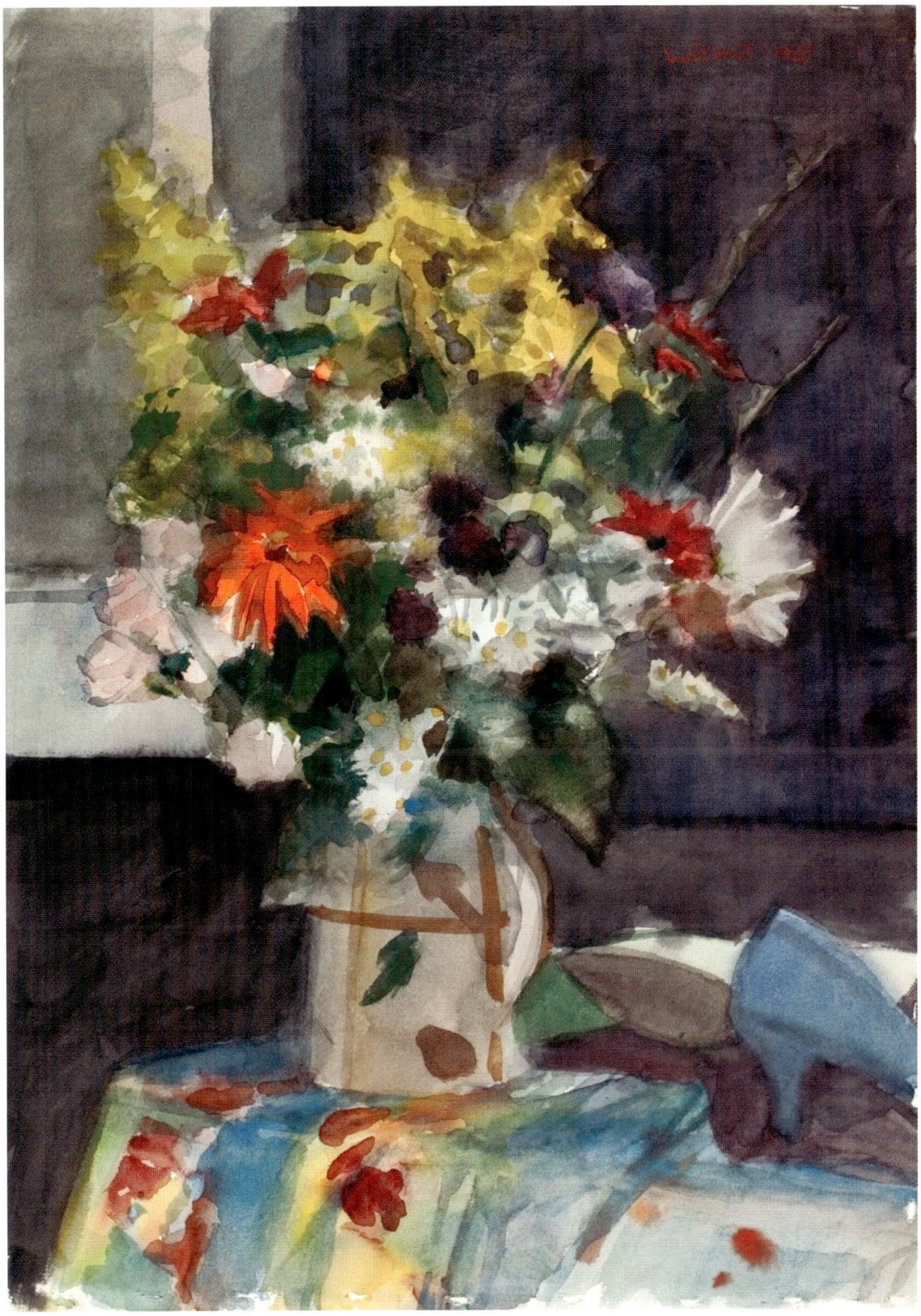

Julie on the Green Lounge

1989, Oil on canvas
56 × 40 inches
Collection of Rose Marie and
Seymour Karbal

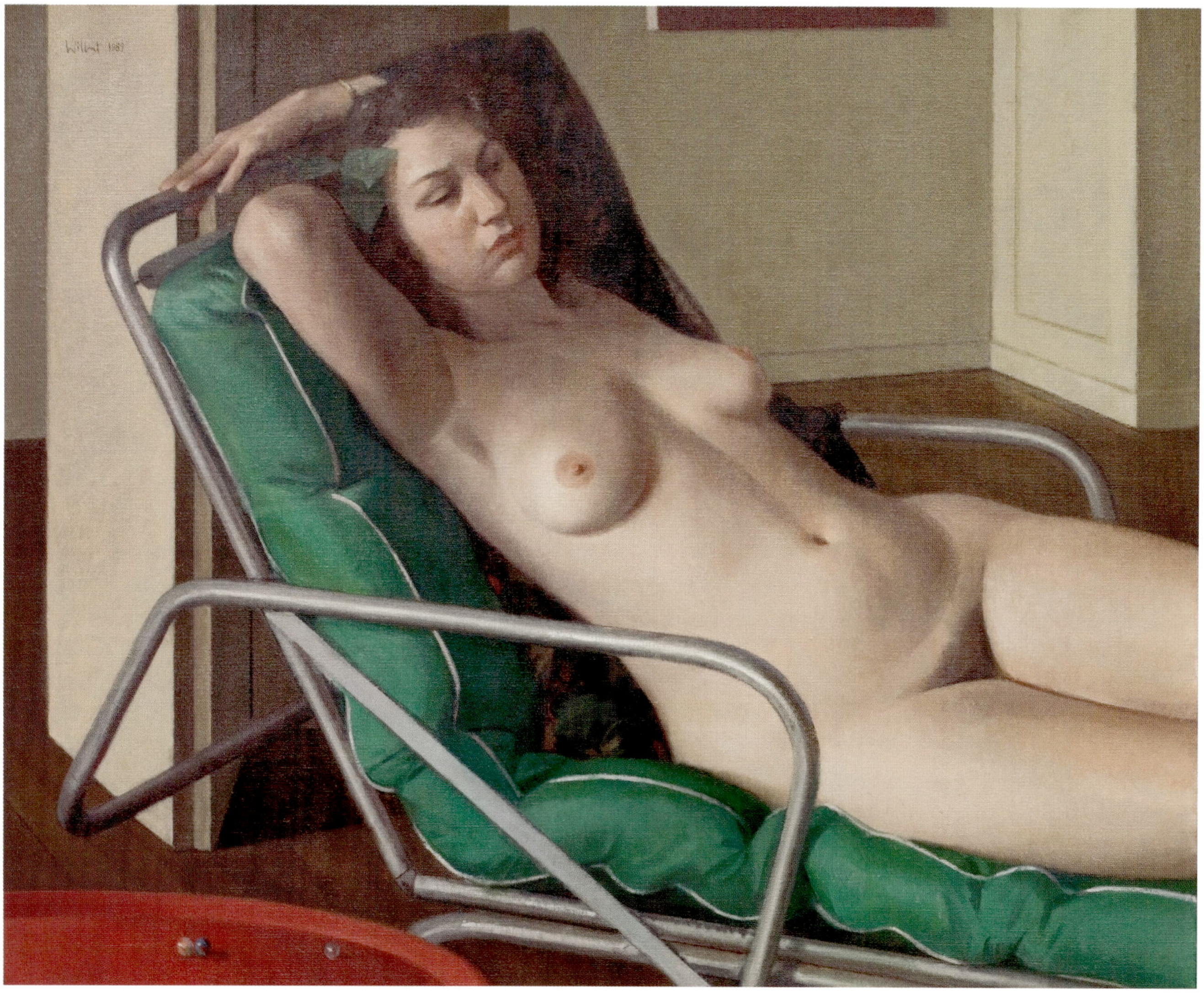

Still Life with Weathervane

1989, Oil on canvas
40 × 50 inches
Collection of the Artist

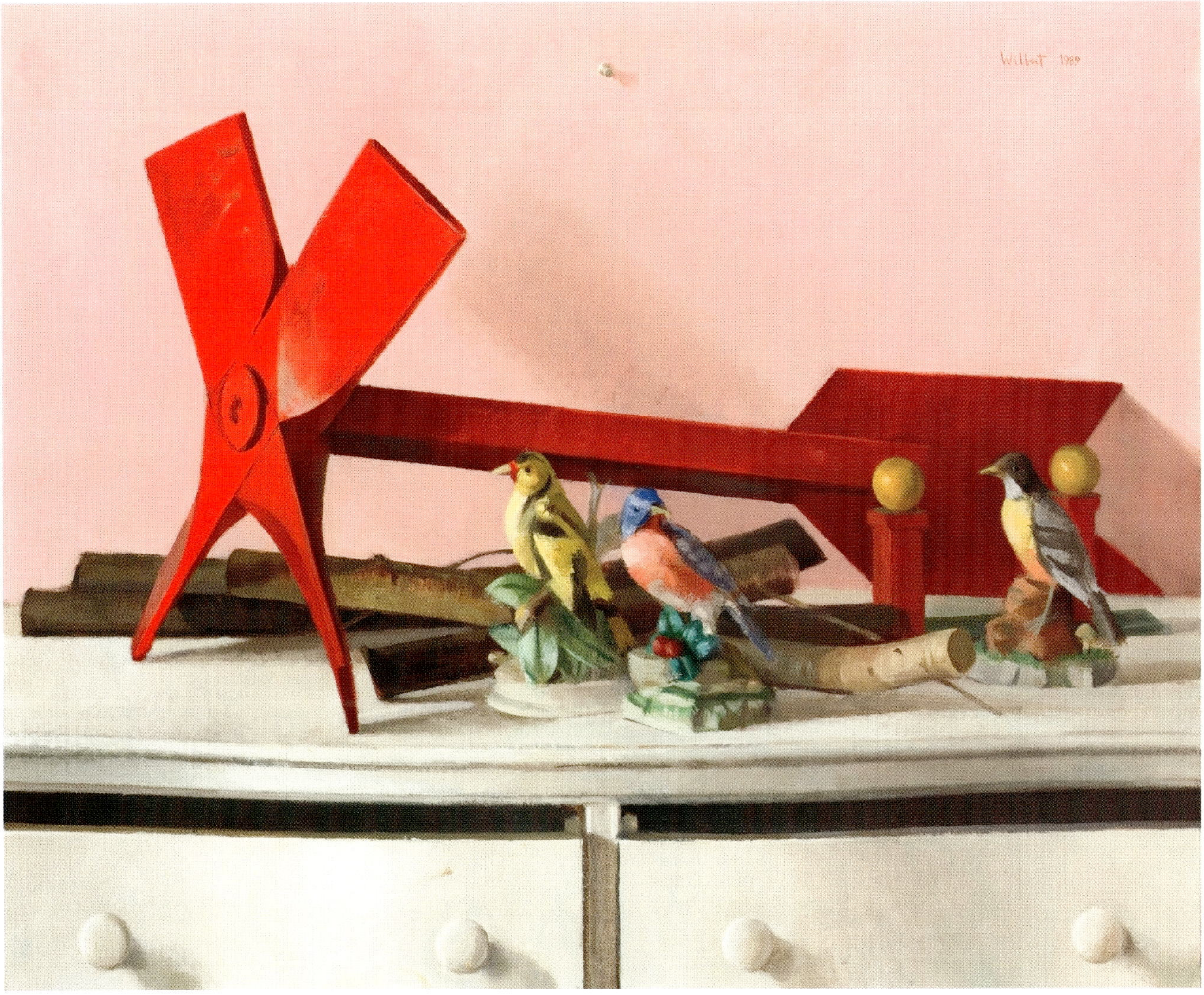

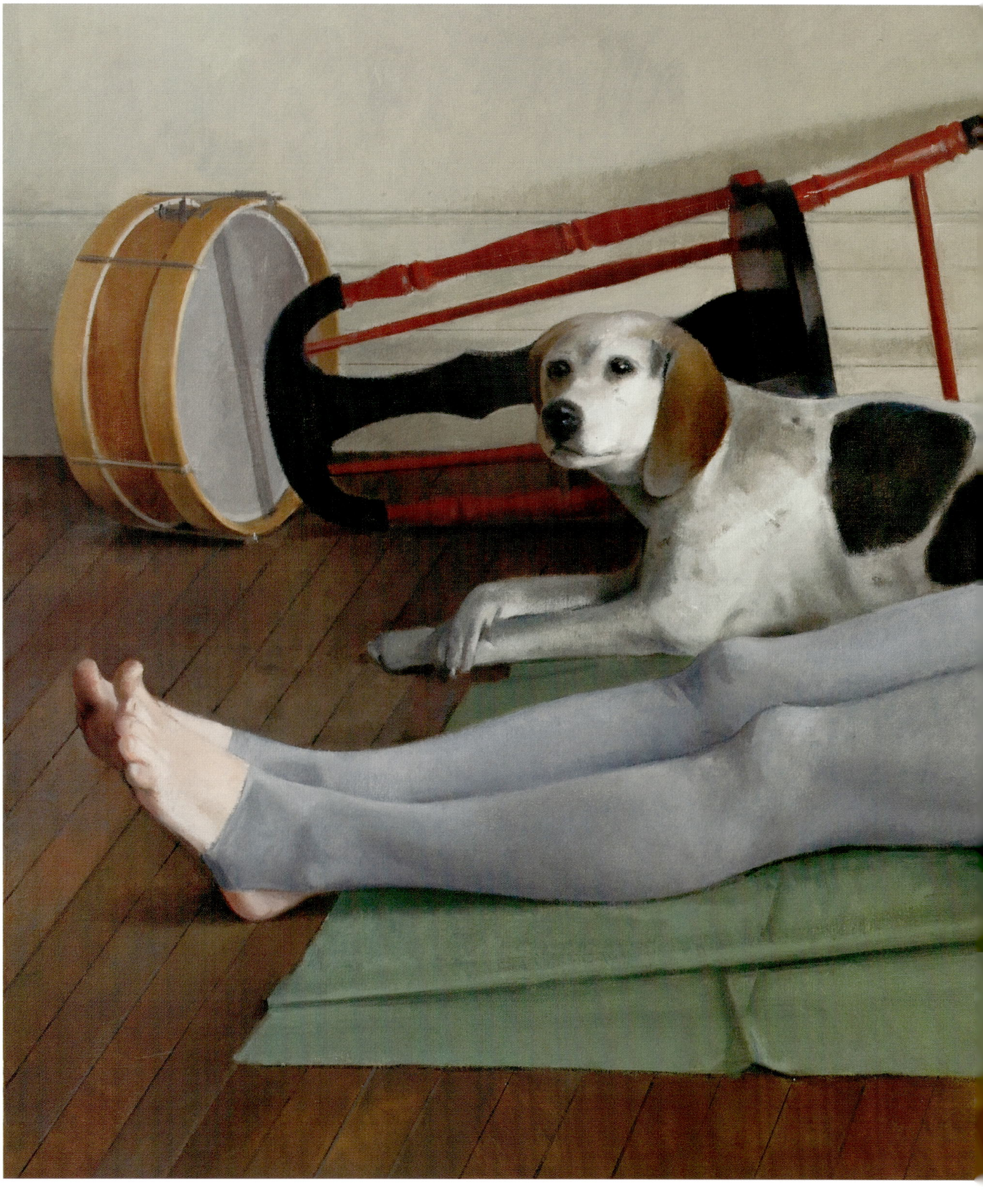

Figure with Dog

1989, Oil on canvas
48 × 92 inches
Collection of Renee E. and
Marty Laker

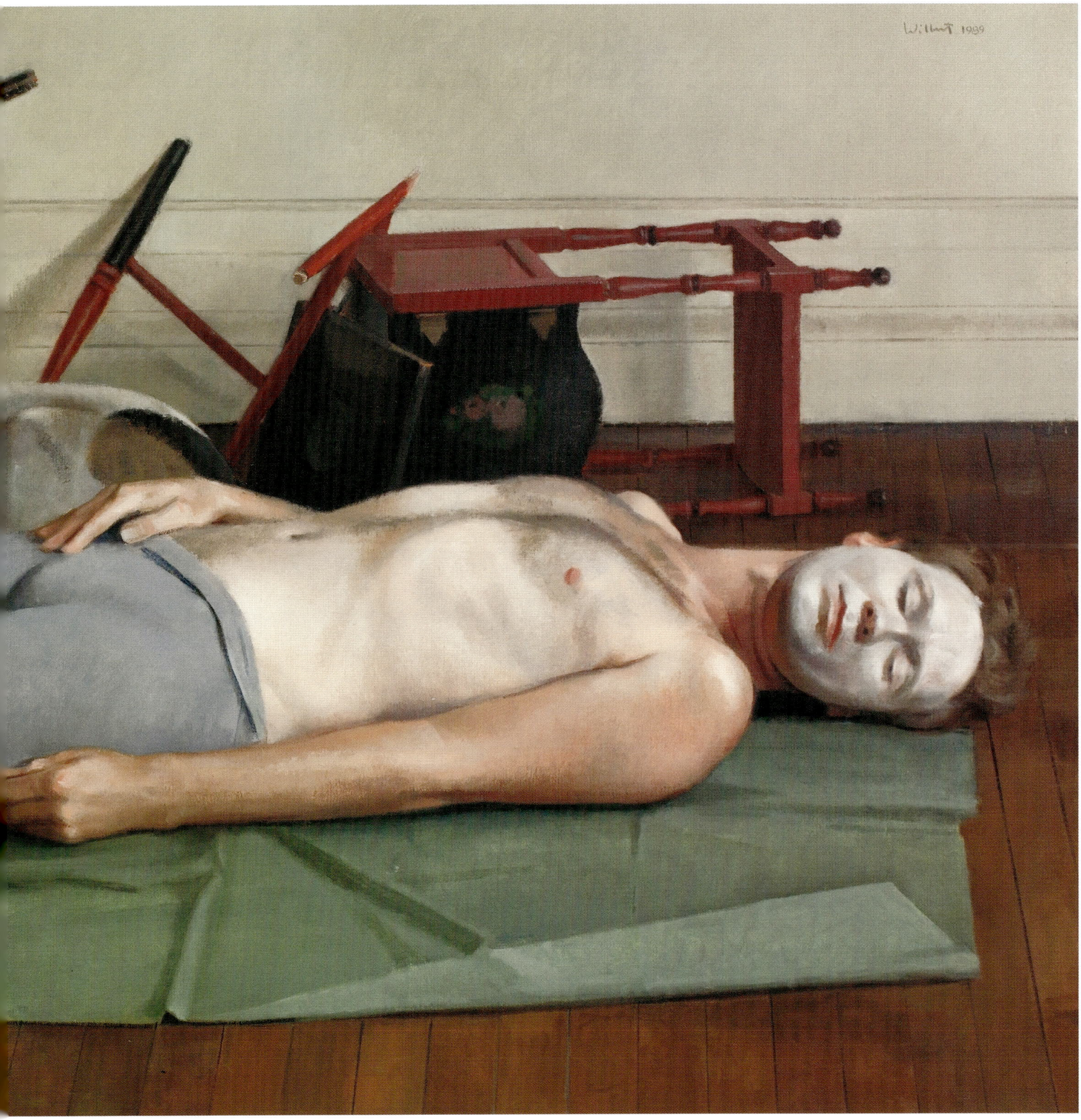

Figures with Folding Screen

1989, Oil on canvas
60 × 48 inches
Collection of Bruce and Joanne Polozker

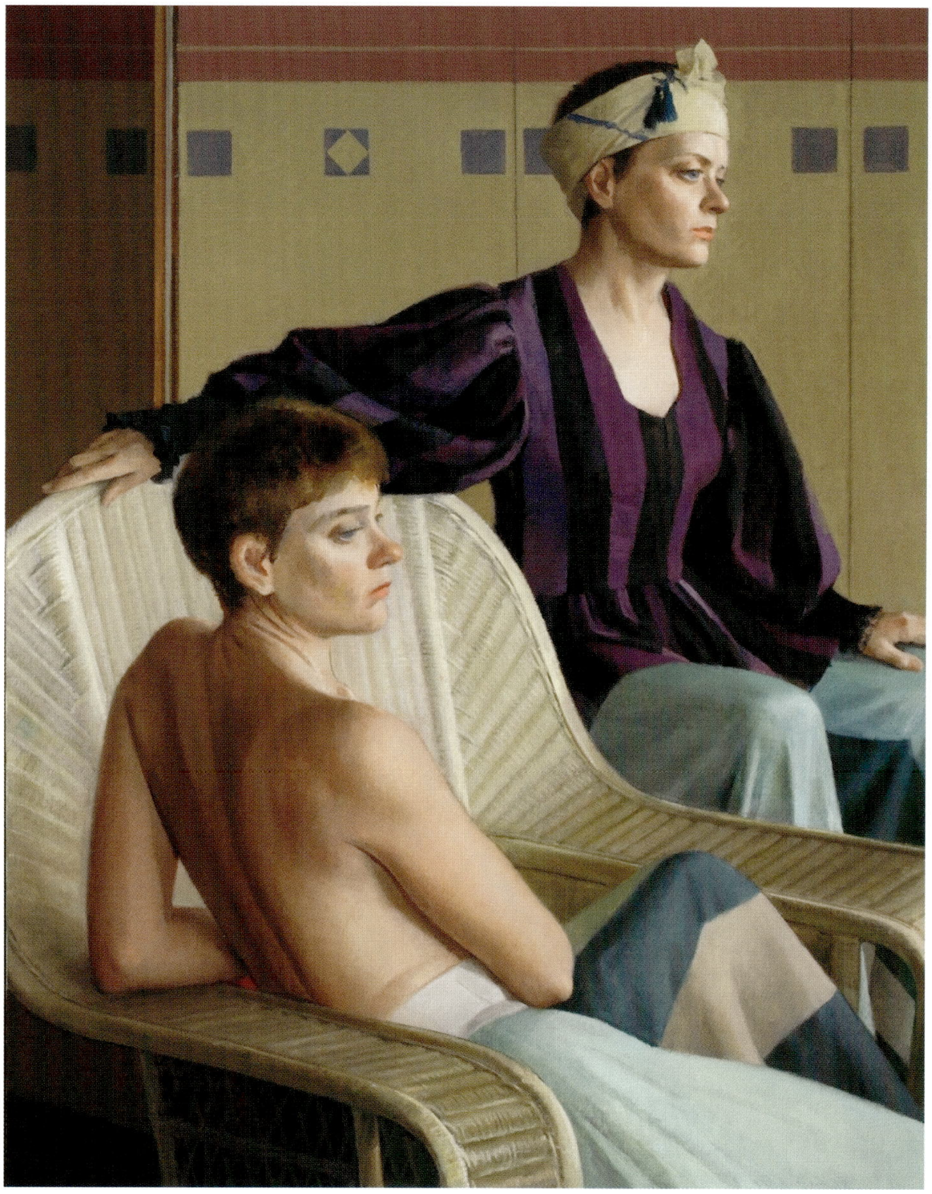

Sunflowers 1992, Charcoal on paper
37 × 26 inches
Collection of Rose Marie and
Seymour Karbal

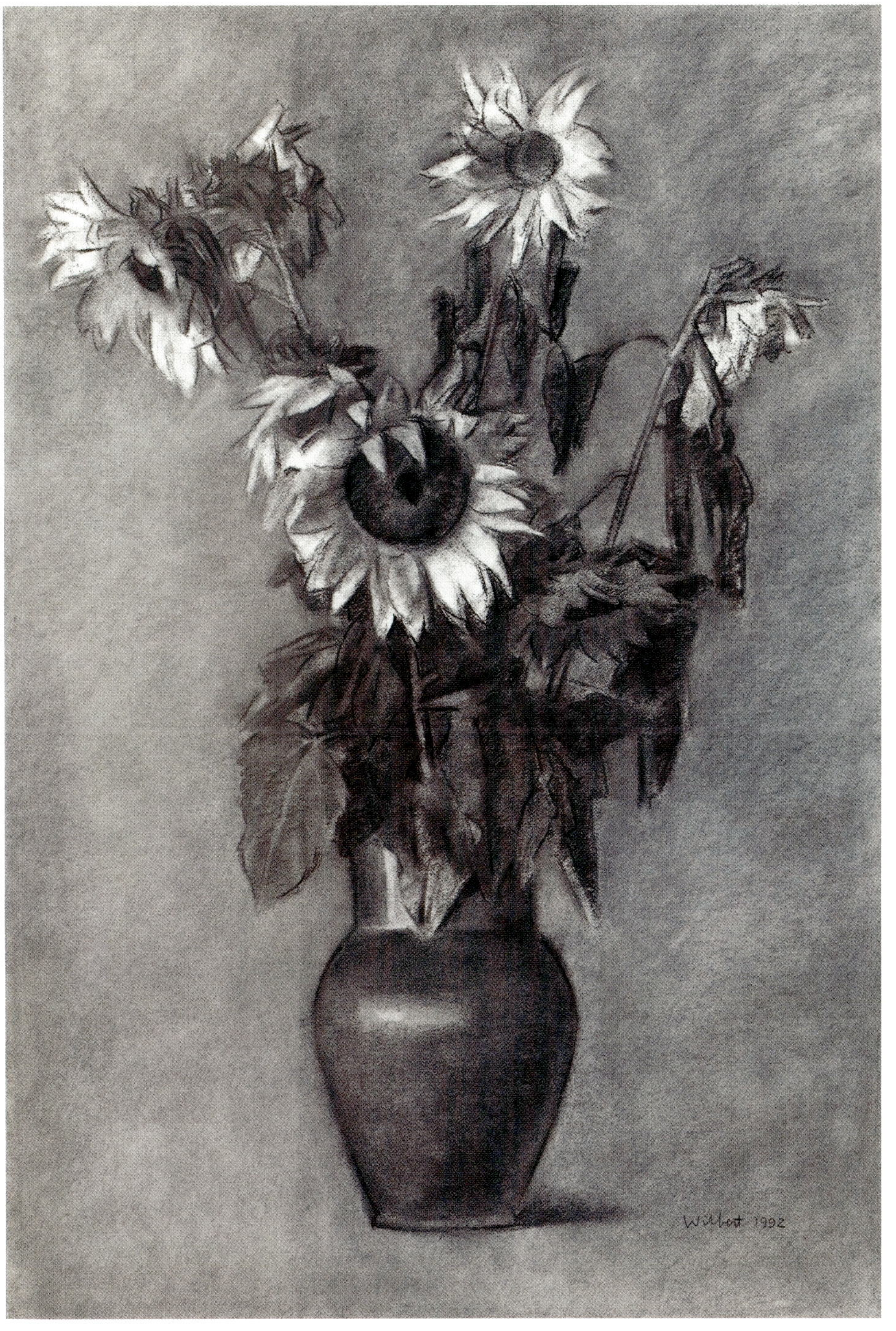

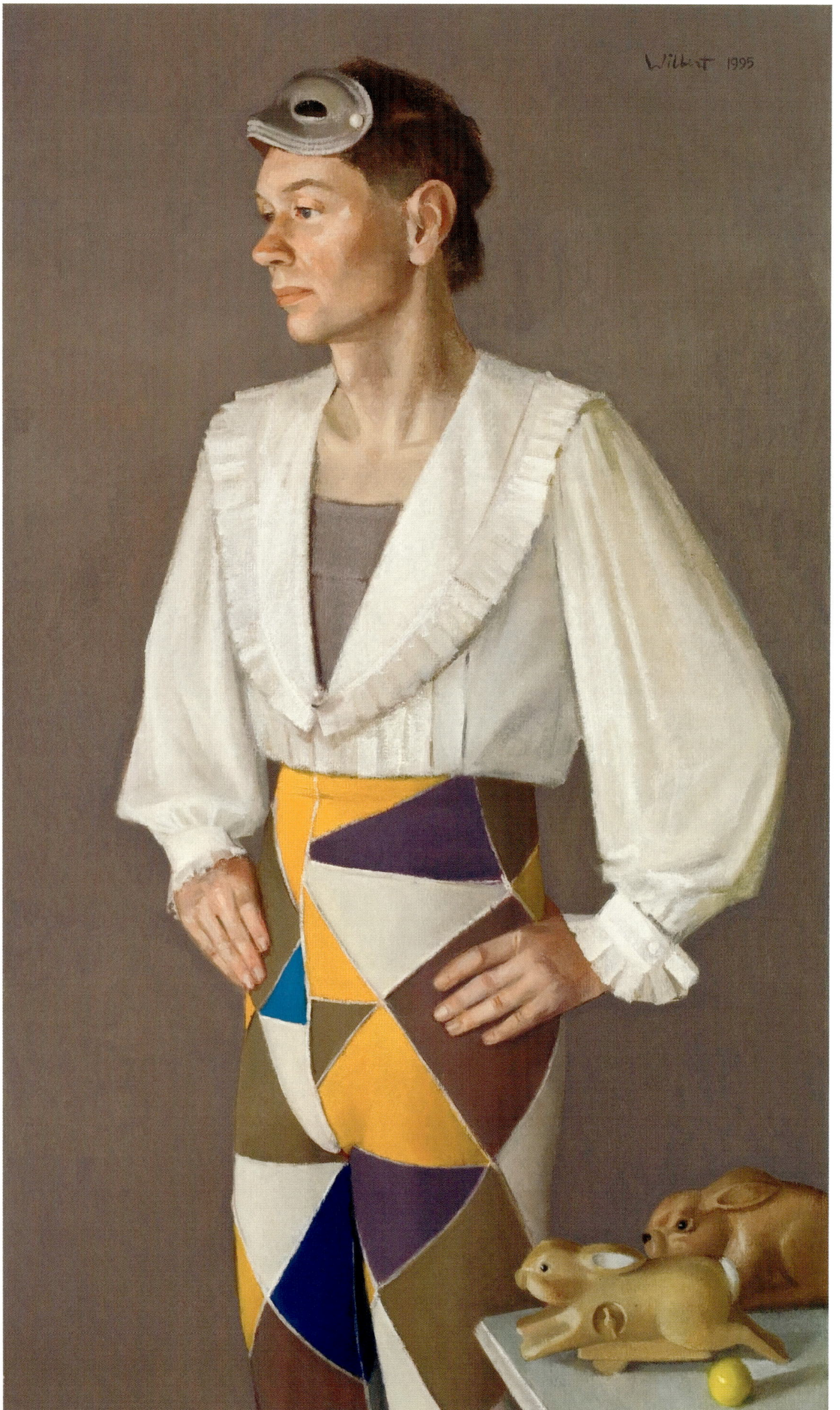
Willert 1995

Gerry as Harlequin 1995, Oil on canvas
60 × 30 inches
Collection of the Artist

Yellow Gladioli with Figured Vase 1997, Watercolor on paper
30¾ × 23⅛ inches
Collection of Marilyn Williamson

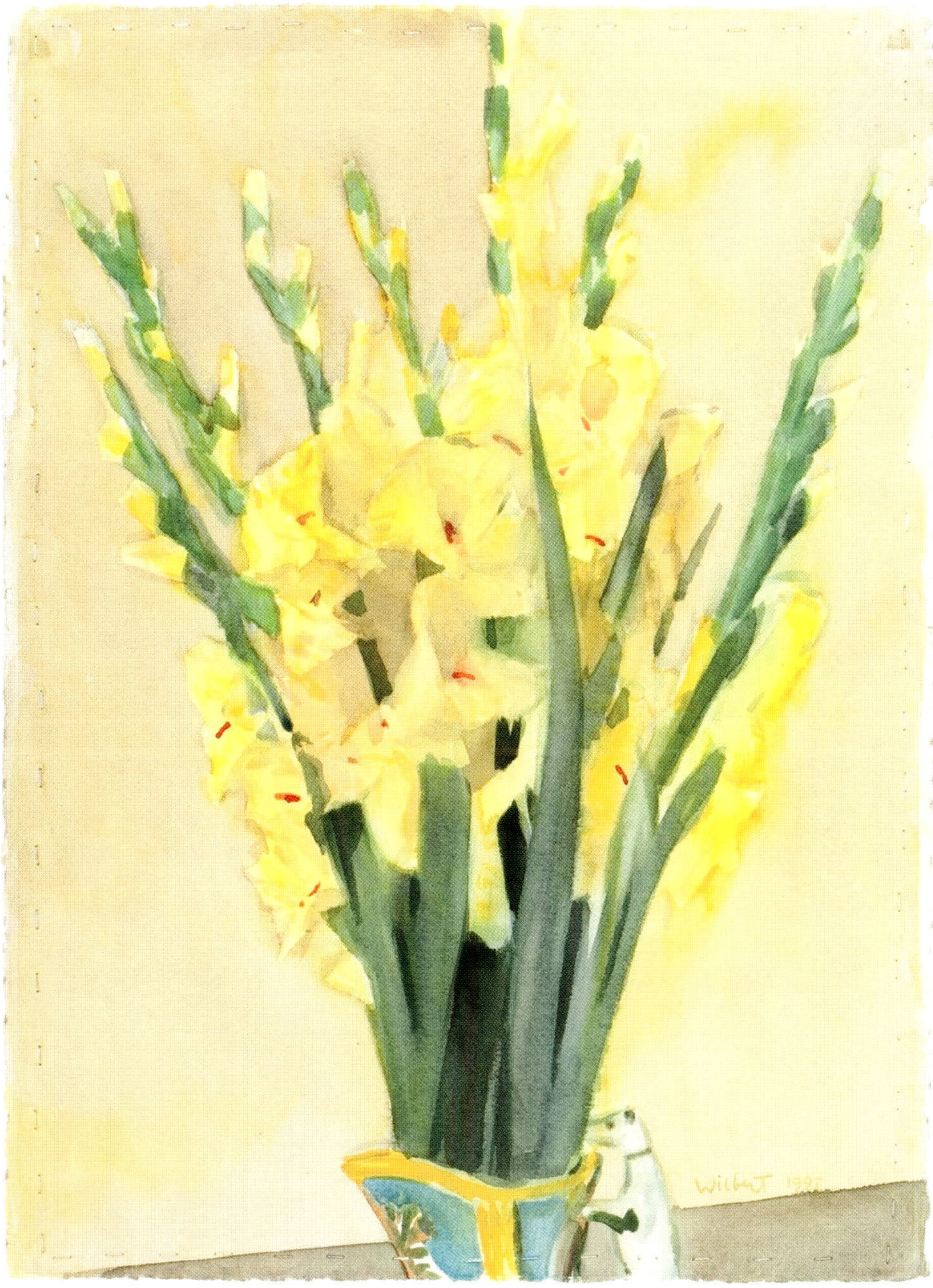

Sunflowers 1997, Watercolor on paper
22½ × 29¾ inches
Collection of the Artist

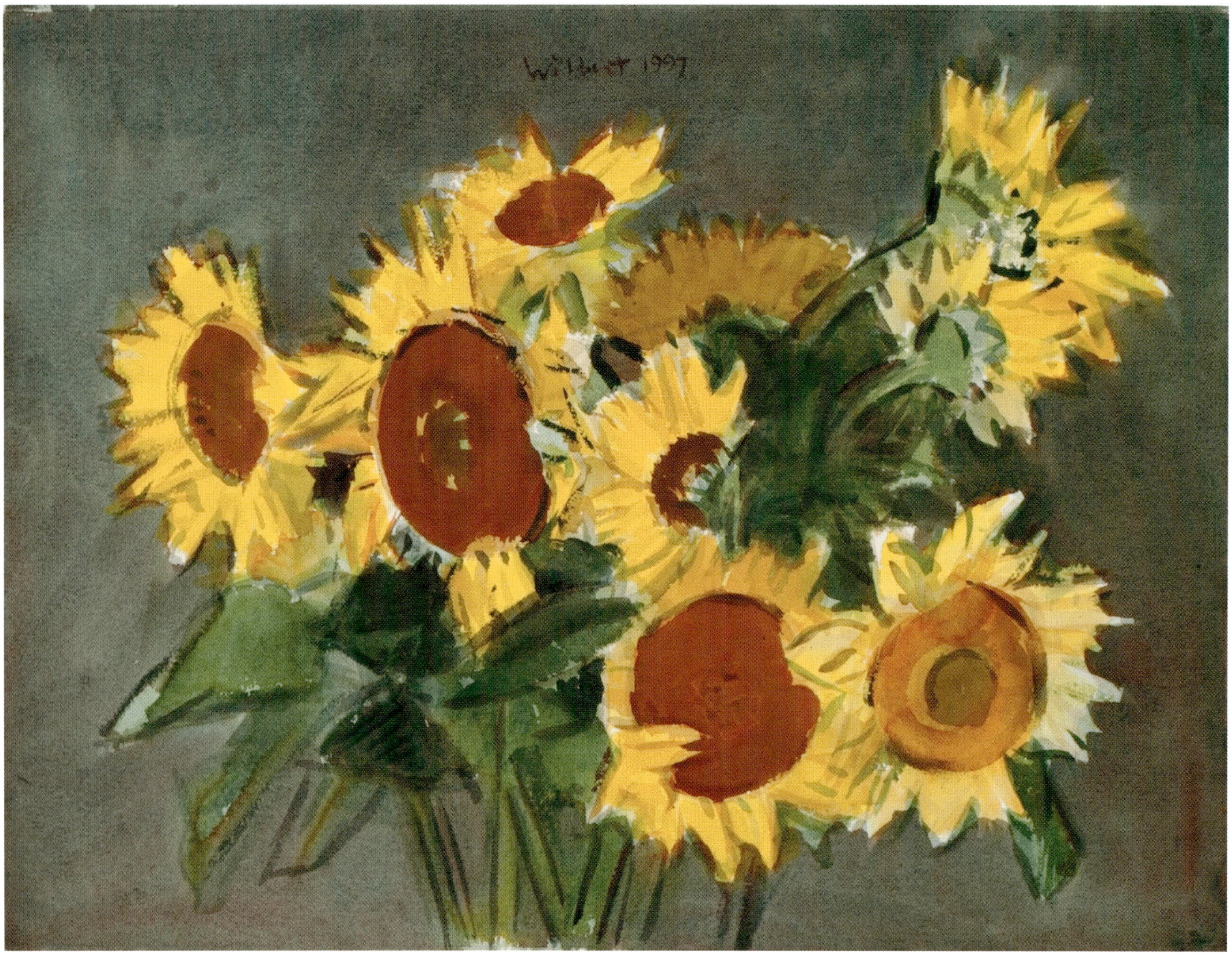

Peonies 1997, Oil on canvas
18 × 22 inches
Collection of Norma Goldman

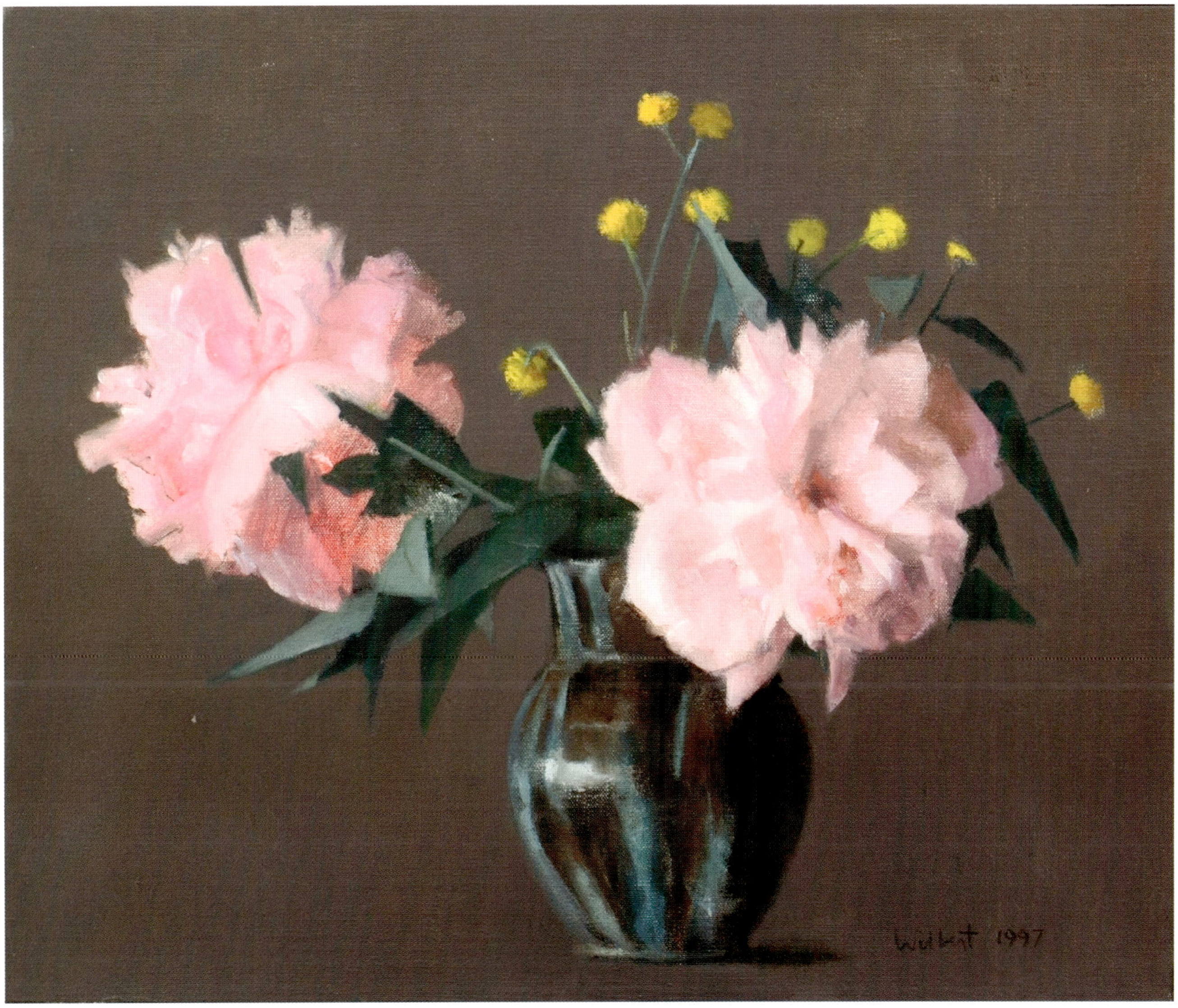

Party Hat with Toy Plane

1997, Watercolor on paper
22 × 29½ inches
Collection of the Artist

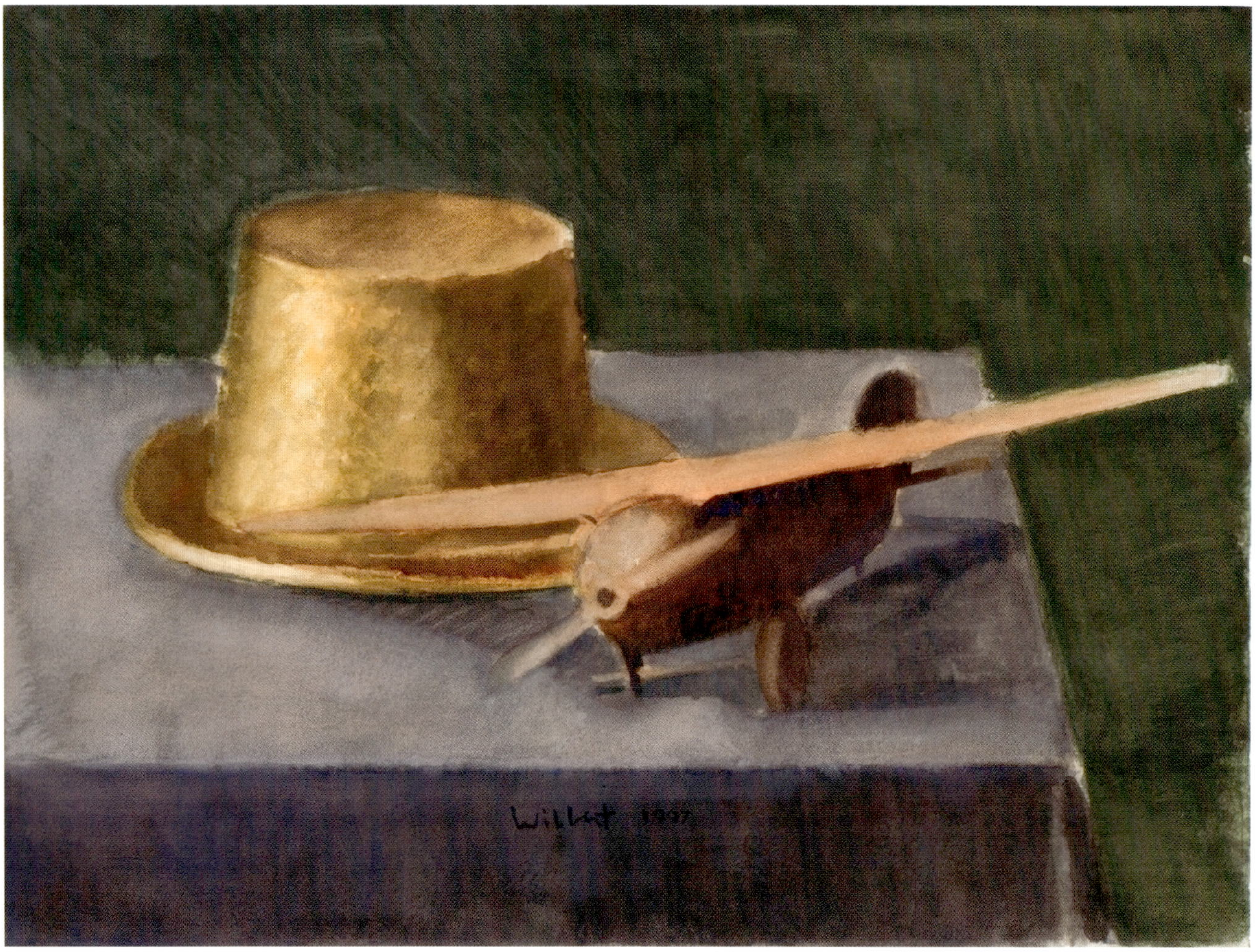

Sunrise–Lake Huron

1999, Watercolor on paper
30½ × 23 inches
Collection of the Artist

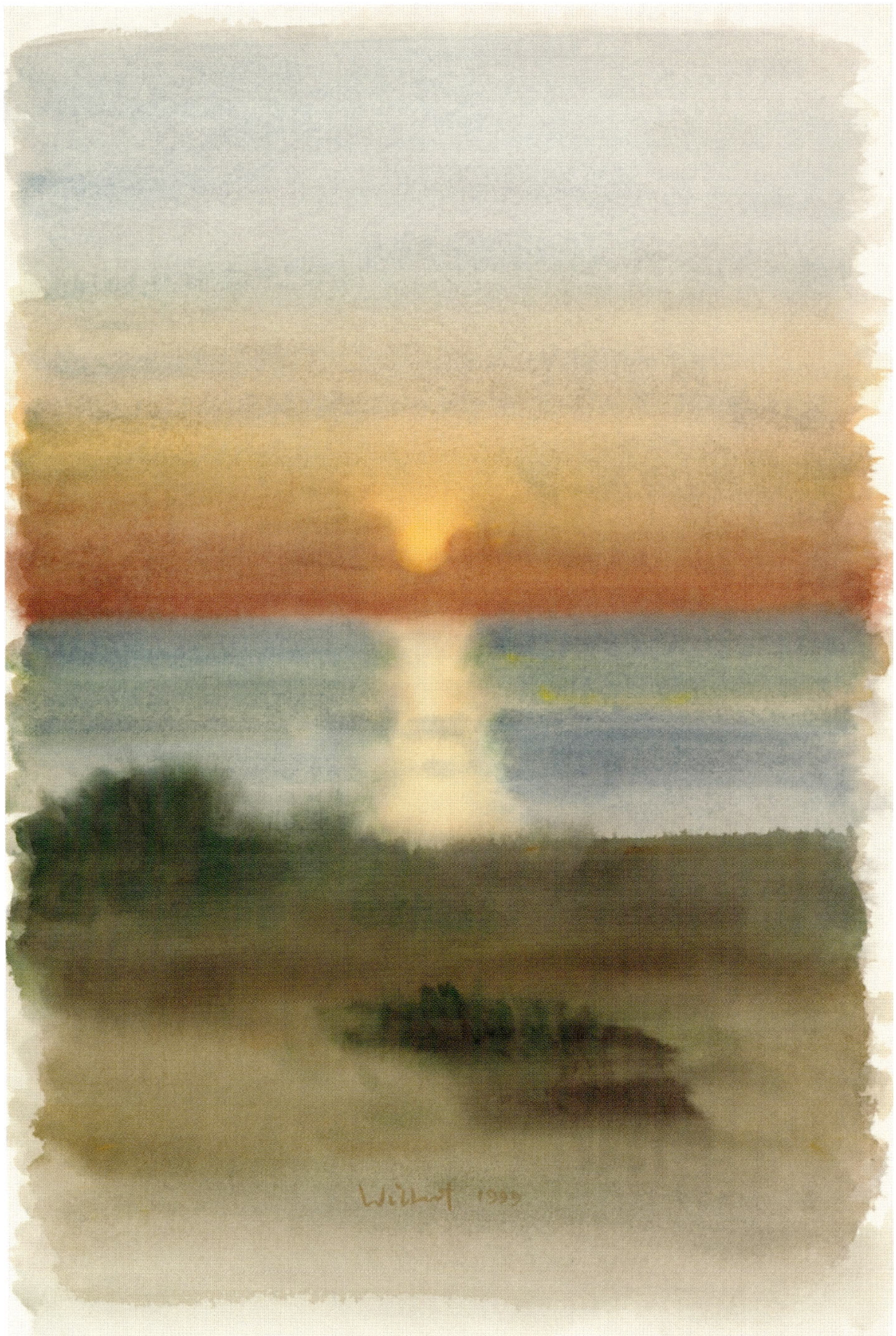

Flowers in Green Vase

1999, Oil on canvas
$31^{1/8} \times 31^{1/8}$ inches
Collection of Marilyn Williamson

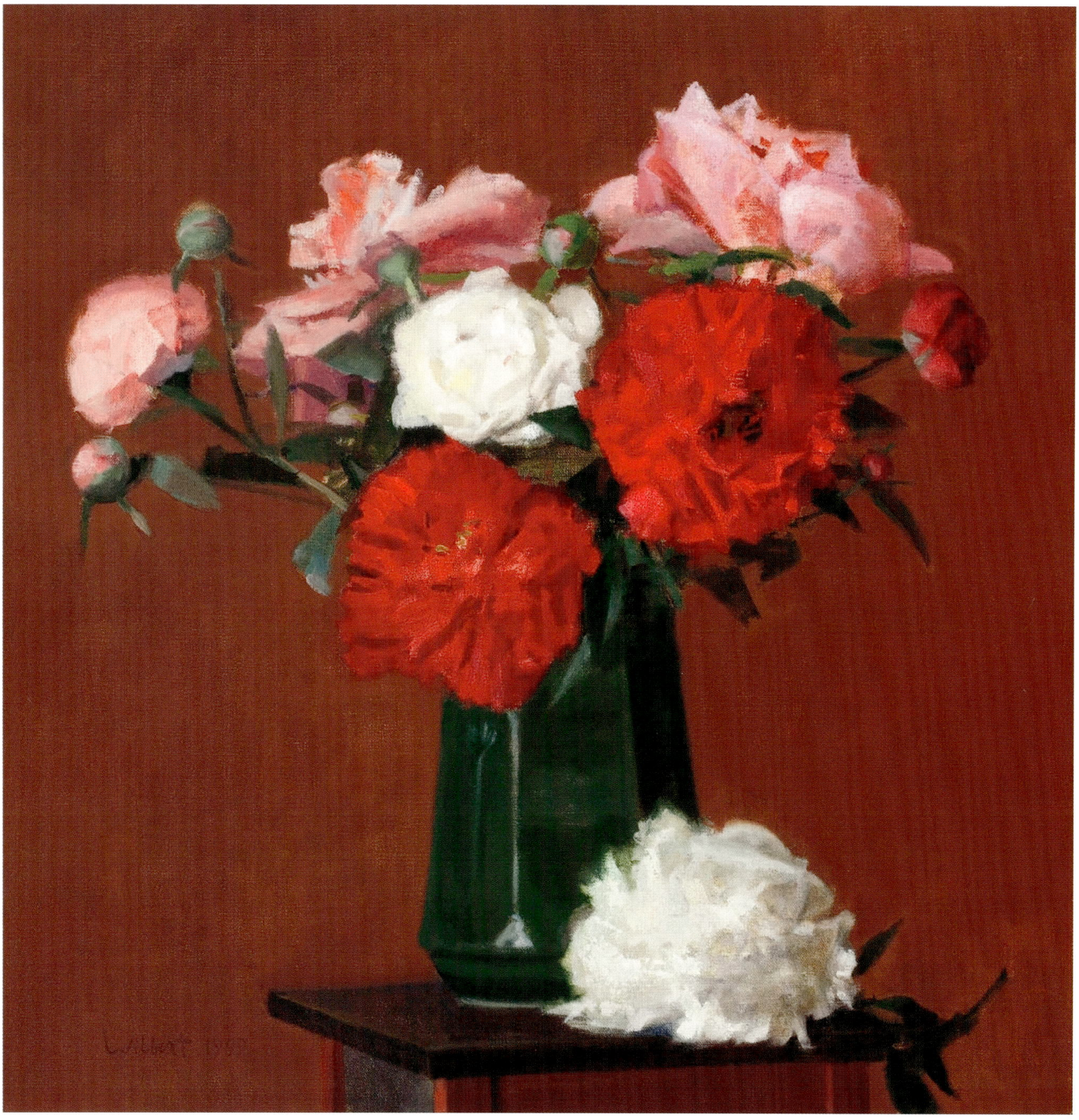

Sunrise 2000, Watercolor on paper
22 × 29½ inches
Collection of the Artist

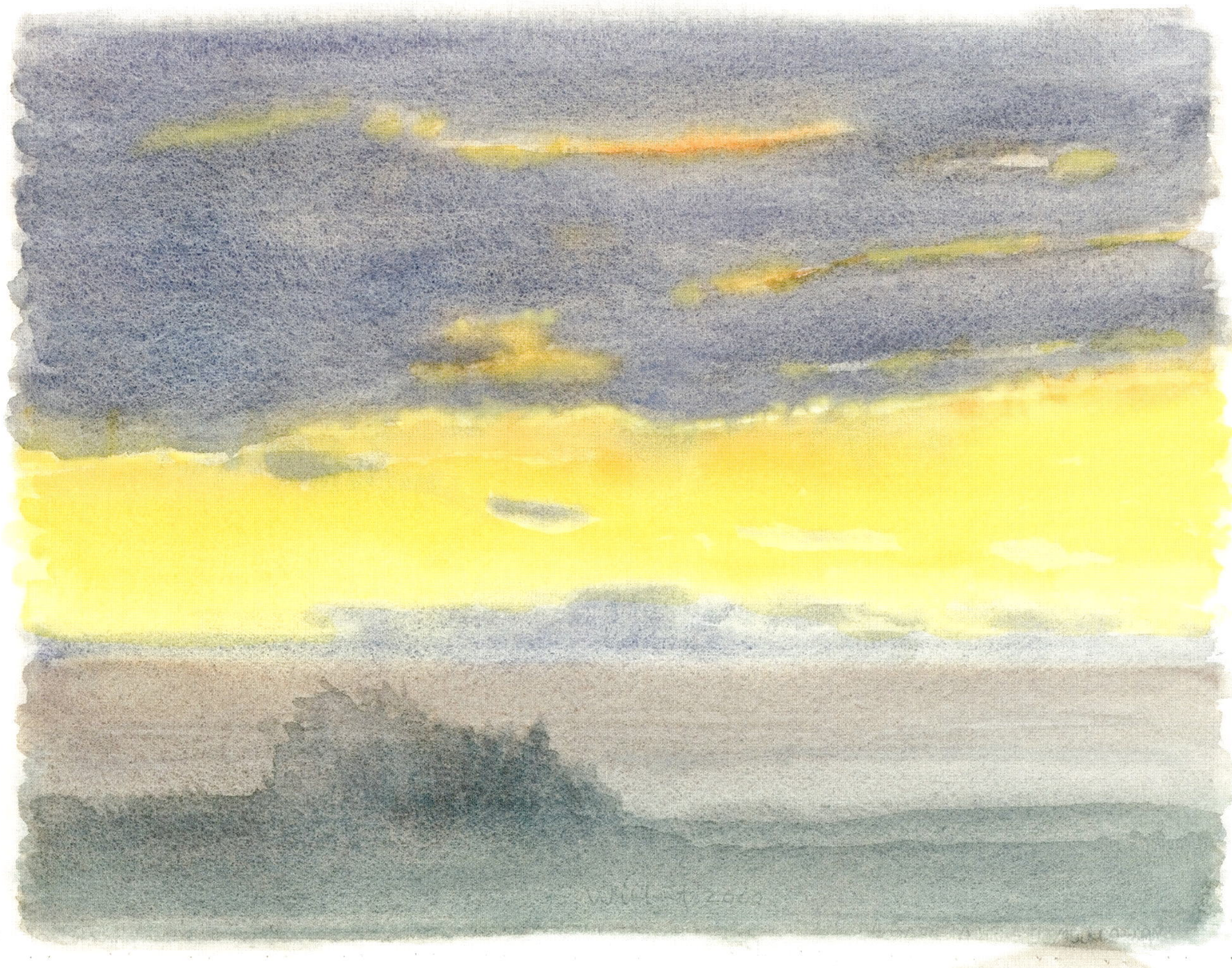

Daffodils 2003, Watercolor and charcoal on paper
27½ × 21 inches
Collection of the Artist

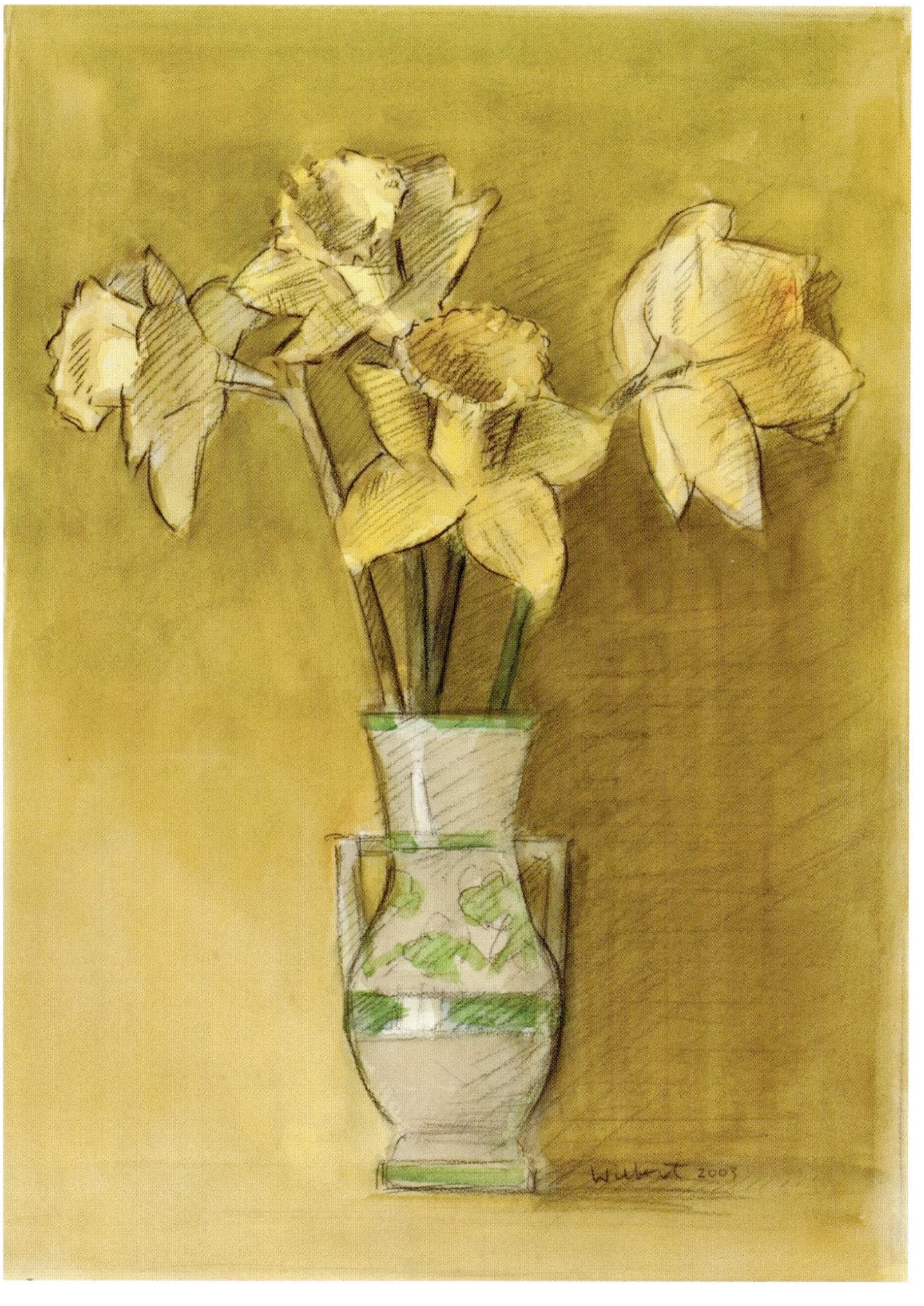

Gerry with Mask and Quoits

2004, Oil on canvas
30 × 36 inches
Collection of the Artist

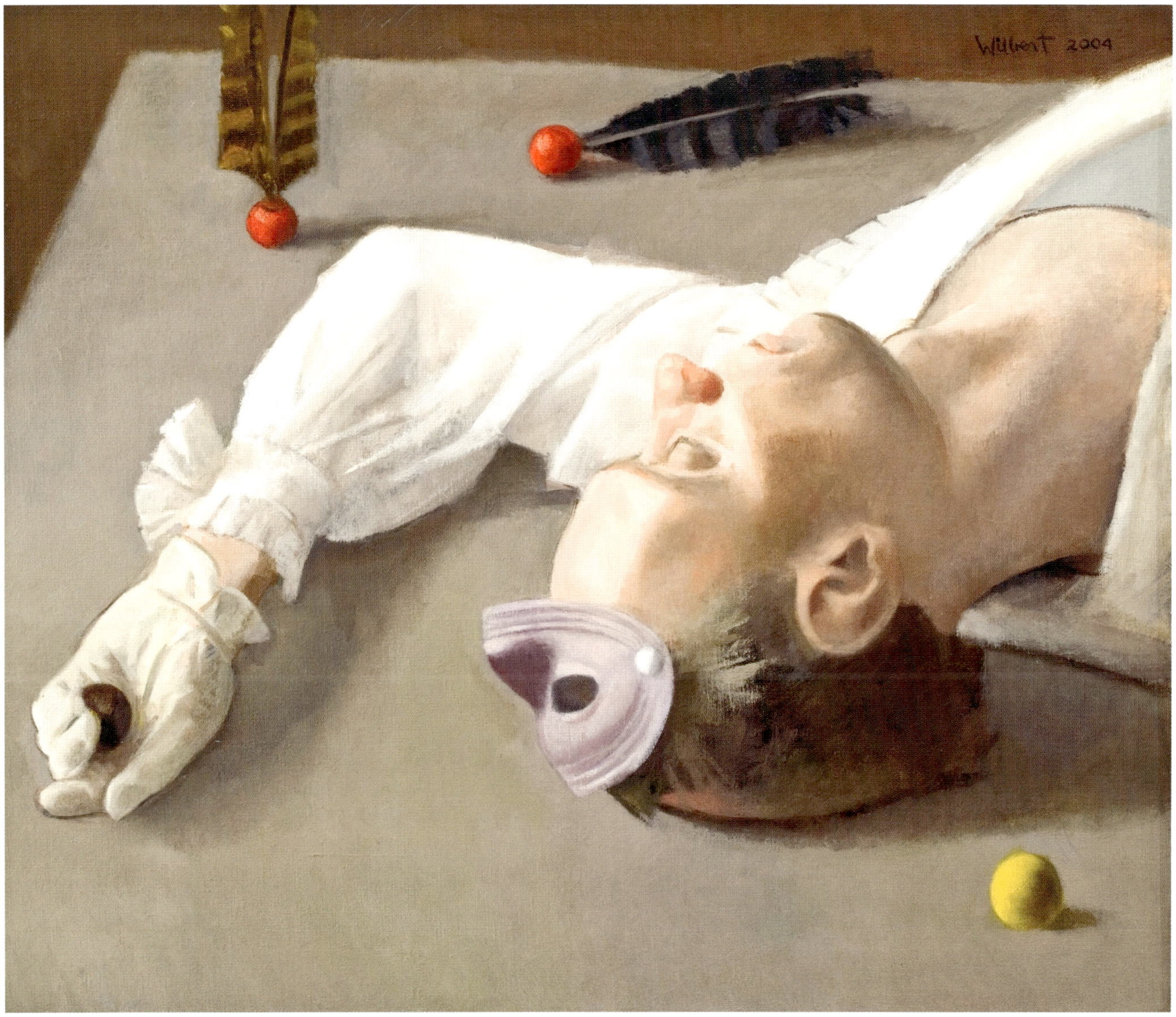

Zinnias with Hat and Mask

2004, Watercolor on paper
22½ × 21 inches
Collection of Marilyn Williamson

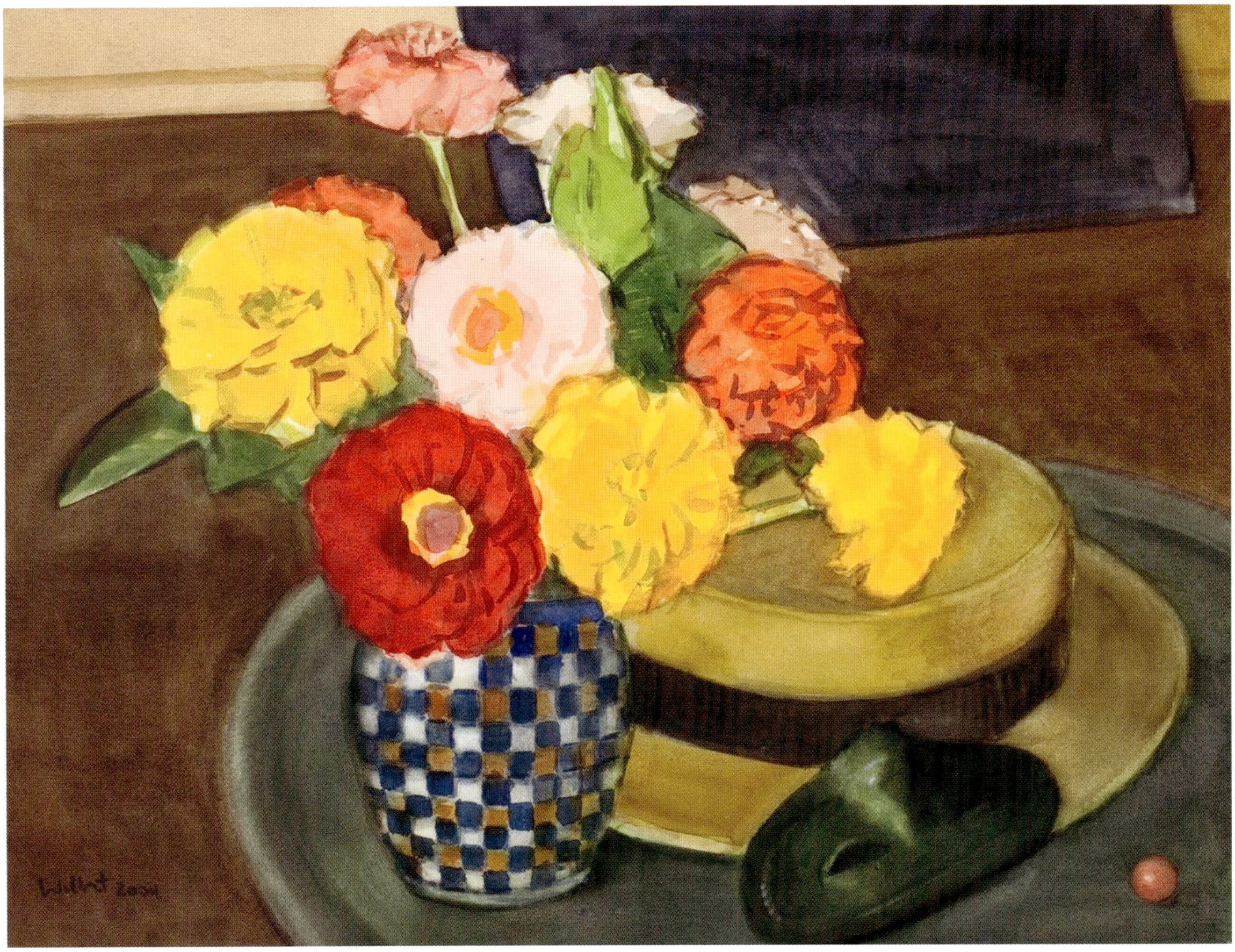

Sarah in Fur Coat 2004, Oil on canvas
40 × 30 inches
Collection of the Artist

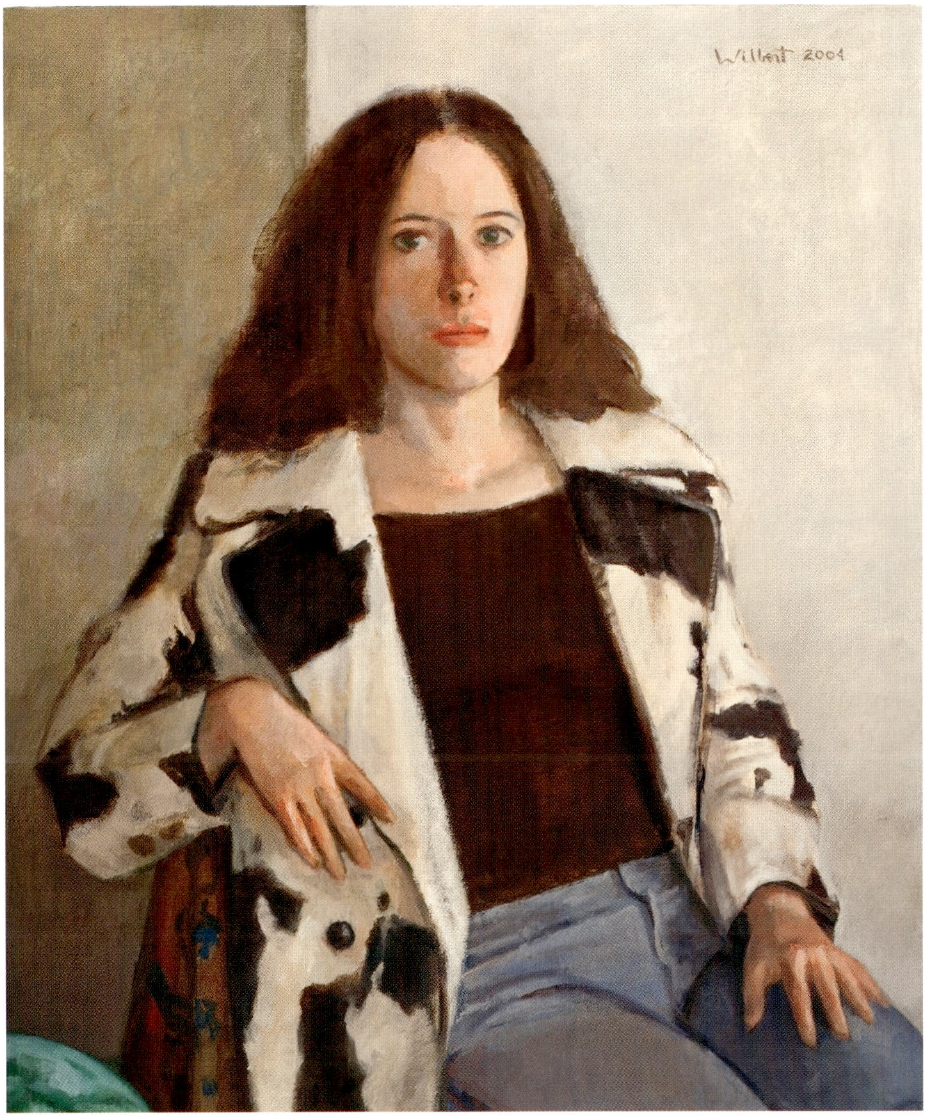

Self-Portrait with Mannequins

1994–2004, Oil on canvas
48 × 60 inches
Collection of the Artist

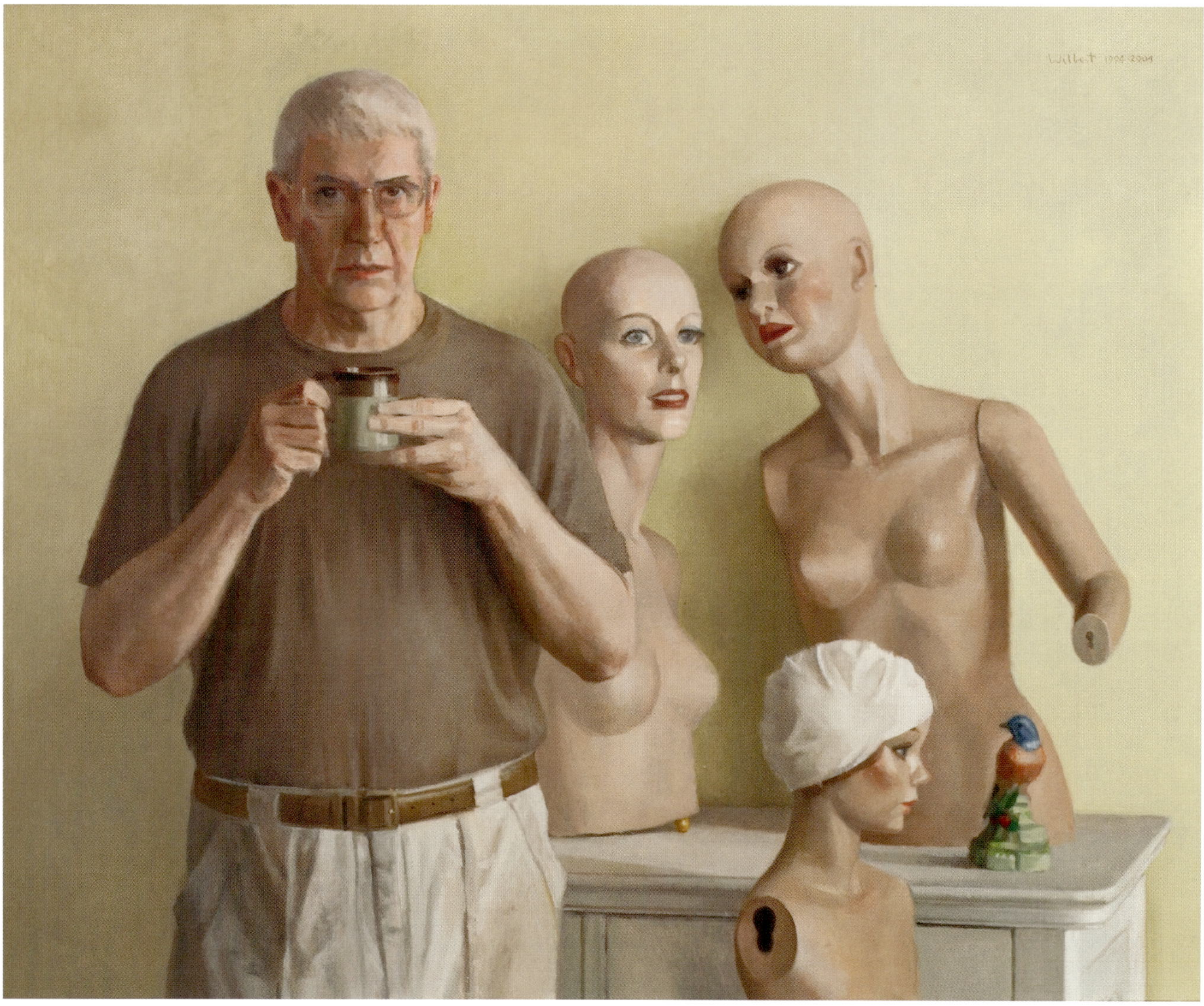

Red Carnations and Pink Chrysanthemums in Black Vase

2006, Watercolor on paper
26½ × 21½ Framed and matted
Collection of the Artist

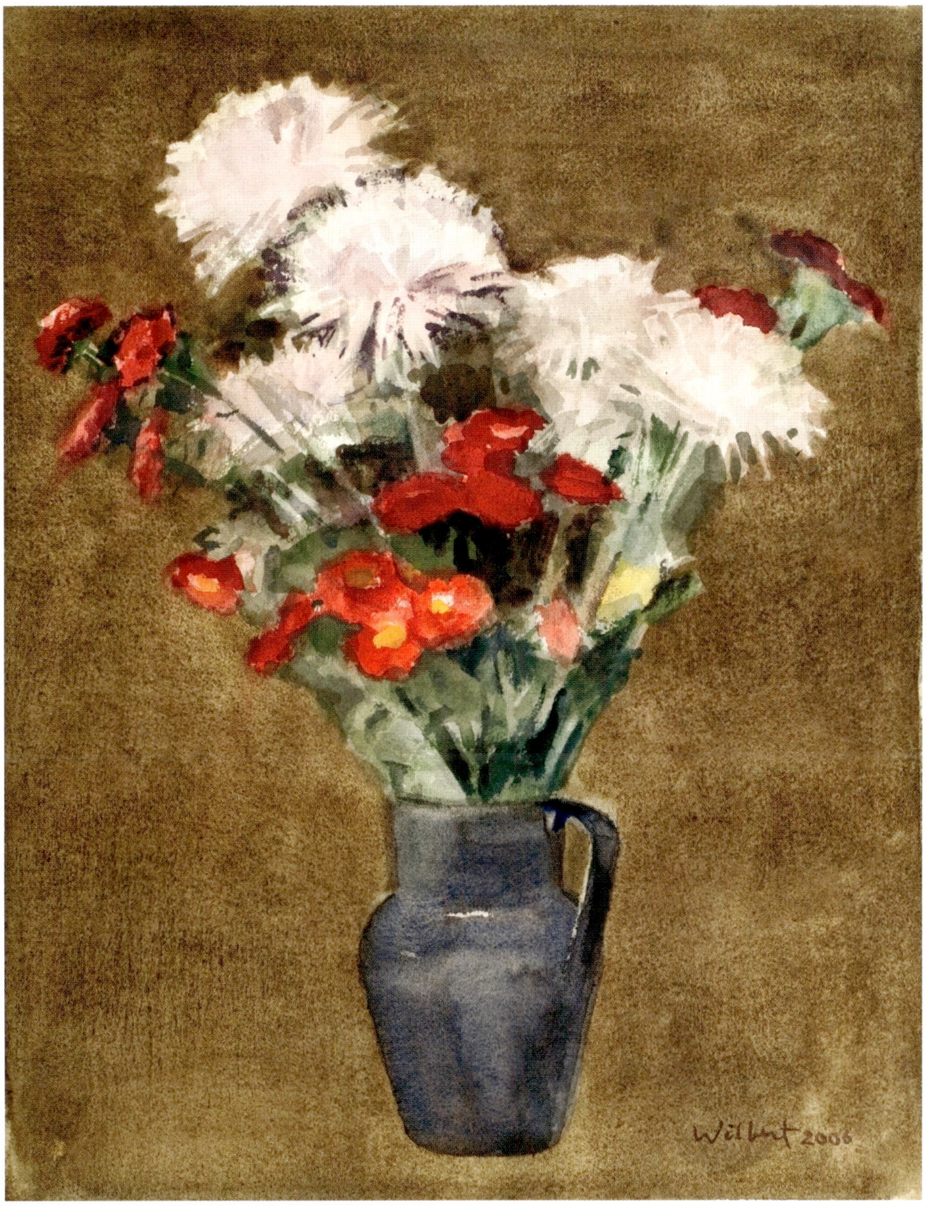

Chronology

1929 Born October 9, 1929, in Chicago, the youngest of two children of Herman and Helen Wilbert.

1939–46 At the age of ten, attends weekly figure sketching classes at the Art Institute of Chicago.

1947–51 Attends the University of Illinois at Urbana, majoring in art. Studies with Warren Doolittle, Nicola Ziroli, C. Earl Bradbury, Louise Woodroofe, and Laforce Bailey. Serves as an art writer for the *Daily Illini*, the student newspaper.

1950 Attends a University of Colorado–sponsored summer painting class in Central City, Colorado, under the tutelage of Julio de Diego. Meets C. E. Van Duzer, who later becomes director of the Flint Institute of Arts.

1951 Awarded a Bachelor of Fine Arts degree by the University of Illinois at Urbana.

Serves as an administrative officer in the U.S. Air Force, Chanute Air Force Base, Rantoul, Illinois.

Begins graduate studies at the University of Illinois at Urbana.

1952 Marries Gretchen Convey of Chicago.

One of his watercolors is accepted for exhibition at the Metropolitan Museum of Art in New York.

1953 Studies painting with Abraham Rattner and art history with Allen Weller.

As a graduate assistant teaches drawing classes for architecture students.

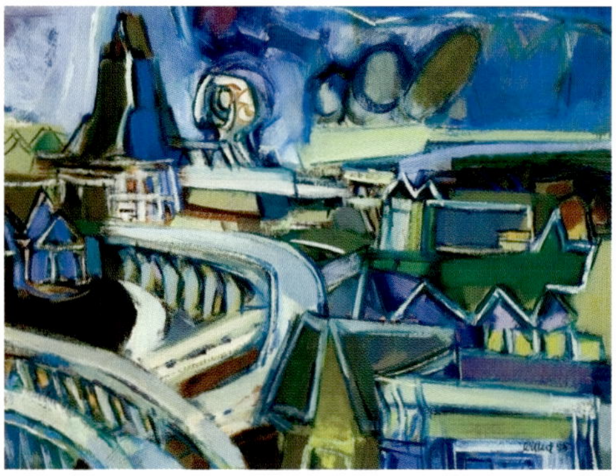

1959

1954–55 Awarded a Master of Fine Arts degree by the University of Illinois at Urbana.

Employed as educational assistant to the director, Flint Institute of Arts, Flint, Michigan. Teaches adult painting classes at FIA as well as classes for Flint Junior College students.

1956 Accepts the position of assistant professor in the Department of Art and Art History at Wayne State University in Detroit. Begins teaching watercolor, drawing, and design classes. Begins exhibiting extensively (see the List of Exhibitions).

1957 Wins award at the "11th Annual Exhibit, Michigan Water Color Society," College Gallery, Eastern Michigan University, Ypsilanti.

1958 Directs and curates exhibitions at the AAA Gallery in Detroit.

Wins award at the "15th Annual Water Color Exhibition," Scarab Club, Detroit.

Wins award at the "12th Annual Michigan Water Color Society," Wayne State University.

1959 Birth of son Matthew.

Granted tenure by Wayne State University.

Wins award at the "13th Annual Water Color Society Exhibition," Rackham Galleries, Ann Arbor, Michigan.

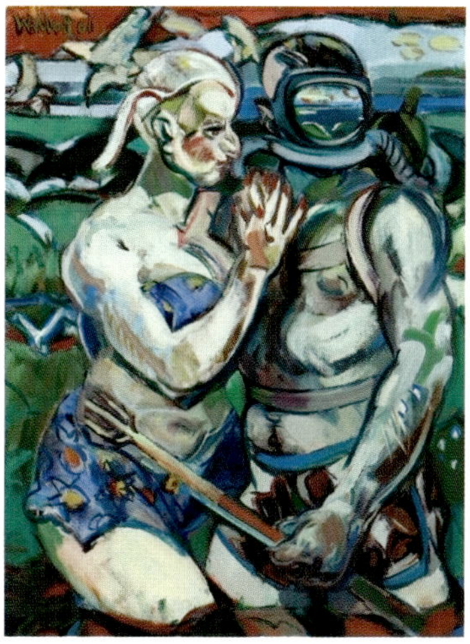

1961

1960 Wins award at the "1st Biennial Michiana Regional Art Exhibition," South Bend Art Center, South Bend, Indiana.

1961 Birth of daughter Laura.

Begins relationship with Donald and Florence Morris at Park Gallery in Detroit (later the Donald Morris Gallery); participates in "New Gallery Members" group exhibition.

1962 Solo exhibition at the Park Gallery.

Wins award at the "2nd Biennial Michiana Regional Art Exhibition," South Bend Art Center.

1963 Continues teaching and exhibits in Ohio and Pennsylvania.

1964 Promoted to associate professor, Wayne State University.

Solo exhibition at the Donald Morris Gallery in Detroit.

Commissioned to paint official portrait of Clarence B. Hilberry, president of Wayne State University.

1965 Continues teaching and exhibits in California, Kentucky, and Tennessee.

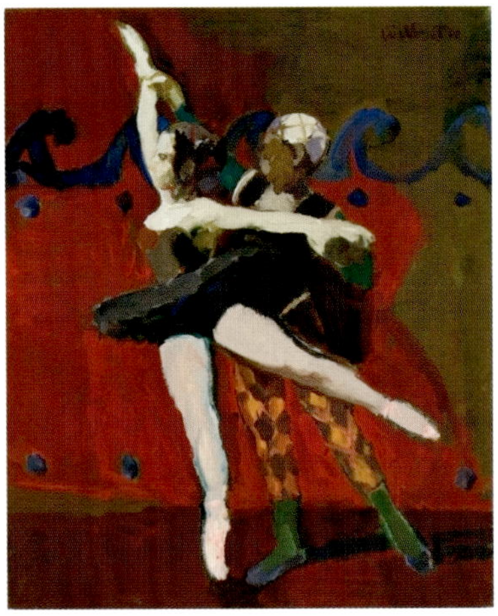

1966

1966 Begins summer visits to Harrisville, Michigan, and creates a series of paintings, "Sunrise–Lake Huron."

Wins award at the "56th Exhibition for Michigan Artists," Detroit Institute of Arts.

Wins award at the "4th Biennial Michiana Regional Art Exhibition," South Bend Art Center.

1967 Birth of son Benjamin.

Solo exhibition at the Donald Morris Gallery.

Wins award at the "Annual Art Exhibition," Michigan State Fair, Detroit.

Appointed coordinator of the painting area, Department of Art and Art History, Wayne State University.

1968 Continues teaching and exhibiting.

1969 Wins award at the "57th Exhibition for Michigan Artists," Detroit Institute of Arts.

1970 Becomes a full professor at Wayne State University.

1971 Begins work on large-scale portrait heads. Continues teaching and exhibiting.

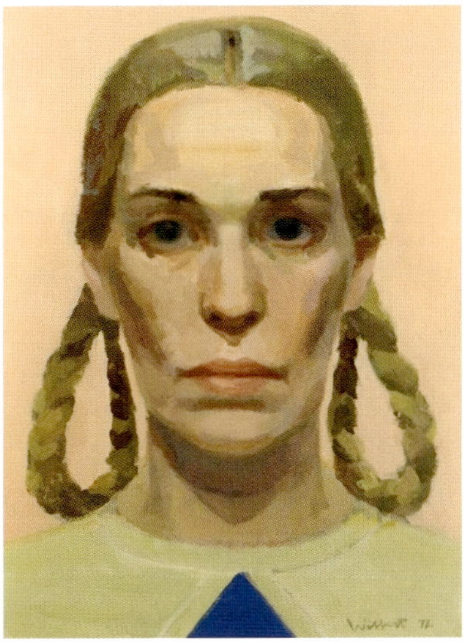

1972

1972 On sabbatical leave from Wayne State University.

After this year paints only from direct observation.

Solo exhibition at the Donald Morris Gallery.

1973 Solo exhibition at the Donald Morris Gallery.

Sabbatical solo exhibition, Wayne State University.

1974 Continues teaching and exhibiting.

1975 Exhibits with Olga Constantine at the J. B. Speed Museum, Louisville, Kentucky.

1976 Invited to participate in "Detroit Area Artists: Works in Progress II," curated by John Hallmark Neff, curator of modern art, Detroit Institute of Arts.

1977 Awarded a National Endowment for the Arts Fellowship.

Solo exhibition at the Donald Morris Gallery (now in Birmingham, Michigan).

Takes a leave of absence from Wayne State University and moves to New York with his family.

1978 Extends leave of absence from Wayne State; works on paintings for a solo exhibition in New York.

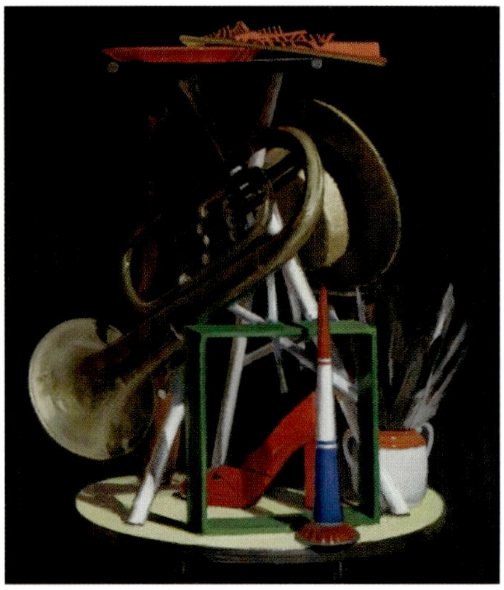

1983

1979 Returns to teaching at Wayne State University.

Successful solo exhibition at Droll/Kolbert Gallery in New York; positively reviewed by Hilton Kramer in the *New York Times*.

1980 Solo exhibition at the Donald Morris Gallery.

Small group exhibition at John C. Stoller & Co. in Minneapolis.

1981 Wins an award from the Michigan Foundation for the Arts.

Sabbatical leave from Wayne State University.

Visiting artist at Ox-Bow Summer School, Saugatuck, Michigan.

1982 Participates in the exhibitions:

"John Egner–Robert Wilbert Sabbatical Exhibition," Wayne State University.

"Contemporary Art in Detroit Collections," Detroit Institute of Arts.

"David Barr–Robert Wilbert," Donald Morris Gallery, International Art Exposition, Navy Pier, Chicago.

1983 Continues teaching and creating new work.

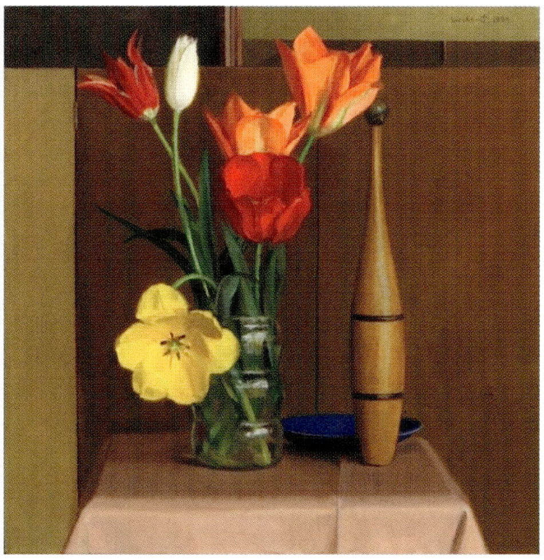

1984

1984 Solo exhibition at the Donald Morris Gallery.

Participates in "Cross Portraits," an activity of the nonprofit group Detroit Focus.

1985 Sabbatical leave, fall semester, Wayne State University.

Commissioned to do seven portraits for Federal Mogul Corporation.

1986 Solo exhibition at Roger Ramsay Gallery in Chicago.

Sabbatical leave, fall semester, Wayne State University.

1987 Commissioned to design the 1987 U.S. postage stamp commemorating the sesquicentennial of Michigan.

Solo exhibition at John C. Stoller & Co. in Minneapolis.

Serves as artist-in-residence with four other non-clay artists, "New Territories," Pewabic Pottery, Detroit.

Invited to participate in "Art in Michigan, 1961–1987," Detroit Institute of Arts.

1988 Continues teaching and creating new paintings.

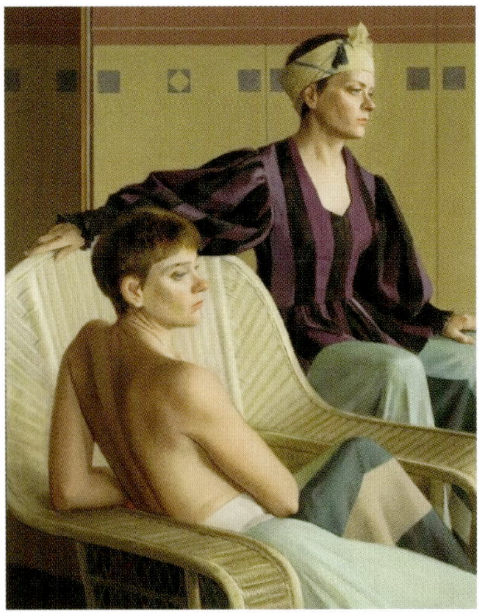

1989

1989 Solo exhibition at the Donald Morris Gallery.

1990 Commissioned to do a portrait for Federal Mogul Corporation.

Solo exhibition at the Roger Ramsay Gallery in Chicago.

Invited to participate in "Eight Michigan Artists," Flint Institute of Arts, Flint, Michigan.

1991 Sabbatical leave, fall semester, Wayne State University.

1992 Solo exhibition at the Donald Morris Gallery.

Invited to participate in "Under the Influence: Mentors/Teachers/Colleagues," Tatistcheff Gallery, Inc., Santa Monica, California.

1993 Three-person show, "Dusk–Firmament–Dawn" (David Barr, Mary Frank, Robert Wilbert), Donald Morris Gallery.

1994 Inducted into the Academy of Scholars, Wayne State University.

Designated Professor Emeritus, Wayne State University.

Invited to participate in "Still Working: Underknown Artists of Age in America," Corcoran Gallery of Art, Washington, D.C.

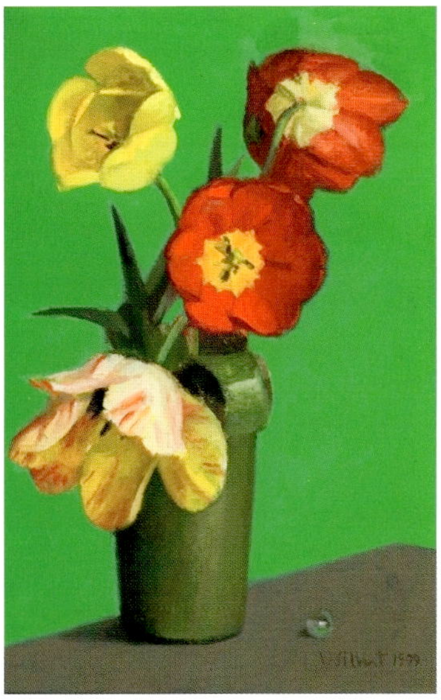

1999

1995 Wins award from the Richard Florsheim Art Fund.

1996 Continues teaching advanced painting, Birmingham Bloomfield Art Center, Birmingham, Michigan.

1997 Begins solo exhibitions at the Susanne Hilberry Gallery, Ferndale, Michigan.

1998–2000 Continues teaching at the Birmingham Bloomfield Art Center.

Commissioned to paint the official portrait of James J. Blanchard, governor of Michigan (1983–91).

2001 Solo exhibition at the Birmingham Bloomfield Art Center.

2002 Continues to create new work and teach at Birmingham Bloomfield Art Center.

2003 Included in the exhibition "Liquid Media: A Survey of Painting from the Permanent Collection," Carmichael Gallery, South Bend Regional Museum of Art formerly the South Bend Art Center.

2004 Continues to create new work and teach at Birmingham Bloomfield Art Center.

2005 Solo exhibition at the Susanne Hilberry Gallery.

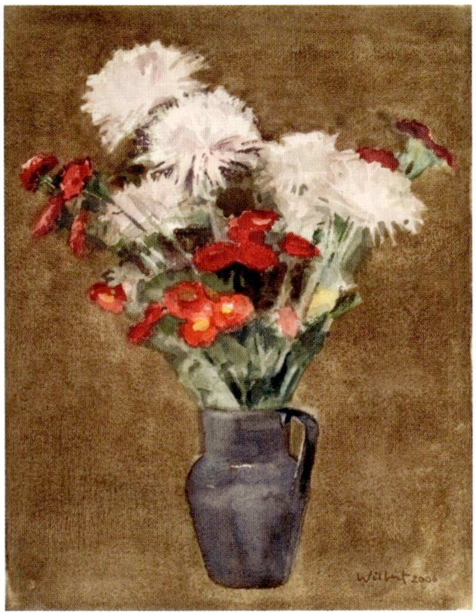

2006

2006 Included in group exhibition, "The 'Super Bowl' Show: Still-Life Prints, Drawings, Photographs, and Vessels." Detroit Institute of Arts.

2007 Included in group exhibition, "Stuff: International Contemporary Art from the Collection of Burt Aaron," Museum of Contemporary Art (MOCAD), Detroit.

Moves studio from Detroit to Ferndale, Michigan.

2008 Commissioned to paint official portrait of Irvin D. Reid, president of Wayne State University.

Continues teaching at Birmingham Bloomfield Art Center.

2009 Invited to participate in "Michigan Masters Invitational," Kresge Art Museum, Michigan State University, East Lansing.

2010 Invited to sign the artists' beam at the Scarab Club in acknowledgment of his contributions as an artist, teacher, and mentor.

Dedication of the portrait of Irvin D. Reid at Wayne State University, Adamany Library, Honors College, May 5, 2010.

Ends teaching at Birmingham Bloomfield Art Center, December 15, 2010.

The Birmingham Bloomfield Art Center establishes the Robert Wilbert Scholarship Fund to be used to assist deserving students with tuition.

List of Exhibitions

"Robert Wilbert: Teacher, Mentor, Friend," February 17–March 28, 2010, The Scarab Club, Detroit.

"Bods: Rethinking the Figure," October 24–December 19, 2009, Robert Kidd Gallery, Birmingham, Michigan.

"2009 BBAC Faculty Exhibit," October 2009, Birmingham Bloomfield Art Center, Birmingham, Michigan.

"Michigan Masters Invitational," May 2–July 31, 2009, Kresge Art Museum, Michigan State University, East Lansing.

"Stuff: International Contemporary Art from the Collection of Burt Aaron," May 12–July 29, 2007, Museum of Contemporary Art (MOCAD), Detroit.

"The 'Super Bowl' Show: Still-Life Prints, Drawings, Photographs, and Vessels," January 25–April 30, 2006, Detroit Institute of Arts.

"Robert Wilbert," November 12, 2004–January 8, 2005, Susanne Hilberry Gallery, Ferndale, Michigan.

"Liquid Media: A Survey of Painting from the Permanent Collection," May 2003–July, 2005, Carmichael Gallery, South Bend Regional Museum of Art, South Bend, Indiana.

"Robert Wilbert: Watercolors," September 7–October 5, 2001, Birmingham Bloomfield Art Center, Birmingham, Michigan.

"New Paintings: Robert Wilbert," November 19, 1999–January 8, 2000, Susanne Hilberry Gallery, Ferndale, Michigan.

"Robert Wilbert: A Selection of Watercolors and Drawings," April 1–May 3, 1997, Susanne Hilberry Gallery, Ferndale, Michigan.

"Land," June 9–July 22, 1995, Alexa Lee Gallery, Ann Arbor, Michigan.

"Still Working: Underknown Artists of Age in America," June 18–August 21, 1994, Corcoran Gallery of Art, Washington, D.C. *Itinerary:* Chicago Cultural Center, October 22–December 23, 1994; The New School for Social Research and Parsons School of Design, New York, January 24–March 10, 1995; Virginia Beach Center for the Arts, Virginia Beach, Virginia, March 26–May 7, 1995; Fisher Gallery, University of Southern California, Los Angeles, September 6–November 8, 1995; Portland Art Museum, Portland, Oregon, January 3–26, 1996.

"The Detroit Show: Objects for and about Detroit," June 10–July 15, 1994, Center Galleries, Center for Creative Studies, Detroit.

"Robert Wilbert: Flowers, Watercolors and Drawing," November 28, 1992–January 16, 1993, Donald Morris Gallery, Birmingham, Michigan.

"The Fine Art of Patronage," January 20–March 28, 1993, Cranbrook Academy of Art Museum, Bloomfield Hills, Michigan.

"Dusk—Firmament—Dawn," November 4–December 4, 1993, Donald Morris Gallery, Birmingham, Michigan.

"Under the Influence: Mentors/Teachers/Colleagues," September 11–30, 1992, Tatistcheff Gallery, Inc., Santa Monica, California.

"Robert Wilbert: 'Huron Sunrises' Watercolor Paintings," October 20–November 17, 1990, Roger Ramsay Gallery, Chicago.

"Eight Michigan Artists," February 11–April 1, 1990, Flint Institute of Arts, Flint, Michigan.

"Flowers in Art," June 27–August 5, 1990, Krasl Art Center, St. Joseph, Michigan.

"Wayne State University Art Faculty Exhibition," January 10–28, 1989, Community Arts Gallery, Wayne State University, Detroit.

"Robert Wilbert: Recent Paintings," October 28–November 25, 1989, Donald Morris Gallery, Birmingham, Michigan.

"Michigan NEA Fellowships, 1965–1985," April 26–May 23, 1986, Detroit Focus Gallery.

"Wilbert at Morris, Twenty Five Years: Paintings 1961–1986," April 19– May 24, 1986, Donald Morris Gallery, Birmingham, Michigan.

"Robert Wilbert: Figure and Still Life Paintings," February 1–March 1, 1986, Roger Ramsay Gallery, Chicago.

"Fifth Anniversary Exhibition," November 7–December 21, 1986, Roger Ramsay Gallery, Chicago.

"Robert Wilbert," May 25–July 31, 1987, John C. Stoller & Co., Minneapolis.

"Art in Michigan, 1961–1986," October 1987, Detroit Institute of Arts.

"New Territories: Allie McGhee, Robert Sestok, Gilda Snowden, Deanne Sperka, Robert Wilbert," September 11–October 10, 1987, Pewabic Pottery, Detroit.

"Cross Portraits," March 17–April 14, 1984, Detroit Focus Gallery.

"Robert Wilbert: Portrait and Figure Paintings," November 24–December 31, 1984, Donald Morris Gallery, Birmingham, Michigan.

"John Egner—Robert Wilbert Sabbatical Exhibition," October 9–29, 1982, Community Arts Gallery, Wayne State University, Detroit.

"Faculty Exhibition," October 9–29, 1982, Community Arts Gallery, Wayne State University, Detroit.

"Contemporary Art in Detroit Collections," January 27–March 14, 1982, Detroit Institute of Arts.

"A Quartet from Detroit—Four Painters/Four Media," February 7–March 16, 1982, Muskegon Museum of Art, Muskegon, Michigan.

"David Barr—Robert Wilbert," May 13–18, 1982, Donald Morris Gallery, International Art Exposition, Navy Pier, Chicago.

"Portraits," May 29–June 27, 1981, Detroit Artists Market.

"Traditions: The Region/World 1981," April–November 1981, Artrain (Transporting Art. Transforming Lives), Indiana, Ohio, Michigan.

"Post Abstract Realism," July 1980, John C. Stoller & Co., Minneapolis.

"Robert Wilbert: Watercolors and Drawings," March 1–20, 1980, Donald Morris Gallery, Birmingham, Michigan.

"Exhibition 1980: Studio Faculty, Department of Art and Art History," March 30–April 19, 1980, Community Arts Gallery, Wayne State University, Detroit.

"Robert Wilbert," May 30–June 23, 1979, Droll/Kolbert, New York.

"At Cranbrook: Downtown—Detroit—Twenty-one Artists," November 20, 1979–January 20, 1980, Cranbrook Academy of Art Museum, Bloomfield Hills, Michigan.

"14th Annual Exhibition, Art on Paper," November 19–December 17, 1978, Weatherspoon Art Museum, University of North Carolina, Greensboro.

"Full Spectrum: Michigan Moderns and American Folk Painters," 1978, Artrain (Transporting Art. Transforming Lives).

"Robert Wilbert," May 14–June 18, 1977, Donald Morris Gallery, Birmingham, Michigan.

"Detroit Area Artists: Works in Progress II," October 8–31, 1976, Detroit Institute of Arts.

"27 Painters [Artists–Teachers]: A Vigorous Sampling," October 6–23, 1976, Slusser Gallery, School of Art, University of Michigan, Ann Arbor.

"Detroit Figurative Artists," December 2–31, 1976, Eshleman Library, Henry Ford Community College, Dearborn, Michigan.

"Two Views of Reality: Paintings by Olga Constantine and Robert Wilbert," May 8–June 1, 1975, J. B. Speed Museum, Louisville, Kentucky.

"Detroit Art Today—Diverse Directions," September 22–October 10, 1974, University of Michigan Museum of Art, Ann Arbor.

"Figure as Image," March 15–April 6, 1974, Detroit Artists Market.

"Robert Wilbert: Watercolors," May 12–June 9, 1973, Donald Morris Gallery, Detroit.

"Robert Wilbert," 1973, Community Arts Gallery, Wayne State University, Detroit.

"Robert Wilbert: Oils," April 8–29, 1972, Donald Morris Gallery, Detroit.

"Source Detroit III," November 7–December 10, 1972, Cranbrook Academy of Art Museum, Bloomfield Hills, Michigan.

"All Michigan," December 12, 1971–January 22, 1972, Flint Institute of Arts, Flint, Michigan.

"Landscape and Figure Painting," February 14–25, 1972, Sill Gallery, Eastern Michigan University, Ypsilanti.

"Eight Michigan Artists," April 4–25, 1971, Kresge Art Center, Michigan State University, East Lansing.

"58th Exhibition for Michigan Artists," December 15, 1970–February 7, 1971, Detroit Institute of Arts.

"57th Exhibition for Michigan Artists," January 15–February 23, 1969, Detroit Institute of Arts.

"Mid-Year Show," June 30–September 2, 1968, Butler Institute of American Art, Youngstown, Ohio.

"Michigan Painting '68," February 11–March 17, 1968, Bloomfield Art Association, Birmingham, Michigan.

"Robert Wilbert: Recent Paintings," April 9–May 6, 1967, Donald Morris Gallery, Detroit.

"Robert Wilbert: Portraits and Figure Paintings," April 14–May 5, 1967, Community Arts Gallery, Wayne State University, Detroit.

"Faculty '67," April 2–23, 1967, Bloomfield Art Association, Birmingham, Michigan.

"Annual Art Exhibition," August 25–September 4, 1967, Community Arts Building, Michigan State Fair, Detroit.

"56th Exhibition for Michigan Artists," November 18–December 31, 1966, Detroit Institute of Arts.

"Annual Art Exhibition," September 1966, Community Arts Building, Michigan State Fair, Detroit.

4th Biennial Michiana Regional Art Exhibition," March 6–27, 1966, South Bend Art Center, South Bend, Indiana.

"The Collection of Mr. and Mrs. James Lofstrom," 1966, J. B. Speed Museum, Louisville, Kentucky.

"Annual Invitational Dogwood Exhibition," April 19–May 9, 1965, Art Gallery, Frank H. McClung Museum, University of Tennessee, Knoxville.

"California Society of Etchers National Print Exhibition," June 30–August 1, 1965, San Francisco Museum of Art.

"A Survey of Contemporary Art," May 11–June 20, 1965, J. B. Speed Art Museum, Louisville, Kentucky.

"Faculty Art Exhibition," February 9–14, 1965, Community Arts Gallery, Wayne State University, Detroit.

"Robert Wilbert," December 1–19, 1964, Donald Morris Gallery, Detroit.

"3rd Biennial Michiana Regional Art Exhibition," March 8–29, 1964, South Bend Art Center, South Bend, Indiana.

"Mid-Year Show," June 30–September 2, 1963, Butler Institute of American Art, Youngstown, Ohio.

"Michigan Art Yesterday and Today," 1963, Flint Institute of Arts, Flint, Michigan.

"158th Annual Exhibition of Watercolors, Prints and Drawings," January 18–March 3, 1963, Pennsylvania Academy of the Fine Arts, Philadelphia.

"Faculty Art Exhibition," January 2–February 22, 1962, Community Arts Gallery, Wayne State University, Detroit.

"2nd Biennial Michiana Regional Art Exhibition," March 11–April 1, 1962, South Bend Art Center, South Bend, Indiana.

"Members of the Scarab Club, Faculty of the Society of Arts and Crafts, Faculty of the Art Department, Wayne State University," April 17–29, 1962, Community Arts Gallery, Wayne State University, Detroit.

"16th Annual Water Color Society Exhibition," April 8–28, 1962, Kellogg Art Gallery, Michigan State University, East Lansing.

"Water Color Panorama," April 26–May 26, 1962, De Waters Art Center, Flint Institute of Arts, Flint, Michigan.

"Mid-Year Show," July 1–September 3, 1962, Butler Institute of American Art, Youngstown, Ohio.

"Robert Wilbert," November 4–24, 1962, Park Gallery, Detroit.

"Faculty Art Exhibition," January 6–February 3, 1961, Community Arts Gallery, Wayne State University, Detroit.

"156th Annual Exhibition of Watercolors, Prints and Drawings," January 22–February 26, 1961, Pennsylvania Academy of the Fine Arts, Philadelphia.

"51st Exhibition for Michigan Artists," May 19–August 13, 1961, Detroit Institute of Arts.

"15th Annual Michigan Water Color Society Exhibition," May 7–21, 1961, Community Arts Gallery, Wayne State University, Detroit.

"New Gallery Members," October 1–14, 1961, Park Gallery, Detroit.

"Robert Wilbert: Watercolors," 1960, University of Illinois Student Union, Champaign-Urbana.

"1st Biennial Michiana Regional Art Exhibition," March 6–27, 1960, South Bend Art Center, South Bend, Indiana.

"West Michigan Art Exhibition," March 27–May 1, 1960, Grand Rapids Art Gallery, Grand Rapids, Michigan.

"Octet Exhibition," January 13–30, 1960, Rackham Galleries, Ann Arbor Art Association, Ann Arbor, Michigan..

"Faculty Art Exhibition," January 15–February 5, 1960, Community Arts Gallery, Wayne State University, Detroit.

"50th Exhibition for Michigan Artists," May 20–August 7, 1960, Detroit Institute of Arts.

"14th Annual Water Color Exhibition sponsored by Michigan Water Color Society," May 22–June 10, 1960, De Waters Art Center, Flint Institute of Arts, Flint, Michigan.

"The Twenty-Fifth Annual Mid-Year Show," July 3–September 5, 1960, Butler Institute of American Art, Youngstown, Ohio..

"Robert J. Wilbert," October 23–November 20, 1960, Studio 23, Bay City, Michigan.

"17th Annual Watercolor Exhibition," November 11–30, 1960, Scarab Club, Detroit.

"Michigan's Finest Artists and Craftsmen," December 3–25, 1960, Quinn Artists Market, Caro, Michigan.

"49th Exhibition for Michigan Artists," March 17–April 12, 1959, Detroit Institute of Arts.

"Robert J. Wilbert: Recent Oils and Watercolors," April 19–May 6, 1959, AAA Gallery, Detroit.

"Paintings by Wilbert; Jewelry by Kuemmerlein," May 17, 1959, Left Bank Gallery, Flint, Michigan.

"13th Annual Water Color Society Exhibition," June 5–26, 1959, Rackham Galleries, Ann Arbor, Michigan.

"Landscape '59," October 25–November 25, 1959, AAA Gallery, Detroit.

"16th Annual Watercolor Exhibition," November 13–30, 1959, Scarab Club, Detroit.

"9th Annual Michiana Regional Art Exhibition," March 16–April 6, 1958, South Bend Art Center, South Bend, Indiana.

"Portrait Figure Exhibition," January 18–February 4, 1958, AAA Gallery, Detroit.

"15th Annual Water Color Exhibition," November 14–30, 1958, Scarab Club, Detroit.

"Watercolors by Robert J. Wilbert," November 6–30, 1958, Saginaw Museum of Art, Saginaw, Michigan.

"12th Annual Michigan Water Color Society Exhibition," June 8–28, 1958, Wayne State University, Detroit.

"Wayne State University Art Department Faculty Exhibition," April 23–May 12, 1958, Detroit Artists Market.

"Group Exhibition," April 27–May 17, 1958, AAA Gallery, Detroit.

"Recent Watercolors: Robert John Wilbert," January 31–February 21, 1958, Rackham Educational Memorial Building, University of Michigan, Detroit.

"Wayne County Annual Exhibition," April 28–May 31, 1958, McFadden-Ross House, Dearborn Historical Museum, Dearborn, Michigan.

"West Michigan Art Exhibition," April 20–May 24, 1958, Grand Rapids Art Gallery, Grand Rapids, Michigan.

"The 4th Annual Drawings and Small Sculpture Exhibition," March 2–30, 1958, Art Gallery, Ball State Teachers College, Muncie, Indiana.

"Drawings by Invitation," February 19–March 9, 1957, Flint Institute of Arts, Flint, Michigan.

"8th Annual Michiana Regional Art Exhibition," March 10–31, 1957, South Bend Art Center, South Bend, Indiana.

"11th Annual Exhibit, Michigan Water Color Society," June 2–June 22, 1957, College Gallery, Eastern Michigan University, Ypsilanti.

"10th Annual Western Michigan Artists 1956 Exhibition," March 4–28, 1956, Grand Rapids Art Gallery, Grand Rapids, and April 2–May 5, 1956, Kalamazoo Institute of Arts, Kalamazoo, Michigan.

"26th Annual Flint Artists Show," May 23–June 9, 1956, Flint Institute of Arts, Flint, Michigan.

"8th Annual Art Exhibition," August 31–September 9, 1956, Michigan State Fair, Detroit.

"13th Annual Watercolor Exhibition," October 12–26, 1956, Scarab Club, Detroit.

"25th Annual Flint Artists Show," May 9–28, 1955, Flint Institute of Arts, Flint Michigan.

"46th Annual Exhibition for Michigan Artists," November 15–December 18, 1955, Detroit Institute of Arts.

"57th Annual Exhibition by Artists of Chicago and Vicinity," October 1953, Art Institute of Chicago.

"American Water Colors Drawings and Prints," December 5, 1951–January 25, 1952, Metropolitan Museum of Art, New York.

Selected Bibliography

Citations are presented in chronological order beginning with the most recent

Periodicals

Crawford, Lynn. "Robert Wilbert at Susanne Hilberry." *Art in America* (November 2005): 188.

Costantini, Giovanna. "Life Painter." *Hour Detroit* (April 2000): 68–70.

Torno, Janet E. "Robert Wilbert: Teacher, Artist." *Birmingham Bloomfield Art Center News* (Fall 1998): 1.

[unsigned]. "The Painter's Painter: Robert Wilbert." *Detroit Monthly* (December 1992): 49.

Carducci, Vincent A. Robert Wilbert." *ARTFORUM* (February 1990): 144.

Yolles, Sandra. "Robert Wilbert." *ARTnews* (February 1990): 166.

Carducci, Vincent A. "Robert Wilbert." *New Art Examiner* 13 (Summer 1986): 55.

Keller, Martha. "Largess of Attention." *New Art Examiner* 4, no. 4 (April 1980): 1.

Cavaliere, Barbara. " Robert Wilbert." *Arts Magazine* (October 1979): 22.

Electronic Sources

Javan, Kienzle. "Artist Developed Talent in Grammar School." *Detroit Free Press* online, February 4, 2007: www: freep.com.

Sousanis, Nick. "Robert Wilbert @ Susanne Hilberry Gallery." *The Detroiter* online, December 28, 2004: www.thedetroiter.com.

Baulch, Vivian. "Detroit is Fertile Ground for Art." *Detroit News* online, January 31, 1998: www.detnews.com.

Howard-Filler, Saralee R. "Robert Wilbert, Artist of the Statehood Stamp." *Michigan History Magazine* online, January/February 1987: www.michiganhistorymagazine.com.

Selected Newspaper Articles

Colby, Joy Hakanson. "Artist Showcases Work in Detroit Gallery." *Detroit News*, December 4, 2004, F1.

Cohen, Keri Guten. "These Still Lifes Make the Dull Seem Bright." *Detroit Free Press*, December 26, 1999, G3.

Colby, Joy Hakanson. "Painter Puts Still Life in a New Light." *Detroit News*, December 3, 1999, D8.

Provenzano, Frank. "Works of a Masterful Painter Resonate." *Birmingham* (Michigan) *Eccentric*, November 28, 1999, C1.

Provenzano, Frank. "Robert Wilbert Reflects on Life of an Artist." *Birmingham* (Michigan) *Eccentric*, November 22, 1998, C1.

Yazigi, Monique P. "The Artists Are Over 60, and in Their Primes." *New York Times* January 22, 1995.

Cantu, John Carlos. "There's Not Enough Land in 'Land' Exhibition." *Ann Arbor* (Michigan) *News*, June 25, 1995.

Heinrich, Rebecca, and Murphy, Maureen. "Former WSU Prof on Display; Highlights Skill, Talent, Local Inspiration." *South End* (Wayne State University, Detroit), October 10, 1995, p. 8.

Colby, Joy Hakanson. "Travel a Colorful Memory Lane with Detroit's Leading Artist in WSU Show." *Detroit News*, October 12, 1995, F1.

Colby, Joy Hakanson. "Keeping at It." *Detroit News*, November 30, 1994, F1.

Miro, Marsha. "Waxing Artistic." *Detroit Free Press*, January 31, 1993, section H.

Colby, Joy Hakanson. "One for the Eyes and One for the Imagination." *Detroit News*, February 5 1993, D11.

Colby, Joy Hakanson. "Male Nude Photos are Revealing Sociological Portraits." *Detroit News*, August 14, 1993, C3.

Miro, Marsha. "DIA Shouldn't Be Abandoning Its Space for Michigan Artists." *Detroit Free Press*, August 30, 1992.

Colby, Joy Hakanson. "A Garden of Watercolors Flowers in Birmingham." *Detroit News*, December 16, 1992, D8.

Miro, Marsha. "Robert Wilbert Paints Flowers with Attitude." *Detroit Free Press*, December 18, 1992.

Colby, Joy Hakanson. "Use of Light Gives Shine to Wilbert's Work." *Detroit News*, November 3, 1989, D9.

Miro, Marsha. "Wilbert Works in Eloquent Romance." *Detroit Free Press*, November 5, 1989.

Abatt, Corinne. "Artist Uses Light, Color, for Outstanding Effects." *Birmingham* (Michigan) *Eccentric*, November 23, 1989, Creative Living section, p. 1.

Schimpf, Sheila. "Wayne State Professor Designs Sesquicentennial Stamp." *Lansing* (Michigan) *State Journal*, January 4, 1987, B1.

Hawkins, Margaret. "Simple Art of Deception: Draftsmanship Synthesizes Complex Visions." *Chicago Sun-Times*, February 14, 1986, Weekend Plus section.

Colby, Joy Hakanson. "25-year Love Affair: Wilbert, Gallery Mark Quarter-century of Growth." *Detroit News*, April 21, 1986, C1.

Miro, Marsha. "Painter Is Building a New Realism out of Abstraction." *Detroit Free Press*, May 4, 1986, G5.

Abatt, Corinne. "Robert Wilbert, 25 Year Retrospective Showing." *Birmingham* (Michigan) *Eccentric*, May 8, 1986, Creative Living section, p. 1.

May, Jeanne. "Detroiter's Art to Grace 150th Stamp." *Detroit Free Press*, December 10, 1986, A7.

Colby, Joy Hakanson. "Wilbert's Latest Exhibit Pulsates with Hidden Energy." *Detroit News,* December 2, 1984, K4.

Miro, Marsha. "Portraits Are Ravishing." *Detroit Free Press*, December 9, 1984.

Abatt, Corinne." Wilbert's Art-Extraordinary." *Birmingham* (Michigan) *Eccentric,* December 13, 1984, Creative Living section, p. 1.

Colby, Joy Hakanson. "Sensational Sabbatical: WSU Profs Return with a Terrific Dual Show." *Detroit News*, September 5, 1982, B3.

Miro, Marsha. "A Portrait Digs Deep into the Personality." *Detroit Free Press*, June 14, 1981, B1.

Colby, Joy Hakanson. "The Smooth, Sixth Solo of Robert J. Wilbert Charms the Jaded Eye." *Detroit News*, March 9, 1980.

Abatt, Corinne. "Wilbert Achieves Strong Identity." *Birmingham* (Michigan) *Eccentric,* March 20, 1980, C4.

Miro, Marsha. "Wilbert's Art, Vision Come Home." *Detroit Free Press*, April 3, 1980, C1.

Miro, Marsha. "Artrain's Theme: Mixing Modern with Folk Art." *Detroit Free Press*, May 27, 1979, C16.

Kramer, Hilton. "Robert Wilbert." *New York Times,* June 15, 1979, C23.

Colby, Joy Hakanson. "From Chicago Roots Two Art Styles Grow." *Detroit News*, May 29, 1977, H4.

Miro, Marsha. "Lush Parting Show by Robert Wilbert." *Detroit Free Press*, June 5, 1977.

Abatt, Corinne. "Wilbert Still Lifes Defy the Traditional." *Birmingham* (Michigan) *Eccentric,* June 9, 1977, C4.

Miro, Marsha. "Growing in Detroit—Art and Artists to Applaud." *Detroit Free Press*, October 17, 1976, D4.

Landsell, Sarah. "The Clouds Are Clouds, the Bananas are Color in 'Views of Reality.'" *Louisville Courier Journal and Times,* May 11, 1975.

James, Douglas. "Detroit Artists' Diversity Emerges at U of M Show." *Detroit Free Press*, October 6, 1974, D4.

[Hakanson, Joy]. "Hakanson: A Crayon 'Painter' Preparing to Make His Mark." *Detroit News,* May 20, 1973, E4.

[Hakanson, Joy]. "Joy Hakanson Reviews Wilbert: A Painter without 'Gimmicks.'" *Detroit News*, April 16, 1972, E4.

Tall, William. "What's a Realist Doing Here?" *Detroit Free Press*, April 16, 1972.

[Hakanson, Joy]. "Joy Hakanson Reviews 'All Michigan' Art: 'Surprising Number of Mediocrities' in Flint Show." *Detroit News*, December 12, 1971, E4.

Tall, William. "Michigan Artists: Slick Ad-man Look" *Detroit Free Press*, January 19, 1969.

Hakanson, Joy. "Wilbert's Two Solos." *Detroit News*, April 16, 1967.

Hakanson, Joy. "'If It Looks Like Art I'll Get Rid of it'" *Detroit News*, May 31, 1967, Talk section, p. 1.

Williams, Kelly. "Avant Garde Look Typifies Works in Faculty Art Show." *Daily Collegian* (Wayne State University), February 10, 1965.

Hakanson, Joy. "Wayne State Professor in Major Solo." *Detroit News*, December 13, 1964, G24.

Braun, Lillian Jackson. " Neutrality Stifles Art." *Detroit Free Press*, February 3, 1963.

Hakanson, Joy. "Young Painter's Exuberant World of Color." *Detroit News*, November 11, 1962, G12.

Hakanson, Joy. "AAA Gallery Has a Solo by Wilbert." *Detroit News*, April 19, 1959.

Hakanson, Joy. "Water Colorists Open State Show." *Detroit News*, June 7, 1959.

Hakanson, Joy. "Landscape '59." *Detroit News*, November 1, 1959.

Hakanson, Joy. "Water Colorists Open 12th Show." *Detroit News*, June 15, 1958.

Hakanson, Joy. "Busiest Painter a Scarab Winner." *Detroit News*, November 23, 1958.

[unsigned]. "Works of Art Are Described: Institute Exhibit Represents 22 Artists." *Flint* (Michigan) *Journal,* January 10, 1956.

[unsigned]. "Staff of Eight at Flint Art Institute Is Offering Wide Training Program." *Flint* (Michigan) *Journal,* October 17, 1954.

Personal Interviews

Yolles, Sandra. "Interview: Robert Wilbert." *Detroit Focus Quarterly* 4, no. 4 (December 1985): 1.

Miro, Marsha. "Wilbert, Robert John: Personal Interview." August 9–19, 1977. Microfilm reel, Box Number OH114, Archives of American Art, Smithsonian Institution, Washington, D.C.

Radio Program

"Robert Wilbert." *Saturday Edition,* National Public Radio, February 8, 1986.

Paintings Reproduced

Wilbert, Robert. "Detroit Cheers." Cover for the *Detroit Free Press Magazine,* December 22, 1985.

Wilbert, Robert. *Bouquet with Postcards* reproduced. "DIA at 100: A Special Issue." *Michigan: The Magazine of the Detroit News,* March 24, 1985.

Wilbert, Robert. *Gretchen with Veiled Hat* (image sponsored by Manufacturers Hanover Mortgage Corporation). *The Detroit Institute of Arts Presents "A Visual Feast."* Supplement to the *Detroit News,* April 10, 1983, p. 11.

Book Fund Contributors

Pauline Angle
Mary and Kit Aro
Lynne Avadenka
Gere and Sidney Baskin MD
Anita and Seymour Baxter MD
Richard Bilaitis
James J. and Janet A. Blanchard
Audrey and Melvin Bornstein MD
Bonnie Brenner and Earl Rudner MD
David and Susan Goethel Campbell
William S. and Angelina A. Davidek
Darcel and James Deneau
Frederick and Michele Oka Doner
Gary W. Eleinko
Dede and Oscar Feldman
Sidney Forbes
Stanley and Marcia Freedman
Dr. Kenneth and Roslyne Gitlin
Joan and Jack Goldman
Robert L. Griess
Jerrine Habsburg-Lothringen
John and Ann Hegarty
John D. Hilberry and Andronike A. Tsagaris
Joseph L. Hudson Jr.
John Hunter
Marion E. Jackson
Robert Kidd Gallery, Inc.
Richard R. and Joanne E. Kinney
David E. Klein Trust
Barbara K. Kratchman
Neil and Jan Layton
Diane and Edward Levine
Pauline and Harvey Y. Lewis MD
Susanna Linburg
Cynthia Mills
Richard Mittenthal
Nancy A. Mitter and Dipankar
Florence Morris
Donald Morris Gallery, Inc.
Dennis A. Nawrocki
Sophie Pearlstein
Corinne Pemberton
Primack Family Trust
Patricia A. Quinlan
Roger Ramsey Gallery
Robert I. and Pearl Rissman
Rivers Conservation & Preservation Services
Linda A and Alan J. Ross MD
Juliet M. Sabit
Marilyn Schechter
Sheila and Ronald M. Schechter
Delores Slowinski and Robert D'Aoust
Claudia M. Shepard
Ellen and Charles H. Tenner
Elaine S. and Harold R. Wagenberg MD
Cynthia T. and Thomas V. Yates
Christine R. and Reese C. Zantop